EcoGothic gardens in the long nineteenth century

Manchester University Press

EcoGothic gardens in the long nineteenth century

Phantoms, fantasy and uncanny flowers

Edited by Sue Edney

Manchester University Press

Published by Manchester University Press
Oxford Road, Manchester M13 9PL

www.manchesteruniversitypress.co.uk

British Library Cataloguing-in-Publication Data
A catalogue record for this book is available from the British Library

ISBN 978 1 5261 4568 0 hardback
ISBN 978 1 5261 7899 2 paperback

First published 2020

Typeset
by New Best-set Typesetters Ltd

Contents

Figures

Contributors

Francesca Bihet is currently engaged in folklore research at the University of Chichester, based at the Chichester Centre for Fairy Tales, Fantasy and Speculative Fiction; in particular, the Folklore Society and changes in academic approaches towards fairies by society members and how far these reflect the changing public perception of flower fairies. Previously she had a career in academic libraries and has specialised in early modern history and witchcraft. Originally from Jersey, her chapter on Channel Island fairies, 'Pouques and the Faiteaux', was included in *Magical Folk: British and Irish Fairies 500 AD to the Present* (2018), edited by Simon Young and Ceri Houlbrook.

Joanna Crosby's work at Essex University is focused on the social and cultural importance of the apple and the orchard in Victorian England, based on her experience in literary studies and heritage management. Joanna is a trustee of the East of England Apples and Orchards Project, which records, conserves and grows heritage varieties of fruit. She is also a founder of Trumpington Community Orchard. Her practical orchard work has given her an appreciation of the endeavours of Victorian orchardists, and of the importance of orchards in communities today.

Sue Edney is a Senior Associate teaching at Bristol University, specialising in Romantic and Victorian poetry, ecocriticism and the relationship of language to place and identity. She has published on dialect, identity and place, John Clare, William Barnes, Tennyson, Philip Henry Gosse, Gothic sea-anemones and environmental justice, plus several book reviews in assorted journals. She is reviews editor for *Green Letters: Studies in Ecocriticism*, the journal for the Association for the Study of Literature and the Environment (ASLE-UKI). She is the ecocriticism representative on the steering committee of the International Ecolinguistics Association. Sue is currently writing on Virgil's *Georgics* and environmental recovery: *The Georgic Environment and Why it Matters*, and co-editing two forthcoming essay collections: *Hannah More in Context* with Kerri Andrews and *Reworking Georgic* with Tess Somervell. She also has a cottage garden and an allotment.

Paul Evans is a nature writer, broadcaster, senior lecturer in creative writing at the Centre for Place Writing, Manchester Metropolitan University, and a wanderer of woods. He is best known as a contributor of 'Country Diaries' for the *Guardian* and *Guardian Weekly* and as a writer and presenter of natural history documentaries, place-based features, radio poems and docu-dramas on BBC Radio 4. His book *Herbaceous* (2014) is a collection of botanically inspired poetic prose, and *Field Notes from the Edge* (2015), a journey into Britain's secret wilderness, achieved critical acclaim. *How to See Nature* was published in 2018. His background is in the UK nature conservation movement, horticulture in the UK and USA, performance poetry in Britain and New York. He holds a PhD in Philosophy (Lancaster University) and is a Fellow of the English Association. He lives in Much Wenlock, Shropshire, with his family.

Teresa Fitzpatrick is a Researcher at the Manchester Centre for Gothic Studies (Manchester Metropolitan University) and an English lecturer at a further education college. Her specific research interests are the ecoGothic and female Gothic, with a focus on plant monster narratives from the late nineteenth to the twenty-first century. She has presented several papers on her research at Gothic conferences, is a member of the International Gothic Association and reviews ecoGothic material for the *Dark Arts Journal*.

Ruth Heholt is Senior Lecturer in English at Falmouth University, UK. She is editor of several edited collections on the Gothic and enjoys writing about the supernatural. She is co-editor of the Edinburgh University Press book series Gender and the Body in Literature and Culture; editor of the peer-reviewed e-journal *Revenant: Critical and Creative Studies of the Supernatural* (www.revenantjournal.com) and assistant editor of the Edinburgh University Press journal *Crime Fiction Studies*. Her most recent publication is her monograph on the Victorian writer Catherine Crowe (2020).

William Hughes is Professor of Literature in English at the University of Macau. He is a past president of the International Gothic Association, a Fellow of the Royal Historical Society, a Fellow of the Society of Antiquaries of Scotland and Visiting Research Fellow at Bath Spa University, UK. Though known primarily for the pioneering collection *EcoGothic* (2013), co-edited with Andrew Smith, he has also written on the plausible connections between ecological crisis and zombie apocalypse, and is a member of the editorial board of the peer-reviewed journal *Gothic Nature*. He is the author, editor or co-editor of twenty volumes, including *Beyond Dracula: Bram Stoker's Fiction and its Cultural Context* (2000); *Dracula: A Reader's Guide to Essential Criticism* (2008); *The Historical Dictionary of Gothic Literature* (2013); *That Devil's Trick: Hypnotism and the Victorian Popular Imagination* (2015); *Key Concepts in the Gothic* (2018); and the co-edited collections *Empire and the Gothic* (2003); *Queering the Gothic* (2009), *The Victorian Gothic: An Edinburgh Companion* (2012) and *Gothic Britain: Dark Places in the Provinces and Margins of the British Isles* (2018). He is currently writing a monograph on Victorian phrenology.

Caroline Ikin is currently researching John Ruskin's designed landscape at Brantwood, at Manchester Metropolitan University. She has lectured on nineteenth-century garden history, and is author of three books on aspects of Victorian gardens and gardening. She writes reviews for *Garden History* and *Museums Journal* and has held positions with the National Trust and the Gardens Trust.

Shelley Saguaro is Emeritus Professor of Environmental Humanities at the University of Gloucestershire. She is the author of *Garden Plots: The Politics and Poetics of Gardens* (2006) and has contributed several articles to *Green Letters*. These include '"Something that Would Stand for the Conception": The Inseminating World in the Last Writings of Virginia Woolf' (2013) and '"The Republic of Arborea": Trees and the Perfect Society' (2013), in the Utopias and the Environment special issue. Among other publications focusing on trees and plants are 'Telling Trees, *Eucalyptus,* "Anon" and the Growth of Co-evolutionary Histories' in *Mosaic* (2009) and 'Tolkien and Trees' (with D. C. Thacker) in *J. R. R. Tolkien* (2013). Her current research focuses on 'the botanical tentacular' in science fiction and in 'abcanny' fiction.

Christopher M. Scott is a Lecturer in English at Utah Valley University, USA, where he teaches academic writing, literature and cinema studies. His research interests lie in supernatural horror fiction and film, rhetorical criticism, and narrative representations of theological iconography and the natural environment. He recently served as a judge for the Global Undergraduate Awards and co-director of the Gothic Bible Project, an interdisciplinary research group based at the University of Sheffield, UK, and in partnership with the University of Auckland, New Zealand. He currently serves as a member of Utah Valley University's Scholarly and Creative Undergraduate Learning Partnership Team (SCULPT), which supervises undergraduate research and creative projects.

Jonathan Smith is William E. Stirton Professor of English at the University of Michigan-Dearborn, USA. He has published extensively on Charles Darwin and on Victorian literature and science; his books include *Charles Darwin and Victorian Visual Culture* (2006).

Heather I. Sullivan is Professor of German and Comparative Literature at Trinity University in Texas, USA. She is co-editor with Caroline Schaumann of *German Ecocriticism in the Anthropocene* (2017); and co-editor of *The Early History of Embodied Cognition from 1740–1920* (2016); author of *The Intercontexuality of Self and Nature in Ludwig Tieck's Early Works* (1997) and co-editor of journal special issues on ecocriticism in the *New German Critique* (2016); *Colloquia Germanica* (2014) and *Interdisciplinary Studies in Literature and the Environment* (2012). She has published widely in North American and European journals on ecocriticism and the Anthropocene, Goethe, German Romanticism, petrotexts and literature and science. Sullivan is also the 2016 recipient of Trinity University's Z. T. Scott Outstanding Teaching and Advising Fellowship, and the annual Goethe Society of North America essay award in 2016. She is currently working on a book project on the *Dark Green: Plants, Spores, and Humans in the Anthropocene.* Sullivan is the vice president of the North American Goethe Society and also serves the Association for the Study of Literature and the Environment both as professional liaison coordinator and as the chair of the Translation Grants Committee.

Adrian Tait is an independent scholar and environmental critic. A long-standing member of the Association for the Study of Literature and the Environment (ASLE-UKI), he has regularly published in its journal, *Green Letters.* He has also contributed to a number of other scholarly journals, including the *European Journal of English Studies* (2018), and to essay collections such as *Thomas Hardy, Poet: New Perspectives* (2015), *Nineteenth-Century Transatlantic Literary Ecologies* (2017), *Victorian Ecocriticism* (2017), and *Enchanted, Stereotyped, Civilized: Garden Narratives in Literature, Art and Film* (2018). He continues to explore the way in which nineteenth-century and early modern depictions of the environment anticipate but also challenge contemporary, ecocritical concerns.

Foreword: On the Gothic nature of gardens

William Hughes

Gardens, ostensibly, represent the antithesis of both the Gothic aesthetic and its associated culture of cruelty, transgression and excess. The very demarcation of green space as enclosed and duly ordered garden – as opposed to untamed wilderness, apparently boundless sublimity or ambivalent marginal landscape – bespeaks a restrictive domestication that militates against the apparent freedom that may be associated with those places less subject to human control and constant maintenance. The garden is a moral space, as it were, in which certain purported vices – disorder, weeds, imperfection – are variously avoided, discouraged or perhaps even eradicated, the very memory of their possibly anarchic or infectious presence recalled only with a shudder of distaste followed by a tentative statement with regard to their inability to return and again corrupt. Gardens stand for everything that is not Gothic. They stand for order aspired to, achieved and imposed. They interpret deviance or departure from an accredited standard in epistemologically moral terms, implicating such departures from design with punitive reaction. Hence, the process and discipline of gardening endows those who police the borders of domestic(ated) space with righteousness as much as with the power and authority to cut and to mutilate, to burn and to poison, to judge and to approve or exclude on the grounds of colour, of gender or of national origin.[1] This same power is, in turn, effectively delegated to those who participate in – that is visit, appreciate or perceive rather than practically order or manage – gardens, for it is through their approval and patronage that gardens are perpetuated as public as well as private spaces, as environments designed specifically for the control and suppression of nature, and for the expression of a specifically human vision of the organic environment. If the garden, in other words, is by definition not Gothic – unless it has been specifically styled to make it express some aspect of the Gothic aesthetic[2] – then the power of those who actively garden, and of those who design gardens, is, by its very oppressive nature, a force very much driven by implicitly violent and repressive preoccupations associated with the genre.

The garden, it would therefore appear, is something of a paradox and embodies, perversely, central Gothic imperatives within its façade of floristic orderliness and managed arboreality. There is more to be said, however, for gardens embody something of a narrative quality also, and one which further aligns them to the characteristics of the genre. Gardens, it must be remembered, are temporal as well as geographical conceptions, and the successive seasons are marked for their active manipulators and more passive perceivers by cycles of virulent growth and gradual retraction, of fecund reproduction and violent harvest, of life, death and decay. If the gardener or horticulturist aspires to impose a sovereign will as ostensible dictator over the chlorophyllic citizens and denizens of this terrain at some time appropriated from nature, then he or she might well be minded not to forget that a deposed hegemony, given time to regroup, may be apt to return. Such returns display, characteristically, a poignant edge in the cultural and literary myths that surround gardens which, having seen the departure of those who once lovingly cultivated them, have been reclaimed by a vivid and fertile nature, an exiled power always waiting at the human-imposed border of wall, hedge or deforested clearing.[3] But above, and indeed beyond, even the creeping return of excluded vegetation, remains the more abstracted and Absolute power of environmental ecology itself, the puissance of impersonal and implacable Nature, overwriting not merely the domesticated space but impacting, with imperious nonchalance, upon the wilderness which both surrounds and seeks to reclaim the fragile, human-nurtured enclave.

The human-managed cycle of the garden is thus subject to the greater tyranny of wind, rain and drought, of extremes of heat and of cold, supposedly predictable but frequently arriving without warning, even without precedent in human memory. The gardener's work is therefore in vain unless these puissant forces may be countered by the artificial stabilising of fragile ground, by drainage or irrigation, by shelter and artificial heat. Artifice, it seems, and industry at a great price of effort and economics, are needed to maintain the persistence, let alone the content, of the garden – though all of these putative safeguards remain subject to greater environmental stability – a stability that has become very much questioned in the current phase of the Anthropocene. Hence, gardens, being human impositions upon nature, are perversely sites of rebellion against the natural world from which they have been carved out. Representing order to human perception, they are interpositions upon what humanity might perceive as chaos – this itself being a place/non-place that by its very impersonal, inhuman nature has no conceptuality of order, chaos or morality. The Gothic garden is a knowing place. Environmental nature, on the other hand, being impersonal, knows it not and sweeps as destructively across its cultivated physicality with as little regard as if it were uncultivated wilderness, desert or tundra.

Given the complex and at times conflicting relationship between the gardens and the greater natural environment, and the implicitly violent nature of gardening as a human activity, it is surprising that there has to date been no significant interrogation of systematic horticulture by way of the genre, its literary conventions and critical preoccupations. In part this is quite simply a consequence of the politics of academic ecocriticism. Despite a long-standing commitment to reading Romantic textuality in ecocritical discourse, ecocriticism has characteristically eschewed the Gothic generally – even where it has paradoxically exemplified, in particular, the work of Margaret Atwood in its exposition of a meaningful wilderness. Perhaps it is the absence of a consistent utopian idealism across the genre that disqualifies Gothic as a subject suitable for interrogation in the eyes of some ecocritics, for where Gothic textuality may be frequently apocalyptic it is, arguably, seldom unequivocally redemptive or regenerative. Possibly, though, the genre has customarily been seen as simply too popular, too demotic, for rarefied and elite scholarship. Certainly, other than the long-standing appreciation of Atwood and the Canadian wilderness, little was said at length – and certainly not within the confines of a single volume – until the publication of the pioneering collection *Ecogothic* in 2013.[4] That volume, as wide as its interpretations of several conflicting and complementary natures might have been, did not address the implications of that most intimate of horticultural spaces – the garden. For this reason, the present collection of original and provocative essays, with its introduction and afterword, should prove not merely a useful supplement to the broader textual and conceptual field of ecocriticism but a significant extension to the specific confluence of theory and genre that is ecoGothic.

The current volume is both timely and overdue. It is, after all, an appropriate extension of the preoccupation with wilderness, shared by both ecocriticism and ecoGothicism, into the cultivated and domesticated environment. This critical intervention comes at a time when, with the global environmental system apparently on the verge of collapse, those fragile human spaces of non-agrarian cultivation are themselves threatened by personal poverty consequent upon macro-economics as much as by wide-ranging climate change.[5] Indeed, gardening itself – admittedly as a small-scale activity when laid against commercial agriculture and industry – might be considered in having its own redemptive function in redressing the damage of global warming.[6] Bearing that in mind, the radical implications of both the garden and the Gothic may once more be reconfigured into a surprising new configuration, where the former may mean so much more than cultivated space, and the latter have greater implications than ephemeral popular culture.

William Hughes
Taipa, Macau, January 2020

NOTES

1 This process of horticultural policing is, in the British experience at least, not confined to the systematic expulsion of unwanted or alien flora, such as the domestic dandelion or the invasive Spanish bluebells: see Royal Horticultural Society, 'Dandelion', www.rhs.org.uk/Advice/Profile?PID=1012 [accessed 9 January 2020]; BBC, *Gardener's World*, 13 August 2019, www.gardenersworld.com/how-to/solve-problems/how-do-i-get-rid-of-invasive-spanish-bluebells/ [accessed 9 January 2020]. Similar programmes of control and eradication are being applied not merely to invasive mammalian species such as the grey squirrel or the muntjac deer but also to insects such as the harlequin ladybird. See, for example, 'DEFRA in the Media', 24 February 2019, https:// deframedia.blog.gov.uk/2019/02/24/the-sunday-times-on-grey-squirrels/ [accessed on 9 January 2020]; BBC, *Gardener's World*, 12 August 2019, www.gardenersworld.com/ how-to/solve-problems/what-can-i-do-about-harlequin-ladybirds/ [accessed 9 January 2020].

2 See, for example, Alle Connell, '35 Eerie Photos of Kat Von D's Pitch Black Garden: Goth Gardening at its Finest', Revelist blog, 27 July 2017, www.revelist.com/bloggers/ kat-von-d-black-garden/8318 [accessed 09 January 2020].

3 See, for example, Frances Hodgson Burnett, *The Secret Garden* (New York: Grosset and Dunlap, 1911), pp. 97–102; 'The Lost Gardens of Heligan', www.heligan.com/ the-story/introduction [accessed 9 January 2020]. Consider also the imagery of the final phrase of Algernon Blackwood's 'The Man Whom the Trees Loved' in *Pan's Garden: A Volume of Nature Stories* (London: Macmillan, 1912), pp. 3–99 at pp. 98–9.

4 Andrew Smith and William Hughes (eds), *Ecogothic* (Manchester: Manchester University Press, 2013).

5 'Hunter Community Gardening' (cached 11 December 2013), http://webcache. googleusercontent.com/search?q=cache:Qy6ox84NofEJ:huntercommunitygardening. org.uk/about/+&cd=16&hl=en&ct=clnk [accessed 9 January 2020]. Tony Russell, 'Storms and Floods: Have Your Trees Been Damaged?', *Daily Telegraph*, 8 March 2014, www.telegraph.co.uk/gardening/plants/trees/10683870/Storms-and-floods-have-your-trees-been-damaged.html [accessed 9 January 2020].

6 See, for example, National Wildlife Federation, 'Gardeners Can Play an Important Role in Reducing Global Warming', *Science Daily*, 19 May 2007, www.sciencedaily.com/ releases/2007/05/070519084046.htm [accessed 9 January 2020].

Acknowledgements

I would like to thank all my contributors for working so patiently on an unusual project, and to thank Matthew Frost at MUP for his encouragement and enthusiasm for the work. Paul Clarke, Lucy Burns and the editing team have guided me through the production with calm understanding. I'd also like to thank my colleagues for advice and support, especially Richard Kerridge, Bill Hughes, Terry Gifford, Kate Rigby and Greg Garrard; Ruth Heholt for giving me the idea, John Parham for backing her up and reviewing my contribution to the collection; Tim Mowl for sending me his own ideas that sparked further investigation and Sue Hayward, curator at Tyntesfield, for similar reasons. Dale Townshend, Cate Sandilands and Jim Endersby pointed me in right directions, for which I am very grateful. My friends Caroline, Pauline, Olive and Mell either prodded me or avoided me at all the appropriate moments. My family are always generous with their practical and emotional support, especially my sister Jo at whose kitchen table I wrote the proposal, Daniel and Jack, and Kenn who reads quantities of prose without complaining.

Introduction: Phantoms, fantasy and uncanny flowers

Sue Edney

Gothic, as a creative medium and a way of seeing, allows us to question human ability to control events, people or even places. Any inquiry into human and nonhuman interaction is disturbing when control disintegrates, especially in the apparent safety of gardens, designed as areas of human dominance over wild nature, yet creating opportunities for uncanny deeds and presences. This collection is a unique interrogation of nineteenth-century gardens, literary and real, examining their many abilities to support and distort human–nonhuman material connections through the dark glass of ecoGothic. Even in the most benign flower border, humans are (blissfully) unaware of gardens' secret knowledge and subversive power. David Cooper describes the majority of gardens, however beautiful, as collections of 'nature-as-affected-by-humanity' (2005: 7); trees that do not grow according to their own forest rules, special kinds of grasses which are not permitted to run wild. Humans are 'collaborators, not observers' in the garden writes Tim Richardson, and as we 'imaginatively co-create the spaces around us, our mental interactions must also influence their nature' (2005: 151). Gardens are also 'porous', as Catherine Alexander points out, 'essentially unbounded and open to the elements'; 'In terms of cultural constructions of domestic space', she adds, 'the garden is an occasional arena' (2002: 861). That term 'arena' signals part of a garden's function: to be on show. The display signifies relationships, with nature and with society, from the intricate, even secretive Tudor and Elizabethan 'knots' to the expanded prospects of Stowe, Hagley Park and Stourhead in eighteenth-century England.

> [T]here is a continuum of perceptions regarding the link between nature and culture, from *nature in the raw* to nature as a *made thing*, an artifact. These relationships, when applied to the garden, become a metonymic shorthand for the means by which people categorize themselves and others. (Alexander 2002: 861, emphasis in original)

The need to control nature 'in the raw' in order to make the 'made thing' part of the cultural arena – inside the boundary of ordered society – is often challenged by nature itself, as Adam and Eve found out in their over-flourishing plot 'eastward, in Eden' (Genesis 2: 8). The Paradise garden, enclosed 'With thicket overgrown, grotesque and wild' ([*Paradise Lost*: IV. 136] in Milton 1998)[1] is a seriously Gothic place as envisioned by John Milton in *Paradise Lost* (1667), where virtue is tested, innocence is betrayed and evil appears in nightmares. An inner circle of 'goodliest trees loaden with fairest fruit' [IV. 147] contains the deadliest beauty of all. The two trees of Paradise, one of Knowledge and the other of Life, are reasons both for being turned away from the Edenic garden and also for returning. This dualistic potential can be transferred to all gardens: potential for good in virtuous labour rewarded by wholesome fruit, but also potential for going astray – not merely, as depicted in bucolic pastoral, in idleness and frivolity, but in active cultivation of seeds of destruction, as has been discovered in garden history to the present day.

The chapters in this collection recognise the importance of duality in ecoGothic, how the web of good intentions becomes entangled, 'as the vine curls her tendrils' in 'wanton' wildness [*Paradise Lost*: IV. 306–7], discussed by Christopher Scott, Shelley Saguaro and Teresa Fitzpatrick. Much that is disturbing in gardens derives from a misunderstanding of exactly how limited humans can be, and how the garden continually empties out its human significance in obedience to insistent nonhuman imperatives. Milton uses the fearsome energy of Gothic storms, before their eighteenth-century time, to depict earth itself as a contested site after evil enters the garden.

> Earth trembled from her entrails, as again
> In pangs, and nature gave a second groan,
> Sky loured, and muttering thunder, some sad drops
> Wept at completing of the mortal sin
> Original [*Paradise Lost*: IX. 1000–4]

The contributors to *EcoGothic Gardens* reveal vacillation between good and evil in textual and horticultural manifestations, acknowledging Milton's Paradise garden as a spectral presence. The Eden of *Paradise Lost* provides one example of the emblematic, yet uneasy status of English garden design. Through the seventeenth and eighteenth centuries, the establishment of great estates achieved national importance in times of political revolution and restoration. They symbolised domestic skill and pride while increasingly revealing dark constructions at their foundations: they were laid out with wealth gained from overseas plantations, from slavery, from war and from reducing land available to labouring families. However, for many visitors to Chatsworth, Claremont and other 'happy rural seat[s]' [*Paradise Lost*: IV. 247] so depicted in *Paradise Lost*, these sites represent a golden past; what is buried among the dahlias can be ignored in the flush of colour and the hum of bees. The historical presence of these gardens and their human organisers are a vital backstory to the chapters in this collection, as they reflect discordant negotiations between human and nonhuman at the pinnacle of garden design. From Ruskin's Brantwood to Wilkie Collins's 'high Victorian' Blackwater Park, and from the Anglo-German Romantic garden to the palimpsest of Powis Castle, these chapters probe the dark shadows and bring out 'something which ought to have been kept concealed but which has nevertheless come to light' (Freud 1957: 13).

A genuine aversion to the homogenising effects of parkland aesthetic, combined with a growing interest in historicising personal and public relationships with culture and society created opportunities for revaluating what garden creations could represent in anxious times. This was combined with an inward turn, 'a movement from registering precise and detailed meanings of ruins … to responding simply to their impressionistic suggestions of decay and loss' (Hunt 1992: 181). The popularity of the Claude-glass sketching mirror and its ability to create and then re-create 'reflections' (178) fed the imaginations of amateur and professional observer-artists, promoting an uncanny 'doubleness' of vision (178), in itself an symptom of self-haunting (Wolfreys 2002: 14–15). 'Picturesque', as a concept and design practice, became the landscape reflection of Gothic, in part because of its own obsession with medieval Gothic architecture and what it represented as it decayed. Roger Ebbatson, in *Landscapes of Eternal Return*, discusses the function of repetition, as demonstrated in nineteenth-century poetry and fiction, in relation to haunting; that 'the principle of recurrence inhabits and haunts nineteenth-century writing' (2016: 10). 'Negotiations with temporality and spatiality in these and other symptomatic texts occur through what have been termed "dynamic thresholds" between actuality and virtuality or the imaginary,' Ebbatson continues (11), which marks out the territory of uncanny. In some cases, as effectively discussed in these chapters, the most dangerous element is the one closest to the protagonist, the completely familiar, therefore the most uncanny. Proximity – ordinariness – reveals uncanniness in the flower next door; Gothic inflection is often associated with the extraordinary, monstrous Other. EcoGothic as an investigatory technique explores the alien *and* the uncanny in these gardens; they can be the same thing. In H. G. Wells's tale, 'The Flowering of the Strange Orchid', the plant, though figured as 'vampiric', has a wider cultural significance as a gendered uncanny presence; 'my orchid', as Winter-Wedderburn calls it (Wells 2013: 63–71), implying a close relationship, like 'my pet', as Professor Jonkin describes his pitcher plant in Howard Garis's 'Professor Jonkin's Cannibal Plant' (2013: 119).

David Del Principe, in his introduction to the ecoGothic-themed 2014 edition of *Gothic Studies*, emphasises the inclusivity of ecoGothic in contrast to classic anthropocentric Gothic themes: 'the EcoGothic examines the construction of the Gothic body – unhuman, nonhuman, transhuman, posthuman, or hybrid

– through a more inclusive lens, asking how it can be more meaningfully understood as a site of articulation for environmental and species identity' (2014: 1). By these means, ecoGothic can also address 'ingrained biases and a mounting ecophobia – fears stemming from humans' precarious relationship with all that is nonhuman' (2). Thus, ecoGothic allows for the subtle infiltration of uncanniness into horror in order to establish a better story to live by (Stibbe 2014) without relying on 'estrangement in panicked, dystopian terms' (Del Principe 2014: 2), in all the literary gardens explored in this collection.

I have chosen these chapters because of their exceptional ability to tap into new materialist and material-ecocritical discourses beyond the aesthetic, necessary to the discussion of anthropocentric ignorance of how the Other ticks. We need to explore all avenues of our connections in this world or any world, part of our everyday experience or quite out of our knowledge, in order to come to terms with our futures and the destructive part we have played in them. Serenella Iovino and Serpil Oppermann note that the world is 'far from being pure', filled instead 'with intermingling agencies and forces that persist and change' (2014: 1). They change us even as they are changed. Material ecocriticism argues that the agency of matter, in any form, is directly related to the discourse surrounding it which in turn serves to 'structure human relations to materiality' (4). Thus, the narrative of matter is of us as well as of itself. Gardens and their occupants, plants or otherwise, are texts; 'there is an implicit textuality in the becoming of material formations' (6). Bodies of nature also create bodies of work, and are productive of cyclical revolution, the return of different kinds of nature, including the immaterial supports of matter, something Jane Bennett regards as 'sympathy', 'an undesigned system of affinities (which persist alongside antipathies) between and within bodies' (2014: 239–40). Another term for these affinities and antipathies might be hauntings, ghosts, apparitions, even fairies, all of which exhibit 'a mode of impersonal connection, attachment and care' (250). Certainly there is a quality of mutual 'yearning' (241) in the stories examined here, a desire to connect or revisit across material dimensions, to make being alive in any sense a timeless, deeply felt dynamism. I consider these affinities, in the context of ecoGothic, to be an expression of ecocritical uncanny, in order to include in the ecoGothic polytunnel all those elements of vegetal sentience, of plant 'monster', of spiritually alive and enchanted gardens. Therefore, sometimes the 'Gothic' concept is stretched here, as is the 'garden' – gardeners know that a pragmatic relativism is the only philosophy that can cope with the unexpected. Of most importance here is how the vegetal agent, as initiator or co-worker with Others, disrupts order for good or ill and shakes humankind out of complacency.

That humans are, now, insecure on the earth they wished to consider a 'garden' is a feature of the resurgence of interest in Gothic as a genre, in practice in the arts and humanities: now is the right moment for this collection. Andrew Smith and William Hughes note that John Ruskin's dystopian vision of atomisation prevails in Gothic, 'the image of fragments', by which 'nature becomes constituted in the Gothic as a space of crisis' (2013: 2–3). These chapters explore how humans fail in the face of extraordinary, yet often subtle, pressures from outside the boundary, as 'nature in the raw' overtakes and destroys the 'made thing' (Alexander 2002: 861). In addition, the garden can represent a flexible container for fluid emotions – hope and joy, fear and grief, anger and jealousy – all of which feature in the various stories told here. They connect bodies to the immaterial, more-than-human to flesh, bones and skin to petals and roots. The otherness of gardens encourages the presence of Others, malign or beneficial.

The garden is a catalyst for story-telling across eras and cultures, yet although there are many books about gardens, historical and literary, there are few that incorporate literary theory with cultural investigation and the stories that gardens enact. In my experience, two books have contributed greatly to critical appreciation of Victorian and twentieth-century literary gardens in terms of their wider affective influence: Michael Waters' *The Garden in Victorian Literature* (1988) and more recently Shelley Saguaro's *Garden Plots: The Politics and Poetics of Gardens* (2006), with Pauline Fletcher's *Gardens and Grim Ravines* (1983) exploring the poetic contexts of Victorian landscape in general. However, these texts do not have any specific Gothic approaches as part of their remit, although they do examine potential human/nonhuman conspiracies in and of gardens. Saguaro's book extends the concept of garden as a 'plot'; that 'plots pertaining to gardens are literal, figural and ... material ... a complex interrelation of *all* these issues' (2006: xiii). Saguaro also visits a wide geographical range of gardens, removing the convention of Englishness attached to many garden texts.

Most recently, Elizabeth Hope Chang's excellent study of the global and imperial connection of plants to fiction during the Victorian period, *Novel Cultivations* (2019), also examines the aesthetics and the environmental significance of British nineteenth-century garden culture beyond Englishness. There is some inevitable overlap with this collection, in her chapters on the place of exotic and native vegetal life in urban and rural Gothic fiction, and on plant sentience, especially. Chang's research is detailed and wide-ranging, and while discussing authors also examined here – Wilkie Collins, Algernon Blackwood and H. G. Wells, for example – her emphasis is not on an ecoGothic or ecomaterialist interpretation of the human–nonhuman relationship. Chang's work is an important and timely examination of genre fiction in the nineteenth century, using writers' engagement with the global world of plant life and plant 'thought' (160) to explore the construction of fiction itself during this period of internal self-reflection and external geographical and botanical discovery.

Smith and Hughes's pioneering overview, *Ecogothic* (2013) has been vital in encouraging the detailed research clearly evident in these chapters, and references to their seminal collection abound. In general, though, ecoGothic has been more interested in nonhuman animal behaviour, rather than plants or gardens, although Lisa Kröger, in *EcoGothic*, considers the garden as refuge or 'perversion of Eden' (2013: 24) in the work of Ann Radcliffe and Matthew Lewis respectively. There are, of course, texts on 'monstrous' plants; for example, Dawn Keetley and Angela Tenga's collection on *Plant Horror: Approaches to the Monstrous Vegetal in Fiction and Film* (2016) and T. S. Miller's 'Lives of the Monster Plants: The Revenge of the Vegetable in the Age of Animal Studies' (2012) among them, and there are an increasing number of studies of vegetal behaviour in connection with animality, sentience and human–nonhuman interaction. Michael Marder's work has stimulated interest in plant relationships with nonvegetal beings – for example, in *Plant-Thinking: A Philosophy of Vegetal Life* (2013) – and combined research into communication has proved plants to live lives both more strange and more familiar than humans have imagined. In particular, Patricia Vieira, John Ryan and Monica Gagliano have created illuminating foundations for further exciting research with their collections, *The Green Thread* (2015) and *The Language of Plants* (2017). The ability of vegetation to extend and transform boundaries in literature and the environment has also created new ecocritical interest in vegetal science fiction, as intriguingly demonstrated in *Plants in Science Fiction: Speculative Vegetation* (2020), edited by Katherine E. Bishop, David Higgins and Jerry Määttä.

Haunting, of people, place and landscape, is also a key quality in current environmental literary/critical thinking and creative writing, noticeable in, for example, Sarah Perry's novel *The Essex Serpent* (2016), in which the place appears to be haunted by itself. Julian Wolfreys' *Victorian Hauntings* (2002) is an example of the application of 'hauntology' (Derrida 2006) to Victorian literature, and is particularly relevant to emerging nineteenth-century media: photography, film, sound recording, as well as improved printing and other reproductive techniques. As Wolfreys points out, 'the spectral is that which makes possible reproduction even as it also fragments and ruins the very possibility of reproduction's apparent guarantee to represent that which is no longer there fully' (2002: 2). Recent texts on these themes have been of particular assistance to me in my own thinking, especially *Haunted Landscapes: Super-Nature and the Environment* (2016), edited by Ruth Heholt and Niamh Downing and *Affective Landscapes in Literature, Art and Everyday Life: Memory, Place and the Senses* (2015), edited by Christine Berberich, Neil Campbell and Robert Hudson. In her preface to *Affective Landscapes*, Kathleen Stewart notes how unstable material interactions become when we recognise the true uncanny affectivity of landscapes: 'Something becomes legible as an object of repulsion or desire, as a thing attuned to, or missed or mistaken for something else' (2015: xv). Ruth Heholt is careful to point out the disadvantages of a too-liberal engagement with Derrida's 'hauntology'; 'hauntings are *placed* and ghosts belong to particular locales', she writes (2016: 12, emphasis in original), but to generalise these processes is to diminish their strength and their function in everyday life. Bringing the 'spectral turn' (Luckhurst 2002) into the flowerbed and greenhouse concentrates affective experience and place, permitting close readings of uncanny in micro-environments that influence and reflect universal conditions and anxieties without diluting their power. These may be uncovered in the vegetal body itself or in the arrangement of vegetation and other material in managed spaces, or in the discomfort felt by human participants in a world seemingly over-filled with Others.

It is my argument here that the distinctive combination of ecocriticism with Gothic and the uncanny, alongside the 'material turn' in cultural theory gives elements of Gothic an agency beyond fantasy and encourages a process of critical reinvigoration. Using these critical methodologies, an emphasis on the domestic yet liminal space of the garden with all its material consequences opens up unique discourses of affectivity in Gothic literature more generally and more inclusively in the context of anthropogenic environmental destruction. In fact, my original inspiration for this kind of collection was an essay by Dale Townshend in 2014, 'Ruins, Romance and the Rise of Gothic Tourism: The Case of Netley Abbey, 1750–1830'. In this essay, Townshend *places* people and events in specific landscapes and their literary representations so that the persistent influence of one upon the other creates a vision that we can recognise in present-day tourism. But it is the stones themselves that haunt these places and their visitors; they are both the material Gothic containers of uncanny and also 'thoroughly textual phenomena' (Townshend 2014: 392).

EcoGothic destabilises our learned habit of anthropocentric organisation, of prime importance to an ordered garden, demonstrated in all these chapters. The poetic design of Gothic (poetic in its widest sense) encourages us to engage with the unknowing. 'Literature is uncanny', writes Nicholas Royle; it is resistant to 'accountability', which is why, Royle argues, we keep returning to it: the 'literary does not permit a settling on one side or the other' (2003: 15). If we view the garden as a collaborated work, a material story, it is, in its production and in its ongoing life force, a 'source of knowledge', as Wendy Wheeler writes about creative activity, 'and one wherein its practitioners consist of a large number of people who feel a close acquaintance with the wisdom of attending to happenstance and the human body's coded but largely unworded life' (2016: 189).

There is a 'web of connections' (199) set up by being-human or being-some-other-being (which might also be human), coded in our internal and external systems, one of which is literature and one of whose offshoots is material entanglement and intrigue as explored in ecoGothic writing. Underlying the positive benefits of entanglement, however, is the counter-effect of ecophobia, that 'a Nature will finally conquer humanity, will reclaim all of the world, and will remain long after humanity is gone', as Simon Estok characterises the 'ecophobic vision' of much present-day media output (2014: 132–3). 'Fear of a loss of agency does strange things to people', Estok muses, adding, 'Fear of the loss of agency and fear of the loss of predictability are what form the core of ecophobia' (134). EcoGothic investigation is well placed to examine the fear as well as the unpredictability presented by the strangeness of garden spaces in these chapters, where agency slips away into fairies, or flowers, or is undermined by the overwhelming presence of more-than-human energy in ancient orchards, trees and even water. Estok quotes Mary Douglas, who wrote in 1966 that it was important to recognise the potential of disorder, even when 'it is destructive to existing patterns … It symbolizes both danger and power' (Douglas 1966: 95, Estok 2014: 135). A disordered garden is unsettling; it is also stimulating, vital and provocative, filled with creative growth at the core of decay.

CHAPTER OVERVIEW

Michael Waters notes that the majority of nineteenth-century British literary gardens are positive; they depict an emphasis on 'old-fashioned and long-established plants' and 'upon picturesqueness by default' (1988: 310). They are in keeping with and illustrative of a gradualist model of social and cultural change, in which the principles 'necessarily legitimized a cautious, not to say grindingly slow, approach to … change' (310). However, the gardens in this collection, the majority of which are not only European but English, are all connected by their inability to provide a stable backdrop for events and beings, human or otherwise. These gardens seem to conspire with or against their human guardians, or to be placed in such an invidious position that they cannot thrive, resorting to resentful decay and wilful disorder instead, with a distinctly un-gradual accumulation of triggers for anxious displacement and disturbance. As Heather Sullivan notes in Chapter 1 – using her own coining, 'the Gothic green' – many of these tales appear to concern 'humanly determined acts' but they are 'tinged by the mysterious physicality and power befitting the ecoGothic' (16, 19).

When Ruskin attempted to apply control to his own local ecosystem in the Lake District at Brantwood, he became dismayed at his garden's unwillingness to conform to a programme he considered to be supremely beneficial for the landscape and the vegetal beings dwelling therein. There appeared to be such a thing as an 'ideal' garden, in spite of Ruskin's own preference for Gothic flaws. Caroline Ikin, in Chapter 2, details how fairly innocuous schemes, such as rearranging woodland for recreational benefit, had exactly opposite results, and 'mirrored the feudal ideals of Ruskin's political economy, an anthropocentric hierarchy that refused to recognise the imperatives of nature' (34). The practical disintegration of Brantwood as a garden in which nonhuman is intended to cooperate with human – and refuses – sets the scene for a range of garden discourses in which human is, in fact, set against or overcome by nonhuman, even when the opposite appears to be the case. A sense of human failure, which can be made to look like success in some of these stories, not least in Ikin's narrative of Ruskin's initial project, imbues many of the gardens described here. Yet, ecocritical uncanny characterises the repetitive persistence of vegetal self-sufficiency. Plant life and its representation returns in these tales; distorted, excessive or diminished; as agents of spiritual vengeance or as indicators and resisters of human self-absorbed irrationality, violence and malevolence, as in Tennyson's *Maud* and Wilkie Collins's *The Woman in White*.

It would be a mistake to assume that ecoGothic signifies distress in all circumstances. Uneasiness is a useful correcting tool for complacency, and an acceptance of unfamiliar-familiar can open imaginations to the wider implications of events and material change that inspire dynamic, responsive actions instead of the narrowed anxieties of predictable thinking. Joanna Crosby's Chapter 3, for example, offers a historical view of the concept of 'enchantment' in the liminal space of orchards, creating encounters that were actively sought in Classical myth and perceived as potentially beneficial throughout European cultural history (49). The 'sacred grove' was a place of between-worlds negotiation, where human and more-than-human could engage, disagree and learn from their confrontations. Freya Mathews notes the literal meaning of 'enchanted': 'it means to have been wrapped in chant or song or incantation. A land or place is enchanted if it has been called up' (2003: 18). In this space, the Edenic apple as a figurative and material presence can create an ambivalent unease that is both disruptive and redemptive, especially when applied to the orchard fruits in Christina Rossetti's 'Goblin Market'. By whatever means the goblins have been 'called up', Laura and Lizzie are enchanted and must endure the consequences in an apparently idyllic 'country cottage' setting. It is tame indeed compared to the wild marketplace, yet its quiet consistency supports the ultimate rejection of marketplace vibrant Otherness, with all the accompanying dangers.

Similarly, the Paradise garden in Eden is both sacred and profane, profaned by the infiltration of evil, as explored by Christopher Scott in Chapter 4 through Algernon Blackwood's tales of transcendence, 'The Transfer' and 'The Lost Valley'. It is very difficult to feel anything other than discomfort when faced with a patch of man-eating lawn, yet the resolution to this tale of horror is one of renewal, even reform, of human–nonhuman relations. In these stories, entities are called up, again in settings of luxuriant abundance, as Scott explores Blackwood's uneasy paradise gardens on earth. Blackwood's theories of supernatural relationships in the natural-material world are also central to his less-than-Edenic garden in 'semi-rural' English Edwardian landscape, determined to resist the Otherness of wild forest in 'The Man whom the Trees Loved'. Alongside this, E. F. Benson provides an alarming altercation between tree, garden and myth realisation in 'The Man who Went too Far', both stories set too close for comfort to the New Forest in Hampshire, England. Ruth Heholt, in Chapter 5, explains that for Benson and Blackwood 'the gardens are always-already a part of the wildness that roars further out' (96) and ultimately these gardens 'collapse and cease to signify the English cottage garden' they are trying to be (94). Unlike Rossetti's cottage-garden resistance, these domestic places cannot endure the challenge of being subsumed into material entanglement. In all these discussions of relations between 'wild' and 'tame' Otherness, the 'slippage', as Heholt says (82), between human and nonhuman matter collapses the terms themselves. Otherness becomes un-strange yet not quite familiar, and the everyday garden is destabilised as a concept as well as in the elemental material itself: grass, trees and flowers; water and wind. Examining the narrative devices of this particular story, Chang concludes that Blackwood 'propose[s] an iteration of the posthuman that is also the more-than-human' (2019: 178); however, both Heholt and Scott are also happy to use the term 'supernatural' in their discussions of Blackwood, which offers an Otherness beyond human that ecoGothic is well placed to interpret in the context of material nature: immaterial things can still have influential presence.

However invoked, more-than-human beings can also be monstrous, a nineteenth-century fear provoked by the speed of technological and scientific developments, even those that appeared beneficial to the common good. Plant and animal experimentation often became the source of ill-informed fears and the target of both parodic and alarmist journalism and fiction. Part of this post-Darwinian concern manifested itself in stories about plant monsters, evolutionary horrors that turn on their scientific carers – stories that fed into racial/cultural phobias, misogyny and anti-intellectual bias in the reading public. Jonathan Smith, in Chapter 6, offers a compelling case for seeing Darwin as an instigator of 'plant monster' tales of the unexpected, with sensation fiction's 'crime, violence and sexual transgression' (103) at the heart of his botanic 'plots'. Sex and death create and re-create both plant and human, yet to be so obviously exposed provided 'a parable of the dangers of the "fast life" … so often depicted in sensation novels' (106). Sullivan's chapter explores sex and death in the German garden settings of Eichendorff's *The Marble Statue* (1819) and Goethe's *Elective Affinities* (1809), late Romantic fantasies that explore gardens as sites of and catalysts for death and its uncanny representations, in spite of – or because of – their lush greenness. 'Green materiality' (Sullivan, Chapter 1: 18) exposes a 'lack of control over unexpected attractions' (19). Darwinian plant proclivities, acted out in the Darwins' own garden, were reflected in the 'melding of the domestic and the exotic' (Smith, Chapter 6: 111) in, for example, the hothouse and borders of M. E. Braddon's *The Doctor's Wife* (1864).

Darwin was able to conduct his experiments as a result of innovative gardening technology, which enabled new relationship hierarchies to be established between human and nonhuman, most noticeable in the predominately male preserve of the greenhouse, and in Padua's sixteenth-century botanical gardens. In these rarefied enclosures, exotic Others could be brought to the peak of their cultivation, providing obvious tropes for a gendered gardening discourse, in which the female and the monstrous are uncomfortably entwined. The peculiar sentience of the dangerous vegetal unfamiliar in Victorian ecoGothic might be considered 'as examples of the growing canon of environmental literature, in which plant life gained a history, a coherent range of cause and effect and a particular scale of engagement', as Chang reads the plant monster (2019: 179). On the other hand, they may also be monsters, and should be respected as such, if we are truly to ascribe agency and sentience to more-than-human lifeforms. In fact, we need monsters. In Chapter 7, as Shelley Saguaro reconfigures Nathaniel Hawthorne's 'Rappaccini's Daughter' in the light of China Miéville's 'abcanny' and Donna Haraway's 'tentacular thinking', 'the figures of hysteria and repression that so readily haunted a Gothic garden sensibility' in the long nineteenth century 'need now to be replaced by something hitherto unimagined' (126). Beatrice, as a hybrid vegetal-human, is not the monster that she is often considered, rather her 'manner amongst the plants is one of intimacy and kinship' (119), to which, Saguaro argues, we should pay attention. 'What does that kinship mean in practical terms, and what demands does it make on us?' asks T. S. Miller (2012: 472), as both he and Saguaro recognise a potentially beneficent kind of monstrous, which is no less unsettling for humankind. 'Attention to ambiguity and entanglement' (Saguaro, Chapter 7: 115) as pursued throughout this collection encourages us to embrace the 'messy, repressed, disordered or disregarded biotic and abiotic beings of the earth' (116), writes Saguaro, making it clear that in our present 'ecological crisis' (Bergthaller et al 2014: 262), scientific culture is still capable of making damage worse, even when trying to address the problem. It is a 'crisis of the cultural and social environment – of the systems of representation and of the institutional structures through which contemporary society understands and responds to environmental change (or fails to do so: hence the crisis)' (262).

Teresa Fitzpatrick argues for a feminist reading of ecoGothic 'monster' plants in Chapter 8, as exhibited in H. G. Wells's tale of orchid violence against human gardener; 'the struggle between conservative and progressive views are portrayed through gender and body' of plant and human alike (137). Fitzpatrick draws analogies between Wells's and Garis's vegetal *femmes fatales* and cultural reaction to the politics of women's movements in Britain and America. These are the true monsters to be feared, according to an emerging twentieth-century androcentric orthodoxy of order and control. Flowers' confinement in hothouses confirms their existence as both demanding and fragile, thus returning to earlier tropes of female Gothic imprisonment; however, Fitzpatrick argues that feminine plant 'monsters' fundamentally 'challenge established hierarchies' (Miller 2012: 262) of gendered vegetal and more-than-human Others.

Darwinian experiments showed that nature was not divine providence working with human at all; nature in all its forms – wild or tame, animal or vegetal, marine or avian – was not to be trusted, unless it could be categorised or even dissected. Thus, for many, the material-natural became disenchanted, either to be mourned or to be ignored, often damaged and degraded. In this diminished world, children became the focus for hopeful return to reciprocal relations with nonhuman; they lived, if they could, in the enchanted world of flower-gardens, fairy tale and sunlight; surely they could be trusted not only to invoke encounter but also to respond positively to that which is called up, and to return humankind to an idyllic Edenic space, even if only imagined. Certainly, Kipling's Puck, an ancient spirit of folkloric mischief in his tales for children, *Puck of Pook's Hill* and *Rewards and Fairies*, engages with Dan and Una in order to teach them how landscape represents human–nonhuman reciprocity and damage alike. Through an eco-uncanny reading of childhood garden stories and the Cottingley 'fairy' photographs, Francesca Bihet's Chapter 9 explores how adulthood reduces garden mystery, instead providing stony containers for grief and disillusion. Frances Hodgson Burnett's neglected 'secret' garden is transformed through the magic of growth and renewal in which '[a] dult disharmony is removed through the occult harmonies played out by the children and their encounters in the garden' (153). However, the fairies at the bottom of Edwardian gardens were not connected to returned children, killed in the Great War, as Arthur Conan Doyle longed to believe – they were tricks, reproduced hauntings, 'uncanny effects of representation' (Botting 2014: 109) created by knowing children resentful of adult disenchantment. Bihet notes how the period's 'crisis of faith' was hijacked by spiritualists, and the Victorian flower fairy 'intersected' with 'attempts to find tangible proof of another realm' (154).

Alfred Tennyson, while not a believer in spiritualist sleight-of-hand, spent the entire Victorian reign searching for this same answer – what was there 'behind the veil' ([*In Memoriam*: LVI. 28] in Tennyson 2007)? In keeping with the century's emphasis on immediacy of image, his poetics of 'sensation' (although different from 'sensation fiction') created a thin line between experience of image and experience of the real. There is a dynamic connection between discourse, or text, and supposed 'real things', an 'ongoing flow of agency through which part of the world makes itself differently intelligible to another part of the world and through which causal structures are stabilized and destabilized' as Karen Barad writes in her exploration of material agency (2007: 135). The sensations produced, in all the texts discussed in this collection, were unsettling. Chapter 10 discusses how Tennyson's obviously Gothic and violent production *Maud* is acted out in her delightful 'garden of roses' ([*Maud*: XIV. I. 489] in Tennyson 2007); his famous neglected garden, that of Mariana in her 'moated grange' (['Mariana': 8] in Tennyson 2007) was to inspire innumerable garden-Gothic descriptions; in Dickens's *Great Expectations*, for example, and Swinburne's 'A Forsaken Garden'. Yet her vegetal submersion, although extreme, was reflected in Tennyson's own attempts to pierce the 'veil' of personal grief after the death of Arthur Hallam; in his childhood garden at Somersby, on the lawn, among trees that enable an empathetic encounter between material and immaterial nature.

That literary gardens should reflect, even cooperate with their human companions might not surprise us; where ecoGothic uncovers new ground, so to speak, is how these gardens and their material occupants, from tiny flowers to towering trees, birds, mammals and insects, in secluded shrubberies and ornamental lakes, work against their human interactors, as comprehensively illustrated in these chapters. Nonhumankind uses its own selfhood, its material ability to change and direct itself and those others with which or whom it comes into contact, in order to reorganise environments. This became despairingly obvious to Ruskin at Brantwood. Plants have an agency beyond human control; even the stones refused to stay where they were put. 'No amount of intellectual resourcefulness could elude the environmental forces determining the vitality of animate nature', comments Ikin (41), and this applies to every aspect of the gardens in these essays. Wilkie Collins's ingenious villains Count Fosco and Sir Percival Glyde, in Chapter 11, are unable to circumvent the resentful nature of Blackwater Park in *The Woman in White*, with its 'sullen' lake, 'characterised primarily by its gloom, its strangeness, and by a suffocating sense of enclosure' (Tait, Chapter 11: 188). Adrian Tait notes the classic Gothic reflection of feminine captivity here; there is almost a gendering of the garden space by which Marian is contained, and yet she also feels the landscape's own depression. Glyde's wish to drain the lake stems from his 'powerlessness to affect it' (188), and Blackwater Park 'dominates the text as a transgressive, even vengeful entity, abnormal by virtue of the way in which it deviates from the domesticated norm of "Nature"' (188). Yet, one thing this collection highlights is that normality is only in the eye of the controller; there is no human-rational normality in garden life, only normal for nature.

Crosby notes how ecocriticism is particularly suited to discussions of uncanny and liminal places because of its invitation to the reader to 'dwell within the landscape of a text, and to see that landscape as part of the natural and created world that is all, itself, within the text' (51). The material world is entangled in texts, themselves created out of matter, reoccurring palimpsests, as are gardens, haunted by so-called 'real' things as well as imaginary.

And so, finally, in an 'Afterword', Paul Evans describes his own encounters of and in the Wilderness Garden at Powis Castle, simultaneously enchanting and uneasy. Evans effectively coordinates the ecoGothic tendrils, bindweeds and rhizomes planted by each contributor in this collection in a personal meditation and elucidation of historical gardening, touching on each theme explored by the chapters, from entanglement to spectral, monstrous to violent, and beautiful to fatally attractive.

The 'Afterword' unites the uncanny aspects of human and nonhuman in gardens, taking us beyond Gothic – beyond gardens – even beyond landscape's temporality, as past events, or non-events, twist into the present, if it is the present, and encourage us not to fear immersion in the garden 'community' for which we have reciprocal responsibility. It is the garden that acts; the gardener (Evans himself) only facilitates, travelling hopefully, never arriving. Hardly surprising, then, other agents can easily hitch themselves to the wheelbarrow and lawnmower, more-than-human presences in this persistent absence of stability.

NOTE

1 Throughout, references to poetry are in square brackets.

WORKS CITED

Alexander, Catherine. 2002. 'The Garden as Occasional Domestic Space', *Signs*, 27. 3: 857–71

Barad, Karen. 2007. *Meeting the Universe Halfway: Quantum Physics and the Entanglement of Matter and Meaning* (Durham, NC: Duke University Press)

Bennett, Jane. 2014. 'Of Material Sympathies, Paracelsus, and Whitman', in *Material Ecocriticism*, ed. by Serenella Iovino and Serpil Oppermann (Bloomington: Indiana University Press), pp. 239–52

Bergthaller, Hannes, Rob Emmett, Adeline Johns-Putra, Agnes Kneitz, Susanna Lidström, Shane McCorristine, Isabel Pérez Ramos, Dana Phillips, Kate Rigby, Libby Robin. 2014. 'Mapping Common Ground: Ecocriticism, Environmental History, and the Environmental Humanities', *Environmental Humanities*, 5: 261–76

Botting, Fred. 2014. *Gothic*, 2nd edn (London: Routledge)

Chang, Elizabeth Hope. 2019. *Novel Cultivations: Plants in British Literature of the Global Nineteenth Century* (Charlottesville and London: University of Virginia Press)

Cooper, David E. 2005. 'Gardens, Art, Nature', in *Vista: The Culture and Politics of Gardens*, ed. by Tim Richardson and Noël Kingsbury (London: Frances Lincoln), pp. 5–12

Del Principe, David. 2014. 'The EcoGothic in the Long Nineteenth Century', *Gothic Studies*, 16. 1: 1–8

Derrida, Jacques. 2006. *Specters of Marx* (1994) (New York: Routledge)

Douglas, Mary. 1966. *Purity and Danger: An Analysis of Concepts of Pollution and Taboo* (London: Routledge and Kegan Paul)

Ebbatson, Roger. 2016. *Landscapes of Eternal Return: Tennyson to Hardy* (London: Palgrave Macmillan)

Estok, Simon. 2014. 'Painful Material Realities, Tragedy, Ecophobia', in *Material Ecocriticism*, ed. by Serenella Iovino and Serpil Oppermann (Bloomington: Indiana University Press), pp. 130–40

Freud, Sigmund. 1957. 'The "Uncanny"' (1919), in *Collected Works, Vol. 5*, trans. by Alix Strachey (London: Hogarth Press), pp. 1–21

Garis, Howard R. 2013. 'Professor Jonkin's Cannibal Plant' (1905), in *Flora Curiosa*, ed. by Chad Arment (Ohio: Coachwhip Publications), pp. 113–22

Heholt, Ruth. 2016. 'Introduction', in *Haunted Landscapes: Super-Nature and the Environment*, ed. by Ruth Heholt and Niamh Downing (London: Rowman and Littlefield), pp. 1–20

Hunt, John Dixon. 1992. *Gardens and the Picturesque: Studies in the History of Landscape Architecture* (Cambridge, MA: MIT Press)

Iovino, Serenella and Serpil Oppermann. 2014. 'Introduction', in *Material Ecocriticism*, ed. by Serenella Iovino and Serpil Oppermann (Bloomington: Indiana University Press), pp. 1–17

Kröger, Lisa. 2013. 'Panic, Paranoia and Pathos: Ecocriticism in the Eighteenth-Century Gothic Novel', in *Ecogothic*, ed. by Andrew Smith and William Hughes (Manchester: Manchester University Press), pp. 15–27

Luckhurst, Roger. 2002. 'The Contemporary London Gothic and the Limits of the "Spectral Turn"', *Textual Practice*, 16. 3: 527–46

Mathews, Freya. 2003. *For Love of Matter: A Contemporary Panpsychism* (Albany: SUNY Press)

Miller, T. S. 2012. 'Lives of the Monster Plants: The Revenge of the Vegetable in the Age of Animal Studies', *Journal of the Fantastic in the Arts*, 23. 3 (86): 460–79

Milton, John. 1998. *Paradise Lost* (1667), ed. by Alistair Fowler, 2nd edn (Harlow: Longman)

Richardson, Tim. 2005. 'Psychotopia', in *Vista: The Culture and Politics of Gardens*, ed. by Tim Richardson and Noël Kingsbury (London: Frances Lincoln), pp. 131–60

Royle, Nicholas. 2003. *The Uncanny* (Manchester: Manchester University Press)

Saguaro, Shelley. 2006. *Garden Plots: The Politics and Poetics of Gardens* (Aldershot: Ashgate)

Smith, Andrew and William Hughes. 2013. 'Introduction', *Ecogothic* (Manchester: Manchester University Press), pp. 1–14

Stewart, Kathleen. 2015. 'Preface', in *Affective Landscapes in Literature, Art and Everyday Life: Memory, Place and the Senses*, ed. by Christine Berberich, Neil Campbell and Robert Hudson (Farnham: Ashgate), pp. xv–xvii

Stibbe, Arran, 2014. *Ecolinguistics: Language, Ecology and the Stories we Live By* (Abingdon: Routledge)

Tennyson, Alfred. 2007. *Tennyson: A Selected Edition*, ed. by Christopher Ricks, rev. edn (Harlow: Longman)

Townshend, Dale. 2014. 'Ruins, Romance and the Rise of Gothic Tourism: The Case of Netley Abbey, 1750–1830', *Journal for Eighteenth-Century Studies*, 37. 3: 377–94

Waters, Michael. 1988. *The Garden in Victorian Literature* (Aldershot: Scolar Press)

Wells, H. G. 2013. 'The Flowering of the Strange Orchid' (1894), in *Flora Curiosa*, ed. by Chad Arment (Ohio: Coachwhip Publications), pp. 63–71

Wheeler, Wendy. 2016. *Expecting the Earth: Life, Culture, Biosemiotics* (London: Lawrence and Wishart)

Wolfreys, Julian. 2002. *Victorian Hauntings: Spectrality, Gothic, the Uncanny and Literature* (Basingstoke: Palgrave)

1

Deadly gardens: The 'Gothic green' in Goethe and Eichendorff

Heather I. Sullivan

Idyllic gardens so lush and blooming as to seem almost mystical take on an ominously Gothic tone when their grounds or plant life are revealed to have startling power over the human beings who enter their space or alter their layout. In this manner, Joseph von Eichendorff's 1819 romantic fairy tale, *The Marble Statue*, with its enchanted yet threatening garden of Venus, and Johann Wolfgang Goethe's famously enigmatic novel from 1809, *Elective Affinities*, with its transformation of the Baron's lands into a vast English garden that results in four deaths, can readily be studied with an ecoGothic approach. While both the fairy tale and the novel depict landscapes that appear at first encounter merely as the green backdrop for indulgent party scenes, the gardens in these two texts turn out to be associated with the re-emergence of deadly forces that escape human control.

While Allan Lloyd Smith explains that the Gothic 'is about the *return* of the past, of the repressed and denied, the buried secret that subverts and corrodes the present' (2004: 1), Elizabeth Parker defines the ecoGothic as 'Gothic stories in which the natural environment, or the elements within it, are eerily ambient and arouse our anxieties' and that reveal 'the monstrous in nature' (2016: 218). Furthermore, Andrew Smith and William Hughes note that such return of the repressed and arousal of anxieties in what should be familiar grounds means that the ecoGothic typically grapples with a 'crisis of representation' where 'the environment is established as a semiotic problem' (2013: loc. 183). Indeed, since lovely pastoral settings embodying a serene space of retreat in many nature poems, nineteenth-century novels and utopian dreams generally provide such soothing calm that Robert Pogue Harrison describes the garden as a near-universal site of 'human happiness' (2008: 1), then the portrayal of gardens as a site with an unexpected and thus terrifying agency creates an inevitable crisis

1 'The North Front of Stowe in 1750', Stowe House, Buckinghamshire. Engraving, George Bickham (1684–1758)

of representation. The characters and readers alike are confronted with the unsettling alteration of a supposedly aesthetic and settled site into a place of horror, as well as the question of what has been repressed and is now 'returning' with sway over our lives. Such a return of the repressed exceeding human directive is especially harrowing in a garden of seemingly domesticated plants that act as the very symbol for lives dictated by human power. As Dawn Keetley and Angela Tenga make evident in their volume, *Plant Horror: Approaches to the Monstrous Vegetal in Fiction and Film* (2016), when plants run amok, it is horrifying. In light of such plant/garden horror, I propose in this chapter a more specific sub-category of the ecoGothic, the 'Gothic green', in which the human is, in some way, subsumed by vegetal forces.

Viewing gardens as scenes of the Gothic green should not surprise since such aesthetic horticultural sites always contain both material and mythological power. On the one hand, gardens represent the visible power of the landed aristocracy (or the state) to create large-scale aesthetic spaces for pleasure while also functioning as physical support of daily food in the widespread kitchen gardens. And on the other hand, all gardens retain a mythological edge related to the supernatural sites such as the Garden of Eden and others. Gardens thus connote potentially both the materiality supporting our existence and the ethereal powers of destiny not entirely in our hands, and are hence readily integrated into the ecoGothic, as Dawn Keetley and Matthew Wynn Sivils describe it.

They compare how the Gothic grapples with forms of 'entrapment', whereas the ecoGothic:

> not only takes up ... questions about our very being (such as who we are) but also more particular questions of determinism and freedom, especially as these questions play out through a long history and on the limit edges of what we think we know about the human – and what shapes or 'possesses' the human. (Keetley and Sivils 2018: 4)

Hence, if the traditional Gothic typically has gloomy castles and landscapes associated with a dark, possibly *supernatural* and definitely *historical* destiny that resituates the human and from which we cannot escape, the ecoGothic tends, in contrast, to trap human beings in uncertain status dominated by long-term *natural* and *physical* forces revealed not only in dramatic storms, flooding and our bodily natures but also in daily encounters such as the never-ending battle against weeds when gardening. Richard Mabey's *Weeds: In Defense of Nature's Most Unloved Plants* makes the case that weeds, as we arbitrarily define them according to our own whims and as the dark side of our *own* 10,000-year history of agri*culture*, will always haunt us with their wild refusal to 'play by our rules' (2010: 20). The very nature of the garden demands that some plants belong, whereas others do not and are hence 'weeds', regardless of their relevance otherwise.

The ecoGothic shows how the presumably clear categories dividing the human and nonhuman are, in fact, artificial and shifting (as with the definition of weeds), thereby undermining our presumed status as fully independent, self-determining beings able to control the natural world from the outside. Consequently, ecoGothic texts tend to grapple with the problem of representing the (re-)integration of the human into the so-called 'laws of nature'. When such 'laws' pertain especially to the vegetal realm, we speak of the Gothic green that constantly eludes our control. Indeed, as cultivated settings, gardens make most visible both the active work of humans in shaping plant life and the startling refusal of nonhuman life to conform to our demands. In this way, gardens can be more Gothic than other more expectedly uncanny landscapes such as a dark swamp or the standard 'wildness' of a vast forest, the supposed antithesis of culture as per Robert Pogue Harrison's formulation in *Forests: The Shadow of Civilization* (1992). The Gothic green seeks to describe and represent how human bodily relationships to the nonhuman vegetal function, especially in gardens. Human beings certainly may seem to dominate such cultivated sites, yet perceiving that we are actually *situated within* the power of green materiality can awaken a sense of ecoGothic doom.

Exemplifying ecoGothic 'fears of more disturbing and unsettling aspects of our interactions with nonhuman ecologies' (Keetley and Sivils 2018: 1) and, in particular, of the vegetal exuberance of the Gothic green, the narratives from

Eichendorff and Goethe uncomfortably re-place the fate of human beings into natural processes and botanical energies beyond human control. Eichendorff's *Marble Statue* features deadly scenes of seduction in the garden when the dangerously alluring and (in his Catholic view) demonic Venus emerges, seeking to lure Florio into a world of the horrifyingly endless cycle of botanic nature that represents the earthly body. Only a properly chaste song wafting over from the poet Fortunato saves Florio, bringing him back into homosocial appreciation and out of the horrifically botanical exuberance of fertile 'feminine' nature that eternally (or at least every spring) threatens to return the human soul to ancient cycles of materiality. The expansive gardens in Goethe's *Elective Affinities*, on the other hand, seem to offer fitting aesthetic and land-shaping activity for otherwise under-tasked aristocrats. Charlotte and Edward's plan to transform his expansive grounds into an English garden mark their late marriage as an exercise in self-determination and the active shaping of their material surroundings; they also mirror Goethe's own landscaping tasks at his house at Frauenplan, Weimar. The novel's famous play with the question of inevitable chemical attractions and repulsions giving the book its title of 'elective affinities' already suggests that the main characters will enter a test-tube of experimental mixings beyond conscious choice (the elective is determined by physical laws, not human whim, or so it seems). Hence it is not so surprising when these very gardens dominating the aristocrats' activities stage not control but rather a lack of control over unexpected attractions as 'natural forces' that eventually lead to four deaths. The gardens are not just idyllic imaginaries, but part of the very materiality essential to the Gothic green and material ecocriticism alike. In both Goethe and Eichendorff, these green sites set the stage for what appear to be humanly determined acts but that are tinged by the mysterious physicality and power befitting the ecoGothic.

In Eichendorff's *Marble Statue*, a palace garden is the dangerous site of Venus's threatening re-emergence every spring as an embodiment of nature's lush and cyclical powers that seek to seduce young naive males. Giving in to the seduction of the Venus garden means losing one's 'Christian' path and falling into nocturnal wanderings among ruins that are the entrance drug for eternal loss of one's soul. Venus's repetitive cyclical return every spring takes on a nightmarish tinge when understood through the lens of 'plant horror' as described by Keetley (2016). Keetley describes the wildly living power of plant life as its most frightening aspect: 'At its most basic, plant horror marks humans' dread of the "wildness" of vegetal nature – its untameability, its pointlessness, its uncontrollable growth' (1). She adds: 'Plant growth always breaks what seeks to contain it, transgressing borders meant to confine and define' (13). Like the untameable plants, Venus and her garden wildly exceed almost any boundaries, threatening to transgress moral sensibilities and vegetal delimitations. Yet it is not just Venus who has botanical associations in Eichendorff's fairy tale; after all, the protagonist's name, Florio, itself suggests the floral. He must experience and overcome his own flowery nature.

One night while visiting Lucca, young Florio cannot sleep and so wanders through the moonlit grounds until he encounters the titular marble statue of Venus in a little lake. Florio's gaze animates Venus's shapely figure, and she seems to gain life and stare back at him until bright moonlight suddenly exposes her cold stone eyes, evoking the Gothic horror of a ghost: 'the statue of Venus, fearfully white and motionless, stared at him from the marble sockets of its eyes, out of the infinite stillness, almost like a phantom' (Eichendorff 1983: 144). Overcome by horror, Florio rushes back to the hotel, yet he is inspired to seek her again the next day. Venus's frightening attributes are clearly Gothic, but we immediately thereafter learn that they are, even more so, Gothic green in tone. Indeed, the garden is her realm and it is a zone of portentous materiality that Florio finally discovers after a long walk in the heat of the day. He eventually encounters a shady entrance to a hidden garden with tall birches, 'golden birds', 'great strange flowers' and innumerable fountains that 'splashed monotonously in the great solitude' behind which was the 'shimmer of a splendid palace with tall, slender columns. No human being was in sight anywhere; deep silence reigned all around' (147). Florio senses the languid danger of this garden: 'he had a strange sensation, as if everything had long been submerged and the flowing stream of time were passing over him with its clear and gentle waves, and the garden were lying deep beneath, bound by a magic spell' (147). In the distance, he sees a mysterious woman (Venus) amid the wildly colourful flowers, her lovely body in a blue dress, singing provocatively about how spring has woken her again. Florio loses sight of her but finds instead her helper, Donati, sleeping as if dead among the inevitably Gothic ruins. Deathly pale, Donati is startled upon waking and cries out, 'How … did you get into this garden?' (149). It is the garden of Venus who cycles awake with each spring; in other words, Eichendorff connects the seasonal flourishing of the botanical to ancient mythological powers. Indeed, Venus's garden draws Florio into her magnificent realm because of its florid, fleshy materiality which includes her body that was stone, but is now reanimating.

The Marble Statue establishes Florio's choice of mates: either the socially determined and chaste Bianca who is described as a young girl or an androgynous figure, or the florid, hyper-feminine Venus who exists in her alluring garden. In the grand Venus finale, it seems that Florio does not so much make a choice but rather is saved by spiritual and poetic intervention. Thus, Florio and Donati return to the garden at the end of the tale: 'They had not ridden far when they saw the palace rising above them, serene in the splendour of its columns, surrounded by the beautiful garden as if by a happy garland of flowers' (160). Venus, dressed in sky-blue, is adorned with roses, herself a garden of risk. All around her, numerous young women hold up a mirror so that she can consider her own beauty while they sing like nightingales in an overly determined poetic vision of lustful materiality, female self-assertion and floral seduction. As Venus's power expands, her pagan garden spirits reawaken, to walk among the alluring 'fields of blossoms', and beautiful girls emerge 'from the flowers as if waking from midday dreams' (161). The powerfully dangerous garden delights coming out of the blossoms manifest themselves with ecoGothic materiality. Yet, the Gothic aspects truly take form when Florio follows Venus into her palace for the final seduction. Eichendorff does not leave Florio to his fate, nor does he allow his protagonist to make his own decision about which female is the correct one, but rather interrupts the seduction with the suggestively divine intervention of lightning that distracts the young man and brings him to the window, where he is fortunate enough to experience the second form of intervention, the poetic and piously Christian tune sung by the poet Fortunato. The music awakens Florio to the dangerous situation he has entered. Startled, he cries out a prayer and becomes aware of the palace's ecoGothic terrors: he spots weeds growing out of the windowsill where a snake slithers by. With the music washing over him, Florio comes fully to his senses, causing Venus to turn slowly back to stone. Her power, however, has not fully disappeared; instead we witness a final surge of disturbing materiality as the palace's wall tapestries begin moving and the statues come to life: 'before long all the statues were rising in fearful silence from their pedestals' (164). The song rises, Florio panics, and Venus slowly petrifies, but she retains enough strength for one final attack of actual vegetal violence that marks *The Marble Statue* as a text of the Gothic green. Florio is overcome with 'deathly horror. For the tall flowers in their containers began to writhe in unison, terrifyingly, like color-flecked snakes coiling to spring' (164). Panicked, Florio escapes, looking back to see that the palace is gone and only the original quiet pond with its marble statue of Venus remain. Rather than choosing to abandon Venus's luscious green allure, Florio has been saved by external forces.

Having survived his deadly dabbling with Venus's Gothic green garden with a little help from friends (and heavenly lightning), Florio decides to leave Lucca and its frightening botanical threats. He is accompanied by Fortunato, who sings moral lessons, and by Bianca dressed as a boy, though it takes Florio a while to recognise her and so allow the tale to shift into a socially acceptable marriage plot and away from the dangerous femininity associated with the vegetal. Rendered distant and with diminished power, we see at the end only a far-away ruin overcome by wild plants, 'the scattered remains of old crumbling walls, beautiful columns, half sunken in the ground, and artfully hewn blocks of stone, all overgrown with a rankly blooming wilderness of green intertwining hedges, vines and tall weeds' (166). Fortunato reiterates the danger twice, once in verse and once in prose, in case we the readers and Florio still fail to grasp the necessary trajectory away from Venus: 'the beautiful pagan goddess never found peace. Every spring, again and again, the memories of earthly pleasure call her from the awful silence of the grave, to rise up into the green solitude of her ruined dwelling and to practice, with devilish deception, her old art of seduction' (168–9). And the doom she brings is not all green material pleasure since the 'young and carefree spirits who then [captured in her green trap], departed from this life, yet not admitted into the peace of the dead, wander about between wild pleasures and terrible repentance, lost in body and soul, their very beings consumed in the most horrible delusions' (169). The return of ancient vegetal powers in feminine materiality is, apparently, a never-ending threat.

Of course, the German romantic fairy tales are often filled with such nightmares in which young men are lured into dark promises of material pleasures in mountains, caves, mines and gardens; such lost spirits returning from the past share much with Gothic horror. For Eichendorff, a poet can, however, 'exorcise and tame the wild earth spirits' (169). Lucky Florio; he is saved by his handsome male poetic rescuer who, in his final songs, contrasts heavenly Mother Mary with babe in arms to the dangerous and earthly pleasures of Venus. Fortunato's song, in fact, is the actual, and perhaps only, force capable of transforming Venus's dark powers into lyrical representations. And indeed, Florio finally declares himself saved precisely by bursting into song, which denotes that he is learning to transform Venus's vegetative powers into verse in an effort to gain control over his own flowery impulses and name. He learns to tame the Gothic green by *representing* it in verse. The gardens in Eichendorff's *Marble Statue* inspire poetry but must also be contained by it lest their powers overwhelm the susceptible. Seen in terms of the green Gothic, the botanical Venus reveals deep unease in our human responses to the nonhuman forces such as seasonal growth and material, bodily and vegetal exuberance that exceed our control and whose realm we also inhabit. Of course, for Eichendorff, no good poet can go *without* experiencing such dangerously enchanting powers of the world. One must, apparently, dabble in these transgressive energies in order to be able to tap into their poetic potential. Representation is not just challenged but demanded by the unsettling of human/natural delineations. And these powers will return next spring, if not before (and likely in new forms in the Anthropocene's obscene ecoGothic).

Unlike Eichendorff's gardens that function as a site of the deadly pagan goddess's recurring reawakening, gardens in Goethe's *Elective Affinities* function instead as the site for creatively bored aristocrats to set the stage for their own death, to fall prey to deterministic natural forces of attraction, and to end up in a harrowing fate not as poets who *represent* but as *representations* themselves (in, for example, the various *tableaux vivants* staged in the novel). Famous for its garden themes, this novel is also full of death, horror (of social restrictions, at least) and convoluted questions of the representability of nature, life, death and chemical attraction when all of these are in flux. As such, *Elective Affinities* works well for a study of the Gothic green, as well as of the ecoGothic more broadly, since gardening drives the action into death.

In the scholarship broadly, however, there is much more attention given to the questions of marriage, morals, art and to the English-garden fetish in early nineteenth-century German-speaking areas, than to death, as Elisabeth Herrmann seeks to correct with her 1998 book entirely dedicated to the 'problem of death' in Goethe's novel. Herrmann and Gabrielle Bersier (1997) provide broad summaries of the vast array of scholarship on *Elective Affinities*; Herrmann notes that the most typical interpretations tend towards two contrasting directions: 'on the one side, the meaning of fate, nature's magic, myth, and the supernatural are emphasised as powers in their own right that dominate human beings who are necessarily and inescapably under their sway. On the other side, is the focus on the rationality and calculations of the novel', which builds on Goethe's ideas of science, moralistic problems, the historical circumstances, etc. (Herrmann 1998: 13–14, translation mine). In other words, both directions attend to challenging questions of fate and self-determination. I suggest building on Bersier's study of death in *Elective Affinities* while highlighting the novel's aspects relevant for the ecoGothic, such as the influence of 'fate' that seems to be more natural – and physical – than supernatural in form. Unlike Eichendorff, however, there is no poet who learns to *represent* in Goethe's novel but rather alarming examples of the human body itself becoming a material site of representational conflict influenced by ominously naturalistic forces.

This enigmatic novel portrays dramatic human efforts to exert control, specifically over the materiality of landscapes as the characters shape their gardens and grounds, or over the body, as when Ottilie pursues total self-renunciation to the point of anorexic starvation. Otherwise, control seems very slippery, as the chemical reference in the title indicates, so that strong attractions – like chemical bonds – are quickly formed without free will when the right components, or rather people, are brought together. Unlike the chemicals that change partners and take on new forms, the people in Goethe's *Elective Affinities* are brought into new connections that begin to form but are finally torn asunder by social restrictions, leaving their unfulfilled desires and feelings of guilt and loss to implode. This devastation is not described in the Captain's famous summary of 'elective affinities' taking A + B and adding C + D to make AC and BD. The vaguely threatening nonhuman powers typical of the ecoGothic thus dominate this novel, questioning the possibility of – and the representation of – human self-determination and (lack of) power over landscapes, relationships and unstable cultural situations (the novel takes place during the radical changes of the Napoleonic wars, as demonstrated by Nicholas Boyle (2015)). If Eichendorff's fairy tale enacts the (attempted) *containment* of spring's powerful vegetative and Gothic excesses through poetic representation, then Goethe's novel

portrays an unravelling of containment and an explosion of uncanny representations that take on an (ecoGothic) life of their own. Hence, much of the novels'
conversations centre around Gothic questions such as how to grapple with the
deterministic fate of 'chemical' attractions and how to represent the dead,
especially when their graves are moved as part of the realignment of the garden
landscapes.

Elective Affinities begins with a pastoral scene, nicely setting the stage for a
Gothic green reading in which gardens reign and individual fates are influenced
by external forces. The wealthy Baron Edward and his wife have married late
in life after having been separated by parents who sought wealth instead of
love for their children. After they both lost their first spouses, the two finally
marry and are now settling into their new life on Edward's vast estates which
they are transforming, English-garden style. Since Edward grafts new branches
onto young fruit trees in the novel's first line, we see immediately that gardening
is the novel's frame and that Edward likes to experiment with hybrid forms
(with ominous implications for their marriage). In terms of the ecoGothic, it
is also relevant that Edward noticeably avoids the churchyard when he is called
to meet his wife on the hill above: 'He avoided the path that led, through the
churchyard, fairly directly to the cliff, and went instead by the other one, which
wound its way gently up through some charming shrubbery' (Goethe 1988: 93).
This choice appears to be a simple matter of selecting this or that path to climb
up the hill, but it actually foreshadows a sense of discomfort that later reappears
with the disturbances of the graveyard during the wild landscaping efforts and,
ultimately, when it becomes his own resting spot after death.

Viewing their vast green lands with pleasure, Edward asks Charlotte to allow
him to invite his dear old friend, the Captain, to come and live with them even
though they are newlyweds. They debate this invitation as they tour Charlotte's
landscaping, new little paths and the little moss hut (of which Goethe provides
extensive descriptions and which all play significant roles in determining their
marital – and material – fates in the novel). The alteration of the physical
grounds reshapes not just the land–human interactions but also the human–
human relationships. Charlotte gives in to Edward's wish, allowing him to invite
the Captain to live with them, and then Edward, in turn, concedes to have
Charlotte ask her niece Ottilie to join them as well. And, so it begins: the
attractions fatefully take form, fatalistically marked by an odd resonance in the
characters' names: the Captain is Otto, as is Edward, though he adopted his
middle name so as not to confuse everyone; hence, Otto, Otto, CharlOTTE
and OTTilie all come together; and, later, Edward's and Charlotte's son is also
named Otto. Such inexplicable doublings – quadrupled plus one more – support
a reading of the novel with an eye for eerie uncanny aspects.

For the Gothic green, one cannot overlook Ottilie's clear association with
both death late in the novel, and with plants and the gardens from the beginning.

The narrator states: 'As the plants began to root and sprout more and more, Ottilie felt herself increasingly bound to the gardens' (218). She is often described with botanical terms, such as blossoming, and she spends much time working with the plants. With the arrival of spring,

> [Ottilie] found the fruit of her efforts in the garden; everything sprouted, leaved and blossomed at once; many plants that had been started in greenhouses and frames were now moved out into the open, and everything that needed to be taken care of was not just a labour of hope as before, but was now a pleasure and delight. (Goethe 1988: 217)

This connection between Ottilie and botany has been duly noted and is the focus in a recent essay of much insight relating her to eighteenth-century botany by Cornelia Zumbusch, who writes: 'Ottilie is retrospectively associated not just with the transplantations Eduard carries out in the opening scene but also with his personal history and the botanical events preceding the novel's plot' (2017: 8). That is, Ottilie's birthday coincides with the date that Edward transplanted the poplar trees on his grounds and under which he and Ottilie later sit together celebrating their forbidden love. With this botanical connection, Ottilie shares with Eichendorff's Venus a textual, and apparently physical, link to plants. Yet, whereas Venus lures men into inescapably material and pagan cycles of explosive life, Ottilie's innocent, yet 'chemical', attraction is like that of a lovely tree drawing you into its shade – that is, if a tree could decide to stop its intake of nutrients and water so as to starve. Her demise appears as a slide into aesthetic representability of death in a form that looks like life (as is common in fairy tales like 'Snow White' where the protagonist remains beautifully visible in her coffin): 'Ottilie's continuing beautiful state, more sleep- than death-like, attracted many visitors' (Goethe 1988: 261). Edward, in despair, soon follows Ottilie to the grave. Goethe closes the novel with fairy-tale motifs and an unsettling emphasis on the two near-lovers as *representations* since they 'rest side by side. Peace hovers above their resting place, smiling angels in *their likeness* look down on them from the vault' (262, emphasis added).

Life-in-death representations, freshly altered gardens, hybrid forms (of love and vegetation) and reorganised churchyard graves fill this Gothic-toned novel in which the many luxuriant sites and happy blooms only seem calmly green in contrast to the unsettled emotions of all the Ott/o/e/ie figures. The gardens in *Elective Affinities* are more than the site of budding romance; they are also the site of drowning death(s) as well as a physical space to be measured and altered with scientific seriousness. From the outset, when the Captain arrives, eschewing mere romantic reshaping of the grounds, he insists instead on proper measurements and large-scale gardening changes, meaning that we cannot assume some kind of simplistic naturalistic glory in their landscaping plans. Things go well after Charlotte finally accepts the Captain's lead, and so he takes over with many grandiose and scientific plans which include expanding and reshaping three small ponds back into a large lake. Such efforts are so expensive that they greatly exceed their budget, which moves the conversation from aesthetics to economics, as Astrida Tantillo notes (1994). The alteration of the estate mirrors both Goethe's own work in his Weimar garden and indicate that the literal grounds (economic, political, social and natural) of these people are shifting. And, indeed, Charlotte begins to enjoy the Captain very much as they work closely together on the transformation of the gardens, and her feelings towards him grow.

Once Ottilie joins them, the novel's two new love stories develop rapidly: Edward falls for the very young Ottilie, and Charlotte comes to love the Captain, just as we knew they would from the title's implications for inevitable chemical attractions. When Edward suggests a divorce to be followed by two happy new weddings, Charlotte adamantly rejects this option. The men despair; the Captain departs and Edward runs off to war, but not before sleeping once with his wife, leading to a pregnancy. During this one-night encounter, Edward thinks only of Ottilie and Charlotte only of the Captain, which produces an uncanny resemblance between the baby Otto and the two spurned lovers: he has Ottilie's eyes and the Captain's facial features. This uncanny element of inexplicable resemblance fits the pseudo-scientific themes of chemical attractions and repulsions, but also an inevitable sense of the not-quite natural fate that will befall them all. Goethe's text, with its pseudo-science-based Gothic contrasts therefore with Eichendorff's primarily Catholic-Gothic overtones.

Disaster strikes in Goethe's novel, just when it seems as if 'fate' is leading them all to new happiness. Edward survives the war and then convinces the Captain to return home with him and to try again to celebrate the divorce/ double marriage. Joyfully, Edward finds Ottilie with baby Otto sitting under the fateful poplars beside the newly created lake. The poplars and the lake are physical manifestations of the gardening work undertaken by the friends, and these altered landscape features now seal the fate of the characters – if only they had left the little ponds instead of re-creating the geologically formed lake! Sitting by the water, Edward re-declares his undying love for Ottilie and convinces her that they can talk Charlotte into marrying the Captain. Since night has fallen, Ottilie unfortunately risks taking baby Otto in the boat so as to reach the castle sooner. Rushing, she accidently drops him in the water. In contrast to the rescues of the two previous drowning victims depicted in the novel, one during Ottilie's birthday party, and one in the inserted dramatic novella about young neighbourly love, baby Otto cannot be saved. At the very moment of a possibly happy love story, Otto's death dictates everyone else's future: Ottilie refuses to speak or eat any more and starves herself to death; Charlotte will neither accept nor decline the Captain's marriage offer; and Edward soon dies of grief after Ottilie's death since he, too, stops eating and drinking. There was also a previous death associated with baby Otto: at his baptism, the old pastor collapses and dies. Deadly love and landscaping; it is an odd fate. Indeed, fate takes various forms in *Elective Affinities*. Ottilie, for example, plans her death while speaking specifically of 'fate': "'Fate has not been kind to me," replied Ottilie, "and those who love me can expect to fare no better"' (Goethe 1988: 247). And, with Gothic emphasis on a 'demonic power', she claims, '[I] have strayed from my path, and I must find my way back again. A hostile and demonic power that has taken hold of me seems to prevent me from doing so, even if I had been able to find peace with myself once more' (253). From plant cultivation to self-induced death, that is Ottilie's Gothic green trajectory.

Charlotte hoped that Edward and Ottilie might overcome the tragic loss of Otto and finally come together even though she sees all of their fates as being connected to the gardens and the artificial lake in which Otto drowned:

> But Ottilie saw things differently ... she had forgiven herself in her heart of hearts under the sole condition of total renunciation, and this condition was binding for all time. Things went on in this way, and Charlotte came to realise how much the house and gardens, the lakes, cliffs and trees only served to renew their sense of tragedy daily. (Goethe 1988: 245)

As Seth Peabody describes it, Goethe critiques with his literary drownings 'a particular way of engaging with the environment, one based on the assertion of control with the oversight that would come from true responsibility' (2018: 227). Furthermore, Peabody writes, 'In Goethe's *Wahlverwandtschaften* [*Elective Affinities*], humans' troubled attempts to control the environment result in an *Umwelt* [environment] that can be best described not through the physical spaces it embodies, but through the unease it engenders' (228). I concur with Peabody's focus on the unease engendered by the gardens and the failed human efforts at control, and add to it a material-ecocritical emphasis on the active, even agentic, vegetal forces in the gardens that impact the fate of the people. The issue is not just that human actions matter, but also, with ecoGothic tones, the active nonhuman powers, including the 'elective affinities' of attractions as well as the transplanted poplars and altered lake.

These fateful deaths are not the only uncanny, Gothic, aspects to Goethe's *Elective Affinities*; I note here several others that feature strange materiality with more specifically Gothic green components integrated with gardening. First, the architect and Charlotte decide to redesign the chapel's landscaping, which involves moving a number of gravestones away from the actual graves, much to the dismay of various relatives who lose the connection to the remains of their loved ones. This situation leads to strange discussions about whether it is important at all to represent the dead with headstones physically connected to the actual location of the remains. Charlotte argues that: 'This matter is not

2 'Visitor to a Moonlit Churchyard' (1790). Oil on canvas, Philip James de
Loutherbourg (1740–1812)

so significant' (Goethe 1988: 177), and she casually offers to pay restitution to
the families who gave money to the church for their gravestones. The architect
agrees with her, noting that 'we should not give up their memory, merely their
actual resting place [with the altered churchyard]' (177). These two accept this
somewhat problematic, one might even say sacrilegious, separation based on

their landscaping desires and then shift the conversation to the question of why the representations made to preserve the memory of the deceased are always the same; Charlotte demands to know: 'why they can never get away from the form of small obelisks, broken columns or funeral urns' (177–8). In other words, they embrace covering the physical graves with new flowerbeds or lawns while moving the gravestones elsewhere, debating only what the connection between body and image should be when separated spatially. In such ecoGothic moments, materiality reigns but its (dis)connection to representations has eerie connotations. In contrast to Eichendorff, Goethe's representations (gravestones, the *tableaux vivants*, and Ottilie's beautiful corpse) do not *contain* the unsettling power of ecological forces but rather *release* them, further destabilising the human–material interactions.

In sum, the Gothic green aspects of Goethe's text include the four deaths, the transplanted trees coinciding with Ottilie's birth, and the displaced graves producing debates about how to represent the dead when the bodies are separated from their gravestones by new elements of the gardens. *Elective Affinities* resonates with destabilised grounds and social settings in the tumultuous time of emerging capitalism, the Napoleonic wars and the changing 'attitudes towards love, passion, marriage, and divorce' that are at the 'centre of the novel', according to Marlis Mehra's discussion of gardening in the text (1981: 253), and also the uncertainty regarding human and nonhuman interconnections in the impending era of modern science. Simultaneously scientific and absurdly mystical, Goethe's novel leaves open the question of fate or self-determination even while blatantly connecting his characters' outcomes to their actions with the gardens. Human beings are (re-)integrated into natural forces, as Jost Hermand says of Goethe generally: 'Goethe was in contrast one of the few in this time who sought to resist the split between nature in the scientific or Christian sense, and [who] created an image of the world that had at its base the principle of a sensible integration of the human being into nature' (1991: 41, translation mine). The ecoGothic aspects of the novel appear in this uncomfortable zone of indeterminate agency such that what is controlling whom and what dictates 'fate' is vaguely and disturbingly unclear. Representations seem to escape containment and take on a life – or death – of their own. Finally, the text's ecoGothic association of fate and materiality take on more specifically Gothic green attributes since the deadly gardens dominate.

With its glorious yet death-producing gardens that embody the combined effects of human and nonhuman actions, Goethe's *Elective Affinities* unsettles the notions of fate and self-determination. Instead of simple choices, his characters grapple desperately with such forces as chemical attractions, emotional attachments (socially appropriate and otherwise), displaced graves, political and bodily destabilisation and, ultimately, the botanical influences typical of the Gothic green. Similarly, Eichendorff's *Marble Statue* appears to claim poetic victory and thus control over Venus's vegetal power emerging in her garden, despite the fact that spring's flowery vibrancy, whether perceived as life-giving or threateningly physical, shall always return and dominate as long as life continues (we must hope). By emphasising the uncanny qualities of human–botanical–land relationships in gardens, Goethe and Eichendorff provide exemplary texts for the Gothic green study of human immersion in the broader ecological energies of our world that all too often escape our representational containment but that finally, however much we resist, contain us.

WORKS CITED

Bersier, Gabrielle. 1997. *Goethes Rätselparodie der Romantik: Eine neue Leseart der* Wahlverwandtschaften (Tübingen: Max Niemeyer)

Boyle, Nicholas. 2015. 'The Composition of *Die Wahlverwandtschaften*', *Publications of the English Goethe Society*, 84. 2: 93–137

Eichendorff, Joseph Freiherr von. 1983. *The Marble Statue*, in *German Literary Fairy Tales*, ed. by Frank G. Ryder and Robert M. Browning (New York: Continuum), pp. 133–71

Goethe, Johann Wolfgang von. 1988. *Elective Affinities*, in *The Sorrows of Young Werther. Elective Affinities, Novella*, trans. by Victor Lange and Judith Ryan, ed. by David E. Wellbery (New York: Suhrkamp), pp. 89–262

Harrison, Robert Pogue. 1992. *Forests: The Shadow of Civilization* (Chicago: University of Chicago Press)

Harrison, Robert Pogue. 2008. *Gardens: An Essay on the Human Condition* (Chicago: University of Chicago Press)

Hermand, Jost. 1991. *Im Wettlauf der Zeit: Anstöße zu einer ökologiebewußten Ästhetik* (Berlin: Sigma Bohn)

Herrmann, Elisabeth. 1998. *Die Todesproblematik in Goethes Roman* Die Wahlverwandtschaften (Berlin: Erich Schmidt)

Keetley, Dawn. 2016. 'Introduction: Six Theses on Plant Horror; or, Why are Plants Horrifying?', in *Plant Horror: Approaches to the Monstrous Vegetal in Fiction and Film*, ed. by Dawn Keetley and Angela Tenga (London: Palgrave Macmillan), pp. 1–30

Keetley, Dawn and Matthew Wynn Sivils. 2018. 'Introduction: Approaches to the Ecogothic', in *Ecogothic in Nineteenth-Century American Literature*, ed. by Dawn Keetley and Matthew Wynn Sivils (New York: Routledge), pp. 1–20

Mabey, Richard. 2010. *Weeds: In Defense of Nature's Most Unloved Plants* (Sydney, Australia: HarperCollins)

Mehra, Marlis. 1981. 'The Art of Landscape Gardening in Goethe's Novel *Die Wahlverwandtschaften*', *Studies in Eighteenth-Century Culture*, 10: 239–59

Parker, Elizabeth. 2016. '"Just a Piece of Wood": Jan Svankmajer's *Otesánek and the EcoGothic*', in *Plant Horror: Approaches to the Monstrous Vegetal in Fiction and Film*, ed. by Dawn Keetley and Angela Tenga (London: Palgrave Macmillan), pp. 215–25.

Peabody, Seth. 2018. 'Goethe and (Um)Weltliteratur: Environment and Power in Goethe's Literary Worlds', *Seminar*, 54. 2: 215–30

Smith, Allan Lloyd. 2004. *American Gothic Fiction: An Introduction* (New York: Continuum)

Smith, Andrew and William Hughes. 2013. 'Introduction: Defining the EcoGothic', in *Ecogothic*, ed. by Andrew Smith and William Hughes (Manchester: Manchester University Press, Kindle edition), locs 147–420.

Tantillo, Astrida Orle. 1994. 'Deficit Spending and Fiscal Restraint: Balancing the Budget in *Die Wahlverwandtschaften*', *Goethe Yearbook*, 7: 40–59

Zumbusch, Cornelia. 2017. 'The Metamorphoses of Ottilie: Goethe's *Wahlverwandtschaften* and the Botany of the Eighteenth Century', *European Romantic Review*, 28. 1: 7–20

2

'Diabolic clouds over everything': An ecoGothic reading of John Ruskin's garden at Brantwood

Caroline Ikin

John Ruskin's vision of the plague cloud – the 'Diabolic clouds over everything' recorded in his diary in 1879 (Evans and Whitehouse 1959: 979) – is a fitting metaphor for his gardening at Brantwood, his home near Coniston in the Lake District. Ruskin bought Brantwood in 1871, aged fifty-two, and lived there until his death in 1900, his last decade passed in the seclusion of mental infirmity. He was seeking shelter in the remembered landscape of his childhood but was ultimately faced with a seemingly malevolent nature mirroring his declining mental health. Although Ruskin experienced moments of peace and contentment in his Lakeland home, and his output of writing never slackened pace until the final decade, his later years were riddled with personal disappointment interspersed with bouts of extreme mental instability.

An ecophobic tension arose from, and contributed to, Ruskin's destabilisation: his reverence for nature was spoiled by the new facts of materialist science, the skies were sullied by the poisonous pollution of industry, and his mountain landscape was haunted by the memory of loved ones, an absent presence signifying unfulfilled love, betrayal and regret. His work in the landscape embodied personal and professional obsessions, and a Gothic reading of Ruskin's garden gives a new perspective on the destabilisation and decay of his later years. By stripping away the anthropocentrism of the Gothic and examining the role of the environment in the construction of Ruskin's fear and oppression, the framework of ecoGothic provides a useful context through which to examine Ruskin's response to the landscape. Employing the language of ecocriticism, particularly Simon Estok's concept of ecophobia (2018), this chapter offers a reading of Ruskin's attitude to nature – manifest in his mature writing and in the garden at Brantwood – as a contribution to ecoGothic discourse. The manner in which Ruskin shaped, and was shaped by, his garden will be examined through the lens of the literary Gothic and the ecoGothic, and in relation to Ruskin's own Gothic paradigm.

Ruskin had reappropriated the concept of Gothic in the second volume of *The Stones of Venice* (1853), in a chapter entitled 'The Nature of Gothic', in which he assigned meaning beyond the standard literary tradition characterised by tropes such as fear, horror, decay and the uncanny. Although ostensibly dealing with architecture, Ruskin's definition encompassed the nature of democracy and the temperament of the northern workers who created the great edifices of Gothic buildings. Importantly, Ruskin reversed the negativity and villainy associated with the pointed arch in Gothic literature by ennobling the form and praising the imagination of its creators. As Richard Adelman has noted, Ruskin reimagined what had been seen as 'signifiers in gothic fiction of human degradation and depravity into an expression of human completeness' (2017: 153–4). Ruskin celebrated the 'restlessness' and the 'strange disquietude of the Gothic spirit' which in his assessment represented animation and freedom, rather than degradation (Ruskin: X. 214). Ruskin's Gothic was as much an expression of his political economy as it was representative of art and aesthetics, yet the 'disquietude' of both the Ruskinian and the literary Gothic persists in his garden, and the two aspects can be explored in parallel.

DOMESTICATING GOTHIC FROM THE GARDEN

It was in a context of despondency and disappointment that Ruskin moved to Brantwood: his household in London had broken down over the preceding decade with the deaths of his parents and his former nurse, and the marriage of his ward, leaving the family home empty. Ruskin was also troubled by his obsessive relationship with Rose La Touche whom he had hoped to marry but was hindered by her parents' opposition and her own fluctuating uncertainty. After a serious mental breakdown in 1871, Ruskin purchased Brantwood without having seen the house, and decided to make the Lake Country his permanent abode, his first home independent of his parents. Ruskin was seeking shelter at Brantwood; it was not merely physical escape from the noise and pressure of London society and work, but represented a desire to be subsumed in the landscape. He longed to 'lie down in Coniston Water' (Dearden 1967: 47), his language echoing the healing rhythms of the Psalms (23: 2) but also hinting at a biophilic urge to become one with nature, to seek the eternal peace of the watery depths of the lake. He craved the familiar topography of remembered family holidays amid mountains, both in the Lake District and in the Alps, a geography intrinsic to Ruskin's well-being and sense of belonging. This reliance on the beneficence of nature was to be Ruskin's undoing: by offering himself to the landscape, he allowed the malevolent potency of the environment to penetrate his consciousness. As in Gothic discourse, where nature 'appears to participate in a language of estrangement rather than belonging' (Smith and Hughes 2013: 2), Ruskin's attempts to find solace in the landscape of home were thwarted, leading ultimately to alienation from the nature he had once revered.

From the outset, Ruskin attempted to shape Brantwood into a place of belonging, shelter and nurture, a sentiment captured in his epithet: 'my own little nest' (Evans and Whitehouse 1958: 750). On taking possession of his sixteen acres of woodland and moor, Ruskin immediately began working the landscape to make a garden; his diary records chopping dead branches, burning weeds and cutting paths on his first days at his new home (Evans and Whitehouse 1958: 712). This work was part physical therapy, part practical fulfilment of the garden ideology that Ruskin had been assimilating since childhood. In the years that followed, he finally had the opportunity to indulge his fascination for the manipulation of water, resulting in ambitious projects to create a harbour, pond, reservoir, cascade and icehouse. Ruskin made a garden of his woodland, enhancing the beauty of rocks and streams, and creating a series of paths to connect the garden spaces and access the beauty of the topography, while cultivating areas of moorland as a model of sustainable agriculture. Pockets of the land had been used for kitchen gardening by previous owners, the rest managed for coppice, pannage, charcoal-burning and other rural industry; the landscape that Ruskin took as the blank canvas for his garden was neither 'natural' nor 'wilderness', having been shaped by centuries of civilisation. In halting the human presence of rural industry, and letting the coppiced trees grow into spindly, Botticellian forms, Ruskin was showing nature both mastery and reverence, freeing the landscape from the domination of industry while imposing his own, equally dominant, aesthetic.

This control of nature mirrored the feudal ideals of Ruskin's political economy, an anthropocentric hierarchy that refused to recognise the imperatives of nature. Ruskin sought to perfect an ideal vision of Botticellian beauty in his landscape, the stasis of a picture within the cyclical flux of nature, an otherness pertaining more to the world of allegory than reality. He would have liked to arrest the blossom on the trees, stating in his botanical study *Proserpina* that 'the flower is the end of the seed, – not the seed of the flower' (Ruskin: XXV. 250); floral beauty was the purpose of the plant, and flowers existed for human delight. To maintain this paradoxical natural stasis, Ruskin walked his landscape with billhook in hand, pruning trees to arrest their fecundity, removing stones washed down his stream from the moor above. He tamed the sublime by laying a path to his precipice rock and surrounding it with spring bulbs, by positioning a seat from which to contemplate comfortably the gushing stream, and by planting a cottage garden sheltered by trees. The harbour offered a safe haven on the lake, the wild moor was drained and cultivated with utilitarian crops, and the drama of the waterfall was made into an entertainment by a sluice gate released on command to surprise visitors with an unexpected cascade. Through these interventions, Ruskin attempted to domesticate the Gothic from his garden by eliminating the potential for fear, oppression, horror and disorder, and constructing instead a landscape of calm, shelter and order. The aesthetic of his contrived landscape was doomed to failure, given the inevitability of seasonal change, the unpredictability of weather, the fluidity of nature and the limitations of Ruskin's own vigour.

DESTABILISATION AND DISTRESS

Ruskin's domination of nature was tempered by his moral opposition to materialist science. In *The Poetry of Architecture*, published in 1837 when he was eighteen years old, Ruskin expressed his distaste at the fashion for exotic bedding plants, a view which remained unchanged in later life and which gives an ideological framework through which to view his approach to the garden:

> A flower-garden is an ugly thing, even when best managed: it is an assembly of unfortunate beings, pampered and bloated above their natural size, stewed and heated into diseased growth; corrupted by evil communication into speckled and inharmonious colours; torn from the soil which they loved, and of which they were the spirit and the glory, to glare away their term of tormented life among the mixed and incongruous essences of each other, in earth that they know not, and in air that is poison to them. (Ruskin: I. 156)

This passage is revealing in the context of Gothic as a condemnation of monstrosity in plant hybridisation. Ruskin derided the human disregard for the laws of nature in the self-serving Promethean quest for progress which had resulted in the creation of monstrous plants of unnatural colour and proportion, fashioned to meet the desires of humankind regardless of moral consequence. His later scepticism of materialist science and Darwinian theory is foreshadowed in his youthful attitude to the application of modern science, particularly the 'evil communication' of the hybridists' methodology: a reference to sexual reproduction, which was a subject problematic to Ruskin throughout his life. With the underpinning of this complex and idiosyncratic logic, Ruskin's preference for plants tended towards native species growing in their own climate in harmony with their surroundings. The paradox of this 'natural' aesthetic was that Ruskin had to master, tame and control nature to achieve it.

Ruskin's book on botany, *Proserpina*, published in part form from 1875 to 1886, reflects the mature, post-Darwinian synthesis of his views on exotic plants and hybridisation, offering an approach to science infused with myth, literature and wonder. In *Proserpina*, Ruskin illustrates his notion of 'distressed wildness', expressing an otherness akin to the Gothic construct of wilderness as an inhabited

space that 'subverts human reason and logic' (Smith and Hughes 2013: 121).
Ruskin offers an example of a neglected area at Brantwood in which,

> I had to cut my way into it through a mass of thorny ruin; black, bird's-nest like,
> entanglement of brittle spray round twisted stems of ill-grown birches strangling
> each other, and changing half into roots among the rock clefts; knotted stumps
> of never-blossoming blackthorn, and choked stragglings of holly, all laced and
> twisted and tethered round with an untouchable, almost unhewable, thatch, a foot
> thick, of dead bramble and rose, laid over rotten ground through which the water
> soaked ceaselessly, undermining it into merely unctuous clods and clots, knitted
> together by mossy sponge. (Ruskin: XXV. 293)

The language of this passage is riddled with images of death and obstruction,
vegetative beauty impeded by the wanton abandonment of nature. This is a
disorienting vision of nature, where stems change into roots and solid ground
is effectively eliminated. Human passage is impeded by inhospitable vegetal
layering, suggesting the eventual annihilation of humanity as nature regains
control. This Gothic outcome is confounded by Ruskin's celebration of the
vitality of nature, concluding the passage with the assertion that all will be well
if nature succumbs to the moral superiority of humanity. Ruskin's dual handling
of the Gothic is demonstrated in the triumph of the Ruskinian Gothic notion
of individual freedom of expression over the tropes of literary Gothic evident
in the disorienting decay of the thicket. He concludes:

> It was all Nature's *free* doing! she had had her way with it to the uttermost; and
> clearly needed human help and interference in her business; and yet there was
> not one plant in the whole ruinous and deathful riot of the place, whose nature
> was not in itself wholesome and lovely; but all lost for want of discipline. (Ruskin:
> XXV. 293, emphasis in original)

Ruskin is struggling with an ecophobic response to nature: at once celebrating
its vitality and condemning its destructive agency. Estok equates the inherent
anthropocentrism of human attitudes to nature with ecophobia, arguing that
'control of the natural environment, understood as a god-given right in western
culture, implies ecophobia as ... animal exploitation implies speciesism' (2009:
5–6). Ruskin's professed confidence in the human ability – and moral right – to
'discipline' nature is representative of a Victorian natural theology in which
anthropocentrism was held as a conviction to counter the tide of evidence
presented by materialist science. That humankind was no longer the dominant
centre of nature, but merely an incidental element within a powerful web of
developing ecosystems – the notion of ecological humility central to ecocritical
theory – was destabilising to Ruskin and his contemporaries brought up in the
Evangelical tradition.

The publication of Charles Darwin's evolutionary theory in *On the Origin
of Species* (1859) and *The Descent of Man* (1871) and the growing acceptance of

the materialist approach to science corrupted Ruskin's view of nature, inflicting an ecophobic horror that struck him to the core and shattered the security of his belief in the unchanging permanence of nature. Ruskin's subsequent frightening vision of a vicious, competitive world, constantly in a state of flux, offers a contrasting perspective to his earlier celebration of restlessness in the spirit of Ruskinian Gothic, outlined above. Ruskin was deeply troubled by the departure from the knowable to the unknowable – the uncanny dissolution of certainty – and his destabilisation was manifest in physical illness; Ruskin confessed to Oliver Lodge, Professor of Physics at the University of Liverpool, with whom he was corresponding on the kinetic theory of gases, that he was 'sick and giddy and could eat no dinner' (O'Gorman 1996: 57). As Ruskin's certainties were undermined, his relationship with nature became more complex, reflecting his internal struggle for truth.

MYTHOLOGY, SYMBOLISM AND NIGHTMARE

To this pervasive environmental unease and disorder was added the destabilising Gothic horror of nightmare. In periods of mental illness, the intensity of Ruskin's dreams compelled him to relocate his sleeping quarters to escape the tangible terror of his visions. He often dreamed of serpents, to which he attached a complex symbolic power: a base symbiosis of earth and death (Hilton 2000: 128–9). Writing in *The Queen of the Air* in 1869, Ruskin described the mythic potency of the serpent:

> It is a divine hieroglyph of the demoniac power of the earth, – of the entire earthly nature. As the bird is the clothed power of the air, so this is the clothed power of the dust; as the bird the symbol of the spirit of life, so this of the grasp and sting of death. (Ruskin: XIX. 363)

The serpent of Ruskin's nightmares was born of the earth, inhabiting the land and strengthened by the evil inherent in its realm, a symbol of the malevolence of nature. However, Ruskin's treatment of myth was clearly separated from his material view of the natural world, stating that the 'horror is of the myth, not of the creature' (XIX. 362). When disturbing 'a good sized viper' in the process of cultivating his moorland garden in 1881, Ruskin reported, 'we've put him with a few comfortable sods under him, and a glass over him, in the greenhouse, and he's made himself a hole and gone to sleep' (Lancaster University, The Ruskin (hereafter R), MS B20). Despite the element of physical danger in a venomous snake, Ruskin welcomed the creature, made it 'comfortable' in his garden domain and referred to it as his 'guardian serpent': the corporeal snake in his garden posing no associative resemblance to the deathly serpent of his mythology. Ruskin's contradictory response to real and symbolic nature allowed him to see nature as both a source of goodness and a source of evil, with divine innocence bestowed on the material flora and fauna and diabolic malevolence on the corresponding mythological constructs. Estok reminds us that nature is itself morally neutral; the construct of evil is relative to our human imagination (2009: 7). Ruskin's imaginative use of mythology empowered him to see the evil in nature; it was the breakdown of this duality, or the blurring of real and imagined, that resulted in the contested nature manifest to Ruskin in the horror of nightmare and mental degeneration. Ruskin's subsequent panic at the 'Diabolic clouds' witnessed in the skies above him, explored later in this chapter, is indicative of the distortion of real and imagined evil in his collapsing rationality.

To counter these troubling thoughts, Ruskin sought certainty and permanence amid the destabilisation of science, industry and the very origins of humanity, turning to mythology for truth. He could no longer compete with the increasing proofs of science exposing the mutability of species, just as he was unable to prevent the spread of capitalist greed, or his horror of industrialisation, but it was within his intellectual power to impose order on the natural world through his own system of plant classification, centred on the moral aspects of flowers, mythology and the innocent wonder of nature. In *Proserpina*, written in parallel with the creation of his garden, Ruskin attempted to re-order a world gone astray, with the premise that, 'Proserpine and Deucalion are at least as true as Eve or Noah; and all four together incomparably truer than the Darwinian theory' (Ruskin: XXVI. 98–9). Ruskin hedged his language carefully to avert accusations of blasphemy, but by placing myth and religion on an equal platform in his hierarchy of truth he hinted at the vulnerability of his religious faith and his need to find solid ground following the disintegration of the biblical certainty learned at his mother's knee.

Ruskin's struggle for assurance amid the destabilisation of his convictions led him towards spiritualism, in which he hoped to find peace through communion with his beloved Rose La Touche. The turbulent years of his obsession with Rose had oscillated between hope and despair, and by the time the news of her death reached him in May 1875, Ruskin was resigned to a life without her. Rose had been an absent presence in Ruskin's life for years before her death, and was memorialised in treasured letters and pressed flowers which took on talismanic form to Ruskin. His friend, Georgina Cowper-Temple, who had acted as intermediary and confidante in Ruskin's relationship with Rose, introduced him to spiritualism, and it was at her home in December 1875 that Ruskin experienced the revelation for which he had hoped when the manifestation of Rose appeared to him in the drawing room at Broadlands (Burd 1982: 26). Believing he had been visited by the spirit of Rose that winter afternoon, Ruskin was thereafter open to her presence. In May 1876, he explored the ruins of Brignal Chapel at Gretna Bridge, where he found the stones festooned with ivy-leaved toadflax, the plant known to Ruskin as 'erba della Madonna' and

3 Ivy-leaved toadflax ('Oxford ivy') *Cymbalaria muralis*. Watercolour, pen and ink, graphite on blue wove paper, John Ruskin (1819–1900), presented to Ruskin Drawing School, 1875

especially assigned to him in the floral symbolism he shared with Rose (Hilton 2000: 134). He described 'the window and wall so overgrown with my own Madonna herb that, – one would think the little ghost had been at work planting them all the spring' (Bradley 1964: 370). The ghost of Rose was a benign presence in the landscape, communing with Ruskin through flowers in an ecoGothic dialogue. The deadened fragility of the pressed flowers preserved by Ruskin as a reminder of the corporeal Rose can be juxtaposed with the vital fecundity of the animate flowers inundating the ruin at Gretna, the vital spirit overcoming the weakened body at last.

The duality of Ruskin's feelings towards Rose is reflected in the symbolism of rose and thorn, echoing the transgression of the binaries of love and hatred, hope and disappointment, trust and betrayal that characterised their relationship. In Ruskin's complex floral iconography, the rose represented more than the traditional attributes of beauty and love, and he often equated Rose with the leaves rather than the flower, perhaps in reference to the serrated edges, sharp like the daggers of betrayal. The thorn's capacity to wound, to draw blood from those who sought to grasp and hold it, mirrors Ruskin's painful pursuit of Rose, his 'thorny girl' (R, MS L7.613). The thorns on any plant in the garden at Brantwood would serve as an uncanny reminder of the betrayal Ruskin suffered when Rose failed to keep her promises. In *Proserpina* Ruskin described the state of his woodland, but he could equally have been describing his inner turmoil: 'The leaves had all perished, and the bending saplings, and the wood of trust; – but the thorns were there, immortal, and the gnarled and sapless roots, and the dusty treacheries of decay' (Ruskin: XXV. 294). The vital green life force of the plants had succumbed to death, like Rose, but the dry and twisted roots and the thorns remained forever, an 'immortal' provocation of the memory of Rose's betrayal. Ruskin's use of the word 'treacheries', relating to his earlier reference to the 'wood of trust', welds the language of his bitterness to nature, hinting at his mounting ecophobia in the perceived malevolence of the ungardened vegetation.

THE DESTRUCTIVE AGENCY OF NATURE

Ruskin's destabilisation is further exposed by his intensifying discomfort in the garden in which he had invested the hope of shelter and quietude. Alongside the fragmentation of his certainties of science, religion and domestic fidelity came the failure of Ruskin's gardening projects, his worthwhile intentions foundering in the inhospitable environment. The complex ovular icehouse, intended to bring succour to local people as well as to provide for his household, leaked and was abandoned. The harbour walls, which were constructed as much in illustration of the rewards of manual labour as to shelter boats, had to be reworked, and the currents of the lake continually washed in silt. The tennis lawn, created by digging out stumps and levelling an elevated area of

4 'Ruskin's Moorland Garden', W. G. Collingwood. 1903. *Ruskin Relics* (London: Isbister & Company Ltd). Illustrations by John Ruskin and others

woodland, was relocated to a more convenient position below the house. These interventions, engineered in the landscape by Ruskin, failed ostensibly due to a combination of practical ineptitude and lack of foresight, but the contribution of the environment to their downfall should not be overlooked.

Ruskin's attempts to intercede in the natural cycle of the seasons suggests naivety in the face of the power of natural forces and their disregard for human enterprise. He persisted with the ceaseless task of removing rocks washed from the moor into his woodland stream and constructed a reservoir to feed his waterfall when the stream dried up, thinking to circumvent nature with human ingenuity. No amount of intellectual resourcefulness could elude the environmental forces determining the vitality of animate nature, however, and Ruskin was tormented and perplexed when his plantings began to fail, writing to his gardener in 1882 while away from Brantwood: 'I am vexed at having no word from you about the one thing I care about most – the moor. Mr Collingwood tells me everything has failed. Will you please tell me to what extent and as far as you know, why' (R, MS L82).

Ruskin's work on the moor on the high slopes at Brantwood was an attempt to repurpose a barren landscape for agricultural use, draining the bog into reservoirs, building terraces among the rocky outcrops and planting wheat and fruit trees. In Ruskin's ideology, embodied in the principles of the Guild of St George and on the pages of *Fors Clavigera*, this was the route to moral salvation. Exemplified by the model at Brantwood, Ruskin could instruct 'the workmen and labourers of Great Britain' (Ruskin: XXVII. viii) to follow his lead and arrest the tyranny of capitalism and the moral degeneration of the nation. When the crops on the moor perished, Ruskin was forced to confront his failure to mediate social and political change, a failure provoked by the negative forces of nature. The intention to work in harmony with the land was now replaced with an ecophobic opposition to natural imperatives.

The anxiety expressed in Ruskin's reaction to his gardener at the outcome of the moorland experiment reflects his helplessness in the face of raw nature and a growing sense that the environment was conspiring against him. Ruskin blamed the weather for the degradation of his garden, placing specific culpability on the sky. He recorded in his diary in August 1879:

> Raining in foul drizzle, slow and steady; sky pitch-dark, and I just get a little light by sitting in the bow-window. Diabolic clouds over everything: and looking over my kitchen garden yesterday, I found it one miserable mass of weeds gone to seed; the roses in the higher garden putrified into brown sponges, feeling like dead snails; and the half-ripe strawberries all rotten at the stalks. (Evans and Whitehouse 1959: 979)

Damp and darkness were held responsible by Ruskin for the mortification of his garden, and the 'miserable mass of weeds' mirrored his own wretchedness. He had not only looked at his rotting plants, but touched them, deliberately and viscerally experiencing their decay. His strawberry crop had been arrested in the liminal state between immaturity and ripeness, a half-state of unfulfilled potential useless to plant or human, while weeds had flourished and seeded with the portent of more weeds to come. Ruskin's 'Diabolic clouds' echo the 'Diabolic pow'r' of Milton's serpent in *Paradise Lost* [IX. 95] and suggest that Ruskin ascribed the malevolence of the weather to the influence of the Devil upon the sky, an influence that encompassed 'everything'. Just as he had identified the 'demoniac power of the earth' in the serpent in 1869, quoted previously, a decade later Ruskin was again seeing malevolence in nature, this time not as a symbol, but as a very real manifestation of evil.

THE 'PLAGUE-CLOUD, SOOTY AND FURIOUS'

The ecophobic resonance of clouds is expressed by Ruskin in c. 1885 in a letter to his neighbour Susanna Beever, in which he states:

> But for all of us, a dark sky is assuredly a poisonous and depressing power, which neither surgery nor medicine can resist. The difference to me between nature as she is now, and as she was ten years ago, is as great as between Lapland and Italy,

and the total loss of comfort in morning and evening sky, the most difficult to resist of all spiritual hostility. (Fleming 1887: 88)

Ruskin's admission of his diminished consolation in nature can be read in tandem with his obsession with clouds. Born of childhood curiosity, Ruskin's interest in meteorology had intensified to a significance more spiritual than scientific. It is telling that when Ruskin arrived at Brantwood to find a small cottage in a state of dilapidation – 'a mere shed of rotten timber and loose stone' (Ruskin: XXIX. 101) – his instructions to his builder included the construction of a glazed turret on the corner of his bedroom. Standing in this projecting space, Ruskin would have been surrounded by the panorama of the sky, witness to the effects of dawn, dusk, storm and sun; however, the positive affirmation derived from experiencing the sunrise and sunset was negated by the growing malevolence of the sky. The environment, from an ecoGothic perspective, had become a source of oppression in the dark clouds and sullied air, and Ruskin's earlier comfort in the quiet wonder of nature was overtaken by fear of the storm cloud.

This response to the sky was expressed in two lectures given by Ruskin at the London Institution in 1884 which were subsequently published as *The Storm Cloud of the Nineteenth Century*. The book begins with Ruskin's meteorological observations in which cloud patterns are described and categorised, but readers are soon aware that Ruskin's purpose was a moral rather than a scientific message. The change in the skies, recorded by Ruskin over several decades of cloud-watching, signified a moral imperative. The environment was punishing humanity for the intrusion of industrial pollution on the climate, but also warning of the apocalyptic consequences of the degeneration of morality brought about by capitalist greed. Such eschatological fears had been troubling Ruskin throughout his years at Brantwood: in 1874, a decade before his thoughts on the corrosive influence of the storm cloud were made public, he wrote to Beever:

There is nothing now in the year but autumn and winter. I really begin to think there is some terrible change of climate coming upon the world for its sin, like another deluge. It will have its rainbow, I suppose, after its manner – promising not to darken the world again, and then not to drown. (Fleming 1887: 7)

Environmental collapse as the punishment for human transgression was recognised by Ruskin in the dark skies of the late nineteenth century as a reverberation of Mosaic tradition. He appeared resigned to the inevitability of this environmental judgement and its aftermath, reflecting his own helplessness; the loss of spring and summer would leave only the Gothic darkness of autumn and winter, robbing Ruskin of blossom and hope.

Through an ecoGothic lens, the weather is central to the construction of Ruskin's dread: both the origin and the manifestation of his horror. The 'plague-cloud, sooty and furious' was fuelling his destabilisation, and his diary entries over successive months at Brantwood in 1883 reveal an internalised correlation between his mental and physical well-being and the state of the sky: 'tired – chiefly however by this demon-blackness', 'black fog and cold – I shivery and valueless', 'I am utterly horror-struck and hopeless about the weather', 'steady south plague wind of the bitterest, nastiest, poisonous blight, and fretful flutter – I could scarcely stay in the wood for the horror of it' (Viljoen 1971: 289–306). The weather was clearly infesting Ruskin's thinking and being, and his reference to the 'plague-cloud' and 'plague wind' suggests that the infestation carried the threat of epidemic or pandemic capacity. Ruskin's biblical language again hints at judgement and apocalypse, but his panic is rooted in the Anthropocene.

The Gothic language of blackness, horror, plague and demon was not restricted to Ruskin's personal diary. In May 1884, he confided to his friend Jane Simon with ecophobic intensity: 'The "Bad Time" is fearfully impressed on me by the sky, all through this May. Worse than ever before. Never a moment of purity or peace. Seldom sun. It shines fitfully to day, with angry wind. I am thankful, but more frightened' (R, MS L99).

Ruskin's fear of the weather mirrored his fear of mental illness, his experience of the 'Bad Time' an agonising episode with the inevitable threat of recurrence. The abrupt sentences recounting his impression of the sky embody the restlessness of Ruskin's mind, his thoughts as fitful as the sunshine that troubled him. This agitation again echoes Ruskin's earlier thoughts on the Gothic spirit, which he identified in *The Stones of Venice* as being shaped by the weather, the hardship of the climate determining the 'wolfish life' of the northern worker (Ruskin: X. 187). The imperfection of the stonemason whose hands were too cold to grip his tools was deemed by Ruskin to be an expression of nobleness, and a truthful response to his conditions (X. 240). By the time Ruskin was reflecting on the weather at Brantwood in the 1880s, the climate was exerting an influence that was not be celebrated, but to be feared.

Added to the Gothic blackness of the plague cloud, the physical manifestation of industrial pollution in the sky was a visual reminder to Ruskin of the moral blight of capitalism. In his 1883 preface to a rearranged version of *Modern Painters* (originally published in five volumes from 1843 to 1860), Ruskin's mature reassessment reveals the capacity of pollution to contaminate the purity of mind which he formerly derived from the landscape:

> the slightest incident which interrupts the harmony of feeling and association in a landscape, destroys it all to me, poisoning the entire faculty of contemplation. From my dining-room, I am happy in the view of the lower reach of Coniston Water, not because it is particularly beautiful, but because it is entirely pastoral and pure. Were a single point of chimney of the Barrow iron-works to show itself over the green ridge of the hill, I should never care to look at it more. (Ruskin: IV. 8)

The privileging of purity in landscape over such aspects as beauty, sublimity and the picturesque – together with Ruskin's association of purity with the pastoral – connects human activity to the environment, and renders society responsible for both the spiritual wholesomeness of the view, through the pastoral tradition, and for its reverse: the capitalist corruption of pollution staining the skies a few miles to the south and threatening further encroachment. What is not explicit in Ruskin's preface, but is apparent to any visitor to Brantwood, is that the view Ruskin described is framed by a window of his own design, the seven Gothic arches of which mirror the seven principles of Gothic architecture expounded in his 1849 book, *The Seven Lamps of Architecture*. Ruskin's thoughts on the imminent spoliation of his landscape by pollution are therefore literally framed by his thoughts on the character of Gothic. Industrialisation and capitalism had blighted the soul of architecture and were now threatening to do the same to nature.

RETURN TO NATURE: THE GARDEN ABANDONED

Ruskin's capacity to garden the landscape at Brantwood was determined by his fluctuating mental illness, his debility characterised by the languid ambivalence of possible intoxication. Throughout the 1870s and 1880s Ruskin employed a local doctor, George Parsons, who administered what Ruskin refers to variously as 'sedative', 'syrup' and 'that tonic', and from whom he requests 'some more terrifying and some more sleepifying – mysterious compounds', suggesting that he may have been under the influence of opiates (Ambleside, Armitt Library, MS ALMS 380 36.2). Ruskin admits to Dr Parsons that he feels,

> a quite unconquerable feeling of idleness, which seems to possess me more and more every day – the more I submit to it the worse it is. The less I do – the less I want to, the more I sleep the more I can; going up the steps at the back of the house must be thought twice on – before I attempt it and the ascent to the moor, a Herculean task. At this moment – I'm as sleepy as can be. (MS ALMS 380 37.2)

That Ruskin was overcome by apathy through taking opium offers a plausible reading of his final decade at Brantwood, where he was seldom seen or heard, and his garden was left to return to nature. The bouts of mental illness which had increasingly inflicted Ruskin in later life had become more frequent and more violent, and his family and friends sought to subdue his unpredictable temperament and protect his reputation (Hilton 2000: 569–84).

Whether by his own weakness or by the prohibition of his protectors, Ruskin neglected the landscape in his last years at Brantwood, allowing it to succumb to the decay of abandonment, and surrendering responsibility for its care to others. For centuries the land had been usefully managed, initially for subsistence farming and rural industry, then for Ruskin's aesthetic pleasure. Now, Ruskin's own absent presence in the garden placed it in a liminal state of non-garden, his trees freed from the bonds of their imposed stasis, his streams filling and emptying as the seasons dictated, and his agricultural experiments given over to nature. Ruskin's biographer W. G. Collingwood described the moorland garden, 'the whole has been left to Nature again. The apple-trees grew, but untended; they still blossom. The cherries have run wild and are left to the birds. The rough steps from the rock-platform to the orchard terrace are disjointed, and fern is creeping through the grass' (Collingwood 1903: 44).

In Ruskin's absence, nature had regained control, fauna taking advantage of the harvest and flora gradually removing the trace of human passage through the garden, following its own purposeful trajectory. Ruskin was alienated from his garden, his otherness manifest in the rewilding of the landscape while he became a bystander to his thwarted ambition, witness to the dissolution of his gardened space. Ruskin's loss of agency reflects the insignificance of human intervention in the biocentrism of ecoGothic, and the role of the environment in the construction of fear and oppression is foregrounded in the failure of Ruskin's gardening endeavours to combat the malevolence he saw in plants, flowers and 'Diabolic clouds'.

WORKS CITED

Adelman, Richard. 2017. 'Ruskin & Gothic literature', *Wordsworth Circle*, 48. 3: 152–63

Bradley, John Lewis (ed.). 1964. *The Letters of John Ruskin to Lord and Lady Mount-Temple* (Columbus: Ohio State University Press)

Burd, Van Akin. 1982. *Ruskin, Lady Mount-Temple and the Spiritualists – An Episode in Broadlands History* (London: Bentham Press)

Collingwood, W. G. 1903. *Ruskin Relics* (London: Isbister & Co.)

Dearden, James (ed.). 1967. *The Professor: Arthur Severn's Memoir of John Ruskin* (London: George Allen & Unwin)

Estok, Simon. 2009. 'Theorizing in a Space of Ambivalent Openness: Ecocriticism and Ecophobia', *ISLE: Interdisciplinary Studies in Literature and Environment*, 16. 2: 203–25

Estok, Simon. 2018. *The Ecophobia Hypothesis* (Abingdon: Routledge)

Evans, Joan and John Whitehouse (eds). 1956–59. *The Diaries of John Ruskin 1835–1889*, 3 vols (Oxford: Clarendon Press)

Fleming, Albert (ed.). 1887. *Hortus Inclusus* (Orpington: George Allen)

Hilton, Tim. 2000. *John Ruskin: The Later Years* (New Haven and London: Yale University Press)

Milton, John. 1998. *Paradise Lost* (1667), ed. by Alistair Fowler, 2nd edn (Harlow: Longman)

O'Gorman, Francis. 1996. '"The Eagle and the Whale?": Ruskin's Argument with John Tyndall', in *Time and Tide: Ruskin and Science* (London: Pilkington Press), pp. 45–64.

Ruskin, John. 1903–12. *The Works of John Ruskin*, ed. by E. T. Cook and Alexander Wedderburn, 39 vols (London: George Allen) (references are given by volume and page numbers)

Smith, Andrew and William Hughes (eds). 2013. *Ecogothic* (Manchester: Manchester University Press)

Viljoen, Helen Gill (ed.). 1971. *The Brantwood Diary of John Ruskin* (New Haven and London: Yale University Press)

Archive sources

Ambleside, Armitt Library, MS ALMS 380 1–40 (Ruskin to Dr Parsons, 1873–88)
Lancaster University, The Ruskin, MS L82 (Ruskin to Dawson Herdson, 13 December 1882); MS L7.613 (Georgina Cowper-Temple to Ruskin, undated); MS L99 (Ruskin to Jane Simon, 14 May 1884); MS B20 (Ruskin to Maria La Touche, 5 December 1881)

3

The Gothic orchard of the Victorian imagination

Joanna Crosby

There are numerous Gothic associations with orchards, from the nineteenth-century reverence for the sacred grove through its connections to the mythology of the wild wood as a place of potentially dangerous enchantment. An idealised orchard carries resonances from earlier ages of the ancestral wild wood and of sacred natural spaces, both imagined and real. Orchards are not gardens, yet they occupy an even more liminal space, between garden and park, between cultivated farmland and wild forest, their uncanny atmosphere often heightened by neglect, with older trees losing their youthful, trained shape and becoming full of character – and characters. That type of orchard is the one most commonly represented in Victorian art, but the garden apple tree has its own Gothic associations, taking on the mystical, spiritual reverberations of the sacred garden of Paradise, or Eden, or the formal Classical temple groves. In the carefully curated space of an orchard-garden, some wild encounters have taken place.

Because the apple is a familiar food, an everyday purchase, it has been given little status as a material thing or a cultural indicator for historians and is often used only as a symbol or metaphor for something considered more important in a text. Its ubiquity as a food of all classes and its consumable, ephemeral nature has faded it into the background. Yet Victorians manifested a complex and often contradictory relationship to the apple, celebrating the orchard, both real and represented, as a space for the sacred, the feminine and enchantment, while acknowledging the dangerous and forbidden side of its associations in their representations of the fruit itself.

The harmony of golden afternoons, and not sinister moonlight, are associated with the serenity of orchards, yet this harmony can be more apparent than real. Among the boughs lies a realm of the uncanny; the orchard is one of the

5 From Eden Phillpotts. 1921. *A Dish of Apples* (London: Hodder & Stoughton). Illustration by Arthur Rackham (1867–1939)

liminal spaces where the unseen, but much celebrated, world of fairy and folktale creep into Victorian art and culture. The apple's domesticity allows it to become a messenger from the real to the imaginary worlds, as well as a symbol of hidden disorder, rotten at the core. Any depiction of an apple tree in a garden resonates with that note of uncanny danger that is perceptible around it, once we look past its comfortable presence in the fruit bowl. Decoding the message of the apple and its contribution to the Gothic undercurrents of particular texts and paintings allows a deeper understanding of how the natural world was used in the highly stylised art of the mid- to late nineteenth century. The work of Christina Rossetti and Millais leads us into a most Gothic space, the enchanted or uncanny orchard, and from there back again to the intersection of the uncanny with the hidden Gothic landscape of London and its fruit sellers in the persona of Rossetti's goblins.

VICTORIAN ORCHARDS AND GARDENS IN THE LANDSCAPE

Victorian commercial orchards were usually small (often an acre or less), but many were highly productive, intensively farmed spaces. They sat within the different managed and wild landscapes of England, each of which carried its own symbolism and economic significance, and in turn touched the Victorian imagination. 'Landscape' became a concept of interest, a metaphor for the unconscious, and an image of the national character. Roger Ebbatson states that landscape in art and culture 'acts as a "carrier" of cultural authority' (2005: 3). Mid- to late-century industrialisation was seen by artists to have created a division between the self and the environment, such that 'any imagined return to a place is fraught with a sense of the ghostly or the archaic' (3). When an orchard or a garden is – by its depiction in art – returned to, visited again by the artist, there must necessarily be a 'sense of the ghostly', of the other orchards and apples that can never be revisited or viewed again. Here Ebbatson's 'cultural authority' should not be defined as 'cultural progress' but a less strident, nostalgic collective yearning. Some of the most important nineteenth-century depictions of orchards and apples convey the era's growing disassociation with landscape as an intense fear of loss. It is this meaning of ghostly, of internal shadows and depths of meaning in a painting such as Millais's *Apple Blossoms* as much as the supernatural encounter in Rossetti's poem 'Goblin Market' (both discussed later) that places the orchard within the ecoGothic landscape.

However, unlike the wilder Gothic landscapes of the imagination, there is a sense of order and purpose within an orchard. They may be fantastic, or disturbing, but they are not chaotic. An orchard has been set out to some kind of plan, usually planting the trees in rows, with the intention of getting a good harvest. Rural historian David Lowenthal states that, 'like the archetypical sacred garden, the English landscape is not natural but crafted', and that 'few features of lowland Britain lack embedded links with those who have held and tenanted and tilled it' (1991: 215–16). Representations of orchards, therefore, were important to Victorians as they functioned as decorative reminders of agricultural work and rural life without showing the realities of it, unlike threshing or ploughing. The orchard was a timeless emblem of England, well-tended, ordered and without any hint of industrial progress or urban growth. Once questing knights slept beneath the apple trees, later came decorous nineteenth-century maidens, but both are distanced from the work of the orchard labourers and from any changes in the wider landscape.

Lowenthal elides the landscape with the garden, and orchards are, culturally and materially, part of both. Victorian schemes to house the urban working classes stressed the importance of gardens that were both useful and productive, providing extra food and keeping men away from the public houses, as Margaret Willes (2015) has documented in her study of working-class gardens and gardeners. Suburban gardens were considered incomplete without a small orchard at the far end and fruit trees trained against the wall. Private gardens, therefore, were considered to be a bounded space where the cultivation of productive and aesthetically pleasing plants could, or should, lead to better health, moral uplift and decency within the home. In this context, as garden historian John Prest argues, the domestic garden came to be identified as a recreation of the enclosed sacred garden, either Edenic Paradise or the *hortus conclusus* of the Virgin Mary, keeping out the moral wilderness beyond (1981: 21). Renaissance representations of Eden and of Marian gardens, seen by Victorian artists as they toured the art of Italy and France, were filled with allegorical flowers alluding to Mary's innocence and her virginity, and in this sacred space the apple is present as a reminder of original sin, but also to show the possibility of redemption. In Victorian art the Annunciation often takes place in a cloistered space or garden, setting the Virgin apart from the impure, fallen world. Surviving 'Mary gardens' themselves were seen as quaint manifestations of Catholicism, but the mid-century revival of interest in medieval art, and in the cult of the Virgin, brought them once more into fashion, so that plants seen as sacred to Mary were again given that symbolic purpose in art, while floral symbolism became a part of popular culture in works such as dictionaries of flowers (Seaton 2012: 3–29).

Gardens, in their romantic, flowery form, became increasingly associated with the feminine as the nineteenth century progressed. Apple trees, and especially their blossom, were depicted as an element essential for the feminised garden, although the trees may have been grown and tended by men. One reason for the high esteem for fruit trees in the urban garden was the blossom, so transient and so pure each year against the soot-blackened buildings. For Ruskin, blossom represented a sacred appreciation of the garden in purity, more important than the promise of the harvest to come, and this belief is one that has been transformed into symbolism in Millais's *Apple Blossoms*, as well as in genre paintings such as Edwin Harris's 1884 painting *Under the Blossom that Hangs on the Bough*, which shows a young woman, dressed in white, leaning against a slender tree in an orchard, contemplating a single bloom.

Ecocriticism, inviting the reader to dwell within the landscape of a text and to see that landscape as part of the natural and created world that is all, itself, within the text, is particularly suited to considerations of the cultural or imagined orchard. Such an orchard, whether part of a walled garden or a farm, exists as both a natural and a managed, contained landscape in itself, a material construction and a symbol of Otherness beyond the material. Societal changes outside its boundaries rarely impact on what happens within. This gives the orchard kinship with other British Gothic-inflected places that stand just outside or beyond the natural order, such as churchyards, castles set in 'sublime' wilderness, and the various mounds, caves and trees that mark the dwellings of fairy folk; all of which also became part of the story of national identity during the nineteenth century.

THE DEEP CULTURAL ORIGINS OF THE ORCHARD

During the nineteenth century the world of the ancient Greeks and Romans was becoming more familiar to the Victorians, as the number and quality of translations of Classical works increased, alongside further archaeological discoveries. Classical associations were woven into Victorian depictions of orchards and thus affected the way in which orchards were represented and regarded, and the importance they were afforded, extending English landscape into sacred forest groves. Scholarly interest was mirrored by a popular Hellenistic revival, which resulted in statues 'in the Greek style' being placed anachronistically in suburban Victorian gardens, and in the introduction of planted groves and newly ruined temples to parks and landscapes across England (Barrow 2007). These were not just re-creations of Hellenistic landscapes but of states of mind, with implied or inscribed moral warnings for those who dallied there.

Nineteenth-century scholarship understood that Classical groves were not only the background to Classical temples, but were sacred in themselves, as places to encounter, through worship or by accident, the otherworld of gods, nymphs, fauns, dryads and other mythical beings living within them. The orchard performed the same function as the grove in Victorian art, as a place where the Other could be chanced upon. The promulgation of the romantic and macabre myths about the origins of the species of trees found in Classical groves – poplars were weeping nymphs, transformed, for example – helped to increase their attractiveness to Victorian readers and gardeners, while the trees themselves were familiar species in the English landscape, which made them particularly popular with painters. Including apple trees in the background of paintings depicting Classical themes was not, therefore, incongruous to Victorian artists or their public. The interest in Classical groves provided paintings of English orchard scenes with an extra importance, a further allusion for the educated middle classes to savour.

The sacred grove was the neo-classical equivalent of the Gothic orchard, but the associations that went deeper into the cultural history familiar to the Victorian audience were those derived from Christian imagery of the first orchard, otherwise known as Paradise, or the Garden of Eden. Indeed the Persian word from which 'paradise' was formed means 'an orchard surrounded by a wall' (Delumeau 1995: 4). Early writers and folk traditions retained the idea of a peaceful and productive garden, somewhere that was always just out of sight, to where man could never return. The hunt for an actual Eden motivated many expeditions (Prest 1981), but by the nineteenth century, when more of the world was known and mapped, this first orchard retreated into metaphor. The orchard, as represented in art, was an achievable version of Paradise, one that could be gazed upon and populated with men and woman, or gods and goddesses alike. Nineteenth-century art is where Eden and the first orchard live on, out of time, held under the enchantment of the artist. An apple tree in the background alludes to Eden, and an apple in the hands of a woman transforms her into a dangerously ambivalent woman, either an Eve, or a Classical goddess.

Mid-century Arthurian revival made the folkloric associations of the orchard more explicit. In artistic representation of Arthur's court and their deeds, events had to be depicted in a location, and very often that location was a forest or a 'greenwood'. The past takes place out of doors, within a landscape where magic survives, untouched by the corruption of industry or urbanisation, which is confined to enclosed, roofed locations or city streets with no green life or sky. Arthur's magician, Merlin, a character from Celtic culture, is deeply connected to the landscape of wild orchards, since he retreated into one to study, and the apples helped him to prophesy. He also conjures a magical orchard which takes existence in reality long after the enchantment has faded (Fabry: 2006). Central to the revived Arthurian landscape is Avalon, first described by Geoffrey of Monmouth (c. 1136) as the Isle of Apples. There, as Tennyson, William Morris and Blake all described, Arthur was borne after his last battle, perhaps to return again. Tennyson wrote a beautiful, simple description of an island Avalon in 'Morte d'Arthur' (1842) which resonates with the imagery of heaven.

> ... the island-valley of Avilion;
> Where falls not hail, or rain, or any snow,
> Nor ever wind blows loudly; but it lies
> Deep-meadowed, happy, fair with orchard-lawns
> And bowery hollows crowned with summer sea. (['Morte d'Arthur': 259–64] in
>   Tennyson 2007)

Pre-Raphaelite painters crowded the backgrounds of their Arthurian works with tangles of foliage, apple trees among them, binding the wild to the garden, the familiar to the uncanny. In the Arthurian landscape the forest and woodland were places of danger and supernatural events, but also somewhere to locate physically the disparate stories. The romance and enticing danger of the endless forest set the myths in some version of England that was never real, but which nineteenth-century writers and artists were forever reaching towards. The mytho-poetic landscape represented a wished-for Victorian England, and a vision of how it would continue to be under the peaceful rule of its Queen. Arthurian and Classical revivals, and the Gothic revival in architecture, provided a strategy for legitimately increasing the artistic distance between their followers, the life of the imagination and the material changes in the Victorian landscape. Urban and rural readers (and non-readers) were aware of the changes that were taking place across the environment: enclosures and the increasing industrialisation and agricultural mechanisation throughout the nineteenth century caused the landscape of England to be visibly, irrevocably, altered. These changes affected responses to real green spaces, and their representation. Ruskin was saddened that the English landscape had lost its connection to the sacred.

> Whereas the mediæval never painted a cloud, but with the purpose of placing an angel in it; and a Greek never entered a wood without expecting to meet a god in it; we should think the appearance of an angel in the cloud wholly unnatural, and should be seriously surprised by meeting a god anywhere. Our chief ideas about the wood are connected with poaching. (Ruskin 2010: 320)

The turn towards both Classical myths and native folklore was, in part, an expression of the need to find the god in the wood again. The concept of the forest as spiritual or sacred place of wonder and enchantment became embedded in the cultural education of the literate and increasingly well-travelled Victorians who were now looking at wilderness and un-farmed nature with fresh eyes, contrasting it more favourably with the urban environment, which they judged to be a moral wasteland, far more desolate and dangerous than any natural one. For those, especially women, who could not walk in the wild places so easily or without disapproval, as the poets did, the 'tamed' landscapes of city parks, gardens and domestic orchards became an important alternative. This separation, between wild and farmed, between rural and urban – a separation that has continued and widened in contemporary culture – gives rise to the anxiety about finding oneself in a wooded or forested area that runs so deep in Victorian Gothic culture.

The cultural and material orchards, therefore, find their significance in the context of other imaginary landscapes. It may seem some distance between the grove, the forest, the orchard and the garden fruit tree, but in the Victorian imagination they were closely related. In art and literature the apple tree, or even the apple alone, fulfilled the function of the enchanted grove, the dangerous wild wood and the sacred paradise.

THE PAINTED ORCHARD AND THE GOTHIC IMAGINATION

Paintings of orchards were often sentimental genre paintings, but among them are some remarkable paintings that tap into the enchanted and dangerous associations of the orchard. Such a painting is Millais's *Apple Blossoms* (also known as *Spring*, and exhibited under that title at the Royal Academy in 1859), which depicts a group of girls and young women relaxing in an orchard, surrounded by the blossom and seated on a bed of wild flowers. Their only activity

6 *Apple Blossoms*, or *Spring* (1856–59). Oil on canvas, John Everett Millais (1829–96)

is to make curds and whey; the three stages of the process being shown from left to right in the painting. However, they do not seem to be particularly bonded by this activity and one girl on the far right seems to be waking from sleep, or perhaps succumbing to it, as she is reclining on her back with one knee bent in an unguarded pose. Propped against the low wall behind her, so that in the composition it points alarmingly at her heart, is a scythe. The use of this symbol is discussed by Allan Staley:

> [The scythe] suggests … the famous 14th-century fresco of *The Triumph of Death* in the Campo Santo of Pisa, ascribed in the nineteenth-century to Andrea Orcagna, which shows an elegant group in a garden and a scythe-wielding figure in black bearing down upon them. Millais's scythe blade is only a vestigial echo of the personification of death in Pisa, but it constitutes enough of an intrusion into this idyllic scene to convey the same message, and it points ominously directly at the heart of Alice Gray, who is the figure in the painting most at leisure, and the one figure who, by making eye contact, addresses us instead of sharing unheedingly the pleasant activity of her friends. (Staley 2004: 4)

Ruskin had a very specific reaction to the painting's orchard setting. For him it showed a place 'carpeted with ghostly grass, a field of penance for young ladies, where girl-blossoms, who had been vainly gay, or treacherously amiable, were condemned to recline in reprobation under red-hot apple blossom, and sip scalding milk out of a poisoned porringer' (Ruskin 1904: 26). This surprisingly cruel imagery echoes the punishments found in fairy tales for false behaviour, as well as the Classical myths of women transformed into trees or flowers. The relationship between cultivated apple varieties, blossom, girl and scythe is penetratingly analysed by Melissa Elston, who sees the scythe as 'as much a symbol of anthropocentric alteration of a landscape as it is a symbol of phallic social "policing"', that gives the message that emergent female sexuality is to be 'culled' or perhaps pruned back, in the way in which the apple trees are contained and managed within the enclosed orchard (Elston 2012: 62–3).

However valid these interpretations of the scythe may be, the object also deserves to have its shock value restored as a Gothic and melodramatic symbol. It is reminiscent of the 'spirit' objects that were made to manifest onto early photographs, and it is a deliberately obvious memento mori, that even these lovely girls will, like the blossom, fall and die. We need to remember that this painting was exhibited alongside Millais's *The Vale of Rest*, which shows two nuns digging a grave. One nun stares out at the viewer in a similar fashion to the girl in *Apple Blossoms*, and men are similarly absent. Although these paintings were not companion pieces, Ruskin, and others, considered them together, and both were unsettling enough to be unpopular when exhibited. The direct gaze of the girls in the orchard provoked disgust. The *Daily Telegraph* described them as 'a parcel of girls inconceivably ill-favoured. One girl sprawls on the turf and leers at the spectator, with her head upside down, as if to say 'Here we are! All alive! What do you think of us?' (Fleming 1998: 180). Although painted by a man, the picture is a reversal of the customary and accepted artistic 'male gaze'.

This description of the girls celebrating being 'alive', and perhaps refusing to be as penitent as Ruskin desired, acknowledges the strength and energy of spring and of the young women, although they are pent up in the confines of the orchard. This vitality itself could be a source of dismay and moral decline, for Ruskin and other commentators, since (women) orchards, gardens and souls required careful tending to keep them in order. The orchard is important as an uncanny background that emphasises the incongruity of the scythe and the poses of the girls; their blasé or even gloomy reaction to the life-affirming, blossoming orchard gives extra significance to the setting in a circular relationship between the elements in the painting.

APPLES AND GOBLINS

Christina Rossetti's poem 'An Apple Gathering' also uses the symbolism of apple blossom and the promise and potential harm in apples. This poem was included in *Goblin Market*, Rossetti's first volume, published in 1862. In this short poem, the speaker mourns her loss, which may be of love, or the opportunity to marry and be a mother, or perhaps of her virginity and reputation. Where other girls come back from gathering apples with full baskets that 'jeer' at the speaker, she has missed the harvest and found nothing. Her admirer, Willie, whom she addresses or calls to in the poem, thought her love 'less worth than apples with their green leaves' (['An Apple Gathering': 18] in Rossetti 1862) and was perhaps faithless or otherwise fell short.

> I plucked pink blossoms from mine apple-tree
> And wore them all that evening in my hair:
> Then in due season when I went to see
> I found no apples there.
> With dangling basket all along the grass
> As I had come I went the selfsame track:
> My neighbours mocked me while they saw me pass
> So empty-handed back. ['An Apple Gathering': 1–8]

But when the blossom was out, she adorned herself with the pink flowers. She certainly seems to have acted as one of the 'girl-blossoms' whom Ruskin tried to warn. Here the apple blossom is subverted from representing purity, innocence and youth to being something that can provide only transient pleasure, its brevity being its attraction. That the blossom made the speaker more sensually or sexually attractive is hinted at by the time of day at which she wore them, since 'evening' carries a suggestion of parties and leisure time, and of course night. In the poem 'Goblin Market', it is 'evening by evening' [32] when the girls see the goblins, and Lizzie warns, 'twilight is not good for maidens' [144]. The use of evening in 'An Apple Gathering', both here and in the last verse, where the speaker 'loitered' in the orchard, although the 'night grew chill' [26–8], adds to the uncanny atmosphere of the poem. Again in 'Goblin Market' Lizzie warns her sister, 'you should not loiter so' [163]. Staying out in the countryside or an orchard in the evening, when all the neighbours have gone home, leads to some kind of transformation – sadness, loss and possibly danger.

> I let my neighbours pass me, ones and twos
> And groups; the latest said the night grew chill,
> And hastened: but I loitered, while the dews
> Fell fast I loitered still. ['An Apple Gathering', 25–8]

Is the speaker a ghost or a spirit, trapped forever in the orchard, doomed to be in an abundant Eden but never to take part in its harvest? There are folktales of the way in which time passes in an orchard – if you sleep under an apple tree for a moment you may wake to find that many years have passed. The poem elides time in the same way – how many years have passed between the blossom and the apples?

Rossetti explores the duality of the promise offered by 'rosiest apples on the earth' in 'Goblin Market', the long narrative poem that gave the title to her first collection. This famous tale of sensible Lizzie, who ignores the temptations of the goblin fruit sellers, and her sister Laura, who tastes the forbidden fruit and wastes away until Lizzie saves her, has been interpreted as anything from a Christian parable to a tale of forbidden love. However, concentrating more upon the way in which the descriptions of the goblins echo those of the real fruit sellers working around Rossetti's neighbourhood in London gives an insight into how those sellers, and their apples, were regarded when they interacted with consumers, and how the uncanny can slide with disturbing ease into a busy, modern urban setting.

London traders who sold apples and other fruit on the street were known as costermongers. Reverend Rogers, who ministered to so many of them that he referred to his East End parish as 'Costermongria', defined them as:

> properly speaking, one who sells apples, but the name ... is applied to all those who, as it is technically termed, get their living in the streets ...The most aristocratic possess a cart and donkey, the next class a truck or barrow, the lowest have their little all contained in a basket. (Rogers 1857: 298)

It is significant that Rogers uses the term 'aristocratic' for the better-off traders, since this gives credence to the sense of some lineage that comes with the name costermonger. It is thought to derive from the large apple, the costard (now lost to cultivation), sold since medieval times. Mayhew's *London Labour and the London Poor* (1861) used quotes from Beaumont and Fletcher and Dr Johnson to emphasise the costermongers' claims to some historical nobility as a trade. However, in 1886 biographer Edwin Hodder noted that the costermongers themselves did not think much of their ancient associations with apples, one explaining to him that 'a Coster is a cove wot works werry 'ard for a werry poor livin'' (2014: 269).

Costermongers represented a strand of working-class life that was part condemned and part celebrated by middle-class observers, that of the hard worker who lived outside the rules of polite or moral society, between social strata, familiar to all yet alienatingly Other. Social reformers such as Mayhew interviewed them, and even worked with them for a short time, in order to write articles drawing attention to their poor living conditions. However, these reports drew a prurient interest from the middle-class readers, and costermongers as a class gained renown for their immoral family arrangements (marriage was optional), their lewd leisure pursuits and rough manners, especially those of the women. The journalist James Ewing Ritchie wrote an account of visiting one of their 'free and easy' entertainments, which was a night of 'turns', singing and drinking. He judged that 'Their notions are not peculiarly polished or refined, nor is the language in which they are clothed, nor the mode in which they are uttered, such as would be recognised in Belgravia' (Ewing Ritchie 1858: 223).

Costermonger culture arose from, and was a function of their trade. It certainly influenced the perceptions of the consumers of apples, already nervous of the associations of apples with sin and with enchantment. The street traders' 'otherness' was acknowledged by commentators – Reverend Rogers describes them as being 'Arabian' in their behaviour, and anxiety within the relationship between the low-class seller and the (slightly) higher-class buyer was implicit in every transaction (1857: 298). When Laura and Lizzie hear the goblins beside the stream, they are listening to something very like the street cries of London costermongers, well known to Rossetti herself. Only the rural setting differentiates.

> Morning and evening
> Maids heard the goblins cry:
> 'Come buy our orchard fruits,
> Come buy, come buy:
> Apples and quinces,
> Lemons and oranges,
> Plump unpeck'd cherries,
> Melons and raspberries,
> Bloom-down-cheek'd peaches,
> Swart-headed mulberries,
> Wild free-born cranberries,
> Crab-apples, dewberries,
> Pine-apples, blackberries,
> Apricots, strawberries; –
> All ripe together
> In summer weather. (['Goblin Market': 1–16] in Rossetti 1862)

The goblins themselves are described as caricatures of eager vendors trying to ingratiate themselves with their customer, in this case Lizzie, who has so far resisted their enticements:

> Mopping and mowing,
> Full of airs and graces,
> Pulling wry faces,
> Demure grimaces. ['Goblin Market': 337–40]

As Melanie Hanson points out, Rossetti was familiar with street cries both in reality and in poetry, since one of the earliest books she read was William Hone's *Everyday Book*, in which the cries of the barrow women, with their chorus of 'come and pick, come and pick' are listed as one of the attractions of London streets (Hanson 2010: 61). This becomes the goblins' customary cry, with its 'iterated jingle / Of sugar-baited words' ['Goblin Market': 234–5]. Hanson also points to trade cards with lists of goods described in a semi-poetic style that resemble the tumbling, pell-mell cries of the goblins and feed into the enticing nature of the goods on offer. In her doctoral thesis on Rossetti and Milton, Katja Brandt notes that the trading methods of the goblins resemble those in John Bunyan's *The Pilgrim's Progress*: 'Rossetti's "Goblin Market", like Bunyan's Vanity Fair, is a worldly market place of delusive distraction. When the goblins call "come buy", this vividly recalls the cry of the merchants of earthly wares … "what will ye buy?"' (Brandt 2006: 22).

Rossetti herself also went shopping in Covent Garden market which, although it was a tourist attraction, was also a place of danger, especially late in the afternoon and into the evening. Throughout the day the costermongers were forced to drop the price of the perishable fruit, so that later in the day the poorer, less respectable, customers came out to see what they could afford. The goblins appear in the mornings to other maids, but to Lizzie and Laura only in the evenings, desperate to sell. The gender of both customer and seller is significant, since Catherine Gallagher notes that Victorian middle class was fascinated with costermongers because they raised to consciousness 'the transactions that are taking place in every building across the city, embodied by what takes place in the open air' (1987: 83). Covent Garden takes its name from the site of a convent belonging to Westminster Abbey, called Covent (or Convent) Garden, acquired by Henry VIII in 1536 as part of his reorganisation of monastic lands 'for the King's use' (Kingsford 1925: 40–1). Victorian Covent Garden was no garden where women walked in sanctity, neither was it an orchard, even though it was filled with fruit. Not only are these hidden transactions suspicious, but those mirroring them are taking place in the Gothicised space of the city, removed in every sense from the golden liminality of enchanted orchards and yet parading their products – apples – to every likely client. The city, especially London, as a Gothic site complete with 'goblins', 'intensifies throughout the century', writes Alexandra Warwick, 'gathering further associations in post-Darwinian thinking about issues of degeneration, race and empire' (2014: 102). Aside from the familiar yet dangerous apples, the fruits in 'Goblin Market' are luscious and exotic, implicated in a poetic discourse on degeneracy in general, 'goblin' men and vulnerable women in the marketplace, away from the safety of the garden or the rustic cottage but aware of all this garden temptation.

REWARDS AND RISKS

The goblins appear male, the girls are in danger, and yet in the real market the *female* fruit seller was 'a visible and audible emblem of the sexual and economic exploitation that goes on behind closed doors and has driven her onto the street' (Gallagher 1987: 83). The fruit sellers could be seen as both in danger, and dangerous in themselves. Erika Rappaport's study of Victorian female consumers explores the physical and moral perils of a woman out shopping alone. 'Perhaps nothing was more revolting than the spectacle of a middle-class woman immersed in the filthy, fraudulent, and dangerous world of the urban marketplace' (2001: 6), especially a market in which 'all … are connected by hidden acts and secrets' (Warwick 2014: 103). Germaine Greer sees 'Goblin Market' as a poem and as a symbol, as an expression of repression, asserting that Rossetti had a 'terror of physical experience' (in Rossetti 1975: xxii). This atmosphere of a sensual, physical danger to Lizzie and Laura as customers of the goblin market is expressed in the way in which the goblins, like the cos-termongers and the women selling apples from baskets, are no respecters of personal space. Shoppers and sellers alike were prepared to ignore the societal separations of gender, class and respectability in order to secure any kind of bargain.

In this enchanted, dangerous trading space, therefore, it is significant that Rossetti begins the goblins' enticing list of 'fruit forbidden' with apples, perhaps projecting her own fears of physicality onto an already ambiguous symbol. The description of the apples in 'Goblin Market' mimics that of the ultimate forbidden fruit that growing on the Tree of the Knowledge of Good and Evil in Eden, described in the Bible as 'good for food' and 'pleasant to the eyes' (Genesis 3: 6), while Rossetti's goblins describe their fruits as 'sweet to tongue and sound to eye' ['Goblin Market': 30]. However good-looking these fruits may be, Rossetti was aware that even an apple could be poisonous. In 1855 Arthur Hassal led a long-running investigation into adulteration of many common foods, finding that some apples were being painted with poisonous colours to conceal blemishes. The press reported his findings with alarm:

> APPLES: Purchased in James Street, Covent Garden. The apples in this sample are coloured yellow, and on one side deep red; … The red consists of the usual non-metallic pigment, and the yellow is due to the presence of CHROMATE OF LEAD in really *poisonous amount!* (Hassal 1855: 248, emphasis in original)

What makes 'Goblin Market' so vivid, and so worthy of inclusion as an ecoGothic text is the simultaneous warping and twisting of two material environments connected with the innocence of orchard fruits – the urban market and the implied, but scantily described, rural cottage idyll. Inside the goblins' market, the familiar apple becomes the uncanny forbidden fruit and desires become deadly. The sweet, fairy story landscape of a rural cottage in a glen, a setting which Ruskin specifically associated with innocence and purity, becomes a place of danger, not of nostalgia. Benign fruit cultivation is subverted so that the trees become unnatural, for 'who knows upon what soils they fed / Their hungry, thirsty roots' [44–5]. Poor Jeanie, who ate the goblin fruits and wasted away, seems to be contaminated by them even after death, as Lizzie reminds her sister:

> To this day no grass will grow
> Where she lies low:
> I planted daisies there a year ago
> That never blow. ['Goblin Market': 159–62]

In order to save her sister, Lizzie must leave her idyllic cottage and take on the marketplace, becoming a conduit or vessel for the sickening juices, but never for a moment becoming, literally, a consumer. Lizzie's virtues of self-denial and self-discipline hold her safe against malevolent goblins and poisoned luxuries, as she dives into the dangers of that busy, jostling market. When she returns to her sister she emphasises the transaction was with 'goblin merchant men' ['Goblin Market': 474]. The sisters remain together in adulthood, bringing up their daughters to beware of the promises made by 'the wicked, quaint fruit-merchant men' [553] even as the girls in Millais's orchard recognise the dangers of change, decay and death within their orchard sanctuary.

Apples and apple trees in Victorian art and literature work, often almost subliminally, to pull the apple's ancient associations with risk and reward into a more contemporary, albeit equally mythic, setting. The particular associations of the apple and its orchard with sin, myth and magic make it a powerfully 'Gothic' fruit, so much so that any transaction between a customer and a costermonger has the capacity to turn into a risky business. If polite Victorian shoppers already saw the urban apple sellers as exotic, untrustworthy 'Arabians', why not go a step further and turn costermongers into goblins? Close reading of Victorian texts, both factual and fiction, draws the orchard out from golden myths of a lost England. While some Victorian writers revelled in progress and urbanisation, depictions of the orchard, and of the domestic garden, as a place of calm, persisted. The orchard in culture has been a refuge, a sacred space, but also a place of mystery and magic. This cultural identity forms a counterpoint to the reality of the nineteenth-century productive orchard, which was a place of activity and change, of human intervention, very different from the enchanted, Gothic scene portrayed in art.

WORKS CITED

Barrow, Rosemary. 2007. *The Use of Classical Art and Literature by Victorian Painters 1860–1912* (Lewiston: Edwin Mellon Press)

Brandt, Katja. 2006. 'Christina Rossetti's "Goblin Market": Milton Revised or Revived' (Abo: Abo Akademi)

Delumeau, Jean. 1995. *History of Paradise: the Garden of Eden in Myth and Tradition*, trans. by Matthew O'Connell (New York: Continuum)

Ebbatson, Roger. 2005. *An Imaginary England: Nation, Landscape and Literature 1840–1920* (Aldershot: Ashgate)

Elston, Melissa. 2012 'A World Outside: George Eliot's Ekphrastic Third Sphere in "The Mill on the Floss"', *George Eliot – George Henry Lewes Studies* 62/63: 34–48

Ewing Ritchie, James. 1858. *The Night Side of London* (London: William Tweedie)

Fabry, Irene. 2006. 'Continuity and Discontinuity: Illuminating and Interlacing the Adventures of Viviane and Merlin in the "Prose Merlin"', *Marginalia*, 3, www.marginalia.co.uk/journal/06illumination/fabry.php [accessed 29 May 2020]

Fleming, Gordon H. 1998. *John Everett Millais: A Biography* (London: Constable)

Gallagher, Catherine. 1987. 'The Body versus the Social Body in the Works of Thomas Malthus and Henry Mayhew', in *The Making of the Modern Body: Sexuality and Society in the Nineteenth Century*, ed. by Thomas Laquer (Berkeley: University of California Press), pp. 83–106

Hanson, Melanie. 2010. 'The Consumed Consumer: Business as Usual for Rossetti's Goblin Men', in *Merchants, Barons, Sellers and Suits*, ed. by Christa Mahalik (Newcastle upon Tyne: Cambridge Scholars Publishing), pp. 57–95

Harris, Edwin. 1884. *Under the Blossom that Hangs on the Bough*, oil on canvas, 91.5 x 60.4 cm, private collection

Hassal, Arthur Hill. 1855. *The London Quarterly Review – American Edition*, ed. by J. G. Lockhart (New York: Leonard Scott & Co.)

Hodder, Edwin. 2014. *The Life and Work of the Seventh Earl of Shaftesbury, K G* (1886) (Cambridge: Cambridge University Press)

Kingsford, Charles Lethbridge. 1925. *The Early History of Piccadilly, Leicester Square, Soho and their Neighbourhood* (Cambridge: Cambridge University Press)

Lowenthal, David. 1991. 'British National Identity and the English Landscape', *Rural History*, 2: 205–30

Mayhew, Henry. 1861. *London Labour and the London Poor, Volume I* (London, Griffin, Bohn and Co.)

Millais, John Everett. 1859. *Apple Blossoms*, or *Spring*, oil on canvas, 123 x 176.3cm, Lady Lever Art Gallery, Liverpool

Millais, John Everett. 1858. *The Vale of Rest*, oil on canvas, 103 x 172.7cm, Tate Britain, London

Prest, John. 1981. *The Garden of Eden* (New Haven: Yale University Press)

Rappaport, Erika Diane. 2001. *Shopping for Pleasure: Women in the Making of London's West End* (Princeton: Princeton University Press)

Rogers, Revd Williams. 1857. 'On the Trade, Habits and Education of the Street Hawkers of London', *Journal of the Society of Arts*, 3. 4: 298–304

Rossetti, Christina. 1862. *Goblin Market and other Poems* (London: Macmillan & Co.)

Rossetti, Christina. 1975. *Goblin Market*, ed. and intro. by Germaine Greer (New York: Stonehill)

Ruskin, John. 1904. 'The Academy Notes', in *The Works of John Ruskin, Volume XIV*, ed. by E. T. Cooke and Alexander Wedderburn (London: George Allen), pp. 1–310

Ruskin, John. 2010. 'Of Modern Landscape', in *The Works of John Ruskin, Volume V*, ed. by E. T. Cooke and Alexander Wedderburn (Cambridge: Cambridge University Press), pp. 317–52

Seaton, Beverly. 2012. *The Language of Flowers: A History* (Charlottesville: University of Virginia Press)

Staley, Allan. 2004. 'Pre-Raphaelites in the 1860s: III', *British Art Journal*, 5. 2: 3–12

Tennyson, Alfred. 2007. 'Morte d'Arthur' (1842), in *Tennyson: A Selected Edition*, ed. by Christopher Ricks (London: Longman)

Warwick, Alexandra. 2014. 'Gothic, 1820–1880', in *Terror and Wonder: The Gothic Imagination*, ed. by Dale Townshend (London: British Library), pp. 94–123

Willes, Margaret. 2015. *The Gardens of the British Working Class* (New Haven: Yale University Press)

4

Gothic Eden: Gardens, religious tradition and ecoGothic exegesis in Algernon Blackwood's 'The Lost Valley' and 'The Transfer'

Christopher M. Scott

Throughout his short stories, Algernon Blackwood forms physical landscapes that frequently feature religious iconography. In his autobiographical *Episodes Before Thirty* (1923), Blackwood admits that at one stage of his life he considered himself Buddhist, albeit an esoteric one, yet this acknowledgement obfuscates a much larger picture. Blackwood never subscribed to any religious creed or dogma. Over the years, he wove a spiritual tapestry thread by thread, replacing and supplementing his faith as he went along. The terrestrial landscape occupied much of that spiritual space, but along with a focus on the physical environment in Blackwood's fiction, something else often surfaces from within that space. Isolated in a mountainous terrain, the protagonist in 'H. S. H.' (1913), Delane, must engage with not only a perilous, tempestuous environment but also the evil therein. Materialising from within the setting, Satan visits Delane with the aim of tempting the latter to worship him. Delane eventually summons the courage to cast Satan away, defeating him with pure love (charity) but in the context of Christian symbolic experiences. The protagonist in 'The Sacrifice' (1913) performs what the title suggests and does so for others in Christ-like fashion atop a Calvary-esque summit after administering the Holy Sacrament in a scene mirroring Luke 22: 19–20. Blackwood's famous story, 'The Willows' (1907), also references the sign of the Cross appearing in the sky. For a supposed believer and practitioner of Eastern mysticism, Blackwood employs myriad Christian references attached to the terrestrial settings in his fiction, especially the garden landscapes in his short stories.

One of Blackwood's earliest critics, Grace Isabel Colbron, published a review in 1915 about a peculiar spatial 'theme' running throughout Blackwood's texts that champions the 'Unknown' and occupies a 'great realm' between it and what is 'Known' or 'Obvious' (1915: 620). This liminal space emerges at the heart of Blackwood's fiction and embodies the physical settings that constitute his narrative *mise en scène*. She concludes that within this constructed 'borderland' space, Blackwood manufactures horror (620). The assembled horrors produce an uncanny phenomenon at the heart of Blackwood's supernatural landscapes.

Blackwood's characters are attracted to the horror in the supernaturally liminal space. In his *Elegant Nightmares: The English Ghost Story from Le Fanu to Blackwood*, Jack Sullivan focuses on Blackwood's characterisation, arguing that his characters are visionaries who seek unknown spaces and discover horror (1978: 113). Sullivan also notes that Blackwood himself served as a pattern for his own characters: 'What binds Blackwood's work together is a distinctive vision' that unifies the narrative (113), and this vision verges on the 'mystical' (117). The various characters deployed in Blackwood's tales vicariously live the outlook and beliefs of their mystical master. Blackwood spent most of his years 'continually seeking new places, experiences, and visions' (117). And like Blackwood, his characters often feel 'oppressed by everyday reality' and 'deliberately seek out other worlds' (113). What they eventually discover advances Colbron's conclusion: horror awaits those who cross beyond the liminal nexus. Yet departing slightly from Colbron's position, Sullivan notes a positive rather than negative experience when protagonists return to the quotidian world from the apparently hostile space. In *Supernatural Horror in Fiction*, Peter Penzoldt first claimed that Blackwood was an anomalously 'positive' author in the genre of supernatural fiction (1952: 228–53). Sullivan appears to extend Penzoldt's assertion. Unlike the characters in the supernatural tales of, say, Joseph Sheridan Le Fanu, M. R. James or Arthur Machen, those in Blackwood's stories find themselves restored to normality at the denouement as opposed to being harmed or obliterated. This journey, Sullivan points out, constitutes an 'unfinished circle', where the Blackwoodian protagonist experiences the horror of an alien dimension before returning safely to reality (1978: 114).

Notwithstanding these developments in literary scholarship about Blackwood's fiction, critics have generally overlooked the ecoGothic function of the garden in Blackwood's short stories between 1907 and 1914, not noticing specifically how and why Edenic settings constitute Gothic spaces and what their *mise en scène* illustrates. Scholars have also disregarded iconographic references to Christianity permeating or emanating from Blackwood's physical settings. This chapter will thus argue that Blackwood's 'The Lost Valley' (1910) and 'The Transfer' (1912) employ the *modus operandi* of the ecoGothic to present supernatural gardens that emit dread deriving from Adam and Eve's fall and subsequent ejection from Eden. Blackwood's fiction during this period in British history anticipates late twentieth-century ecotheology by elucidating an extant liminal landscape separating the terrestrial/celestial or mortal/immortal worlds where humankind might transcend postlapsarian paranoia through embracing rather than subduing the fallen world. How to 'understand the nature of another, particularly when that other may be ... multiple, obscured, invisible', as Elizabeth Chang notes (2019: 179), was a pressing concern for Blackwood, demonstrated here.

Depictions of Eden enjoy a rich history within Occidental literature, although bearing little resemblance to the sparse account of the garden in Eden as described in Genesis. The proposed Edenic landscape was conjured through subsequent texts and paintings, from Dante Alighieri's *Divina Commedia* (1320), for example, through Edmund Spenser's *Faerie Queen* (1590) and most famously John Milton's *Paradise Lost* (1667). Dante's Edenic Paradise is a spiritual habitation in an 'ancient holy wood' at the summit of Mount Purgatory ([*Purgatorio*: XXVIII. 1–21] in Alighieri 2001); Spenser depicts an Arcadian landscape; and Milton re-creates English landscapes and georgic virtue in his *Paradise Lost*. Edenic construction also permeates the settings in Blackwood's 'The Lost Valley' and 'The Transfer'. When the protagonists experience and interpret their respective settings, the *mise en scène* reflects an atmosphere generally considered 'Edenic', as mentioned in the fourth book of *Paradise Lost*. The garden in 'The Lost Valley', for example, consists of lush but recognisable vegetation: 'Lawnlike grass, wild lilac bushes, willows, pines, beeches' and 'flowers; ... tall, graceful blue flowers' (Blackwood 2014b: 3996–7).

David Del Principe states that ecoGothic observes nature from a literary Gothic perspective by 'taking a nonanthropocentric position to reconsider the role that the environment, species, and nonhumans play in the construction of monstrosity and fear', and he also identifies the ecoGothic inclusion of the Gothic body to explore how that site relates with 'environmental and species identity' (2014: 1). Blackwood's employment of the supernatural arrives after a Gothic resurgence in *fin-de-siècle* literature with such publications as Arthur Machen's *The Great God Pan* (1894) and Richard Marsh's *The Beetle* (1897), among others. Although occasionally employing the Gothic aesthetic in his narratives, Blackwood prefers instead to implement it in the light of his own interpretation of spiritual and ecological ontologies. Blackwood's nuanced presentation of the Gothic aesthetic cultivates an ecoGothic parterre within which Blackwood's physical landscapes evoke dread through a mystical conflation of gardens and the otherworldly.

BLACKWOODIAN MYSTICAL LANDSCAPES

When he observed the natural landscape, Blackwood viewed it beyond its mere exterior characteristics. He recognised the spiritual, magical forests of ancient lore in those actual forests he beheld around him, as during a train journey across rural Canada in 1894: 'I saw Panthea', he records in his auto-biography, *Episodes Before Thirty*, meaning 'all deity' (Blackwood 1923: 238). Viewing a physical landscape replete with the marvellous casts a supernatural hue upon the features of the terrestrial landscape, and this interpretation of the biosphere colours the natural settings in Blackwood's fiction between 1907 and 1914.

Though he mentions a spiritually interpretive experience with the physical landscape in *Episodes*, Blackwood's journey to the Rainy River District in Canada did not initiate his understanding of the material environment as anything more than natural. His nuanced interpretation of the natural world occurred after his father relocated the family during Blackwood's childhood from the Manor House in Crayford to Shortlands House near Bromley, England, where the new residence boasted a more expansive structure as well as ample land for the children to play. Blackwood recalls one such momentous experience. During the night, he surreptitiously climbed out of his bedroom window to explore the grounds. In *Episodes*, Blackwood shares his childhood excitement during these nocturnal excursions when he ventured through the gardens before discovering a secluded pond. Completely concealed by trees, the pond served as a preternatural place for Blackwood: 'All sorts of beings watched me silently from the shore, crowding among tree stems, and whispering to themselves about what I was doing' (33–4). Blackwood's opening clause with the determiner 'all' followed by the nebulous description 'sorts of beings' places rhetorical emphasis on the variety and innumerable possibility of entities amid the forested pond. Rather than referring to a specific form of existence among the trees, Blackwood leaves open the possibility for a host of supernatural potentials to arrive. About these ethereal members of the natural terrain, Blackwood later reveals, 'Night and stars and trees and wind and rain were the things I had to do with and wanted. They were *alive* and personal' (34, emphasis added). For Blackwood, the variety of beings within the landscape around him constitutes an alternate reality, and the garden serves as a nexus between his worldly and otherworldly existence (represented by his house and pond, respectively). These positive childhood experiences reflect a gestational period for an interpretation of physical landscapes that emerges in narratives with ethereal settings springing to life.

Blackwood reveals his view of the terrestrial world by infusing elements of the celestial into his fictional settings: the supernatural space in his fiction ostensibly reflects his own interpretations of what constitutes the physical environment. 'The Lost Valley' depicts this type of setting through the pro-tagonist's perspective. Walking alone during his descent into the heart of the eponymous valley, Doctor Stephen Winters (referred to throughout the text simply as 'Stephen') observes myriad elements of floral beauty surrounding him. From 'patches of lawnlike grass' to 'wild lilac bushes' to 'clumps of ... tall, graceful, blue flowers nodding in a dream', Stephen encounters botanical elements that paint a colourful landscape comparable to a floral garden (Blackwood 2014b: 3996). Yet despite a natural presentation of beauty, this ostensible garden space functions as a nexus between Stephen's familiar world and the unfamiliar essence of the valley. Stephen experiences a strange characteristic of the landscape he neither expected nor ever experienced in his life. Whizzing and fluttering around him, the trees of the eponymous valley make themselves known: 'From the whole surface of the woods rose a single murmur; like the whirring of voices heard in a dream, he thought. The individual purring of trees was merged' (3996). The forest erupts into what Stephen describes as a cacophony of murmuring, whirring voices and purring. Stephen's unnatural experience in this supposedly natural terrain mirrors Blackwood's childhood excursion in and around the gardens at his Bromley house. Like Stephen, Blackwood described his vegetal surroundings as sentient entities. These similar experiences with the cohabitation of familiarity and unfamiliarity evoke Sigmund Freud's concept of *unheimlich* (the uncanny) where an observed object causes momentary dissonance in the viewer's mind because it simultaneously embodies something familiar and unfamiliar (2003: 1–2). Particularly in Stephen's case, the familiar appearance of botanical materials conflicts with the unfamiliar behaviour they exhibit. Unexpectedly for Stephen, trees are seemingly audible. The notion of arboreal audibility resurfaces in another of Blackwood's short stories titled 'Pines' (1914a). In this tale, the protagonist believes sound emanates from adjacent pine trees, but he then rationally attributes the aural source to the wind in the trees (4771). Narrative situations in which sound emanates from material objects and elements exist in canonical Gothic texts. Ann Radcliffe, for instance, personifies the wind in her novel *The Romance of the Forest* (1791), in which Adeline finds herself alone in an ominous passageway where the wind's contact with the physical structure of the building emits lifelike sounds throughout its interior (155). Like Radcliffe, Blackwood accentuates the sound of wind in 'The Lost Valley' but does so through a cooperative relationship between the wind and the trees. In contrast to Radcliffe's narrative, 'The Lost Valley' depends on the understanding that the trees function without rational explanation. Tzvetan Todorov proposes that, in an empirical reality,

> there occurs an event which cannot be explained by the laws of this same familiar world. The person who experiences the event must opt for one of two possible solutions: either he is the victim of an illusion of the senses, of a product of the imagination – and laws of the world then remain what they are; or else the event has indeed taken place, it is an integral part of reality – but then this reality is controlled by laws unknown to us. (Todorov 1975: 25)

Todorov describes a phenomenon occurring during the moment of narrative ambiguity: the 'fantastic' (1975: 25). S. T. Joshi sees Todorov's conception of the fantastic (*le fantastique*) as belonging to the supernatural horror category of weird fiction (2003: 7). A 'child' of the literary Gothic mode, weird fiction amplifies fantastic moments where the otherworldly irrational thing irrupts into the mundane rational space to arouse feelings of dread (Lovecraft 1973: 14). During Stephen's experience with the fantastic in the forest, neither he nor the narrator attempts to explain the outlandish events, oscillating between supernatural phenomena as they occur and a description of Stephen's dreamlike recognition of the forest sounds. This weird uncertainty lingers until the story's climax when Stephen discovers an inherent connection between the supernatural events and those in the 'real' world, something natural and material. Todorov explains that this literary function highlights what he calls the 'fantastic marvellous', an embodiment of the narrative's ability to suspend certainty until the end, when supernatural phenomena are accepted as connected to reality (1975: 41). 'The Lost Valley' finally pivots on this concept and does so to tether the mystical phenomena associated with the physical landscape to authenticity. Trees in this weird story are audible because they possess emotions; they move because they are alive.

The concept of a fantastically marvellous liminal setting resurfaces elsewhere in Blackwood's oeuvre. Towards the end of the nineteenth century, unexpected physical movement among plant species became a known topic of scientific investigation. Following such publications in 1875 as *On the Movements and Habits of Climbing Plants* and *Insectivorous Plants*, Charles Darwin presents theories on plant mobility in *The Power of Movement in Plants* (1880), in which he concludes that plants react to external sources, namely the sun, and exhibit movement for survival. Plant locomotion became part of the 'monstrous' as demonstrated in such literary examples as Phil Robinson's 'The Man-Eating Tree' (1881) and H. G. Wells's 'The Flowering of the Strange Orchid' (1894). A decade later, Blackwood's fiction replicates this literary botanical trend. 'The Transfer' (1911) depicts a physical landscape through the perspective of Miss Gould, the protagonist, governess for the Frene family, and would-be 'professional clairvoyante' (Blackwood 2014c: 4470). The story's plot hinges upon events connected to a prohibited portion of the family's garden, referred to as the 'Forbidden Corner' (4471):

> It stood at the far end of the magnificent rose garden, a bald, sore place, where the black earth showed uglily in winter, almost like a piece of dangerous bog, and in summer baked and cracked with fissures where green lizards shot their fire in passing. In contrast to the rich luxuriance of death amid life, a center of disease that cried for healing lest it spread. But it never did spread. Behind it stood the thick wood of silver birches and, glimmering beyond, the orchard meadow, where the lambs played. (Blackwood 2014c: 4472)

In the narrator's description of the 'sore place', a notion of spatial liminality already surfaces. Located at the border of the garden, a bald patch represents a threshold between two influences. The description, ostensibly from Miss

Gould's perspective, highlights a broad juxtaposition between an idyllic garden space and a repulsively deserted one; there are other oppositional points that straddle the overarching liminality of the scene: winter and summer, death and life, fire-breathing lizards and frolicking lambs. Even the positioning of the words delineates the location of the patch in relation to the rest of the garden. From the perimeter, the reader is led across the garden with another description of the hideous bald patch that lies beyond the beautiful section before concluding with another peaceful image of a blissful orchard meadow. There are metaphorical Christian elements in the fire-breathing lizards and galivanting lambs. Leviticus 11: 29 designates lizards as 'unclean' creeping things whereas in the New Testament, lambs are associated with Christ. The employment of these oppositional Judaeo-Christian metaphors along with a physical presentation of their description demonstrates the relational topography of the garden. Though each individual piece stands opposite to its neighbouring one, collectively they form the expanse of the garden. There are borders and boundaries that function to structure the textual description of the garden's various thresholds which may or may not be transgressed. Liminality, then, permeates the setting in 'The Transfer' and affects not only the appearance of the garden's elements but the latter's behavioural characteristics as well, especially that of the barren patch.

In spite of Gould's own ability to sense the notorious patch, it connects personally with the seven-year-old family heir under her care: Jamie. On several occasions, for instance, he 'heard it crying' and 'swore' that the spot 'shook its surface … while he watched it' (4473). Jamie is the main witness to the garden's physical activity, but because of Gould's age, position and confidence within the Frene family, she occupies a place of credibility in the story; her conveying of Jamie's experiences testifies to the ominous garden's unfamiliar qualities. The garden's uncanny characteristics – mirroring those of the trees in 'The Lost Valley' – resist rational explanation and become grafted into the narrative's fantastically marvellous reality. But unlike 'The Lost Valley', the supernatural garden patch bears deeper anthropomorphic qualities. Blackwood's garden patch demonstrates an ability to cry and react to human interaction, and this evolving presentation of borderland establishes a new level of consciousness inherent in Blackwood's narrative settings.

Blackwood was familiar with the conflation of consciousness and nature, sharing his inspiration in *Episodes* for understanding the mystical features of nature in this light. An influential figure from Blackwood's pantheon was Gustav Fechner and his theory of the natural world in relation to the cosmos. Fechner's *Zend-Avesta: On the Things of Heaven and the Hereafter* (1906) examines the intersection of consciousness and nature and ultimately argues that all nonhuman terrestrial life bears – together with humankind – an innate form of consciousness. William James, whose own philosophical positions also

7 Tailpiece to 'The Transfer', Algernon Blackwood. 1912. *Pan's Garden: A Volume of Nature Stories* (London: Macmillan). Drawing, W. Graham Robertson (1866–1948)

demonstrate Fechner's influence, echoes the latter's idea that the 'whole universe ... is everywhere alive and conscious' (2012: 70). Crediting Fechner as one of his main sources of inspiration, Blackwood perceives nonhuman nature as 'alive' and with a 'consciousness' (1923: ch. 5). This interpretation of the world informs Blackwood's fiction in which terrestrial landscapes emit a palpable sense of cognisance. When Stephen, in 'The Lost Valley', finds himself detached from society and alone within the physical setting, his senses awaken among a multitude of conscious nonhuman life around him. Likewise, Jamie's interaction with the garden in 'The Transfer' demonstrates cognisant qualities otherwise believed to be non-existent in a landscape. Blackwood's interpretation of Fechner's theory of nature-consciousness translates into fictional settings that stand apart from those in other weird stories and emphasise the living characteristics of nonhuman objects typically viewed as static and bereft of feeling.

Though the nonhuman atmosphere assumes otherworldly characteristics in Blackwood's tales, nothing depicts a mystical setting in the light of Fechner's theory as explicitly as the garden in 'The Transfer'. The story's emphasis on the diabolical garden patch directs attention to the qualities that separate it from other entities – human and nonhuman – in the plot. Even though Gould represents the source of information in the narrative, Jamie constitutes the point of contact with the ostensibly nefarious portion of the garden. After experiencing the unknown life force in the ground by way of its sounds and movement, Jamie 'secretly gave it food in the form of birds or mice or rabbits he found dead upon his wanderings' (Blackwood 2014c: 4773). Not only is he aware of the garden's unique features, but Jamie also understands that the nonhuman entity – whatever it may be – experiences hunger and yearns for something to satiate its appetite. Darwin's *Insectivorous Plants* primarily examines the carnivorous plant species *Drosera rotundifolia*, the common sundew, and discovered that it, along with other carnivorous plants, digests its prey using a similar process to animals and humans (1875: 135). Though Blackwood never explains the digestive process of the garden patch, Jamie slakes its hunger by fetching it prey. Jamie's connection to this nonhuman being becomes real through its own consciousness. Nobody besides Jamie understands the strange phenomena in the garden, but in the light of Fechner's nature-consciousness, 'The Transfer' reveals a mystical space in which the fantastic marvellous inverts logic through the presentation of an alternative understanding of the physical landscape – presented as reality – where the setting is consciously alive, experiences hunger, and must eat to survive.

Dead animals, however, are not the only prey that this garden consumes. Upon the arrival of the reprehensible Uncle Frank, known for his scheming and manipulation of innocent people, the garden patch exhibits behaviour that supersedes any occurring earlier in the plot. Jamie, standing on one side of the garden patch, maintains his distance from Uncle Frank, who approaches him from the opposite side and attempts to lure Jamie into the patch. Meanwhile, the patch mysteriously pulls Uncle Frank directly towards it:

> One moment on the edge he wobbled horribly, then with that queer sideways motion, rapid yet ungainly, he stepped forward into the middle of the patch and fell heavily upon his face. His eyes, as he dropped, faded shockingly, and across the countenance was written plainly what I can only call an expression of destruction. He looked utterly destroyed. (Blackwood 2014c: 4481)

Such words as 'destruction' and 'destroyed' describe Uncle Frank's final condition after his fall, for the 'emissaries of the two kingdoms, the human and the vegetable, had met' (4478). But was his destruction due to physical collapse? The text is not explicit yet offers a clue as to the true nature of his experience. After Uncle Frank's fall, Gould hears a 'gulp' that sounded 'deep and muffled' as it 'dipped away into the earth' and senses a 'pungent smell of earth' (4481). The garden patch apparently consumes Uncle Frank as a sundew digests its insectile prey, and all the vitality that Uncle Frank had leeched from his innocent victims has now transferred from him into the garden patch. Uncle Frank never returns to the house; the narrator, Gould, confirms, 'It seemed as if he dropped suddenly out of life. The papers never mentioned him. His activities ceased, as it were' (4481). The garden patch, on the other hand, flourishes: 'It had changed. It lay untouched, full of great, luscious, driving weeds and creepers, very strong, full – fed, and bursting thick with life' (4481). Unlike in the setting of Blackwood's 'The Lost Valley', vegetal material in 'The Transfer' consumes the human-ness of beings without killing the body. Although he also toys with this idea in the story 'The Man whom the Trees Loved' (1912), Blackwood never places such a robust emphasis as he does in 'The Transfer' on the ability of a vegetal being to digest and reform a human or nonhuman animal while its material body survives. This focus on material ground and its appetite attaches a palpable level of consciousness to Blackwood's mystical landscapes.

In the light of eating, falling and (psychically) dying within a mystical space, let alone garden, these Blackwoodian landscapes conjure up biblical imagery of Earth's first ecological locus. Familiar to Blackwood through his strict Christian upbringing, Eden constitutes the root element of the landscape within which converge physical and supernatural characteristics. A spiritually charged Edenic landscape would primarily stimulate the locations in Blackwood's oeuvre between 1907 and 1914.

HOW 'THE LOST VALLEY' AND 'THE TRANSFER' PRESENT AN ARGUMENT FOR EDEN

Finally, I would like to reconsider both these stories in the light of how uncanniness, through the process of revelation and defamiliarisation, leads to redemptive conclusions for human collaborators and works with ecoGothic tropes in order to 'expose the monstrous anthropocentric gaze' (Del Principe 2014: 2). One major Christian influence in Blackwood's life was his father. Stevenson Arthur Blackwood experienced his life-altering conversion to Christianity while serving in the British military during the Crimean War. A firm adherence to the Bible embodied the atmosphere in which young Algernon and his siblings were raised, and his childhood memories retrieve mixed feelings. Like many of the protagonists in his texts, Blackwood found himself straddling borders. Despite his parents' suffocating zeal, he admired them affectionately, especially his father. Blackwood expresses that he had a 'special loving adoration [for him], for he really *lived* his beliefs' (1923: 33, emphasis in original). Notwithstanding a loving familial relationship during his youth, Blackwood felt pulled in diverging directions. He confesses, 'I never shared the beliefs of my parents with anything like genuine pleasure. I was *afraid* they were true, not glad' (23, emphasis in original). Young Blackwood's devotion to his parents' faith seemingly rested on a foundation of fear rooted in the negative aspects of Christianity (sin and damnation) rather than positive theology (forgiveness and salvation). Ultimately, he feared that his parents were simultaneously 'right' and 'wrong', leaving Blackwood to mature with a nagging feeling of guilt that followed him throughout his working life (Ashley 2001: ch. 1). Blackwood neither renounced nor denounced Christianity, which is why it is odd when critics state that he was a Buddhist in the strict sense of the word, as if he inflexibly confined himself to that faith alone. Blackwood incorporated into his belief system various spiritual concepts, and as his mystical landscapes demonstrate, he constructed his fictional settings using biblical scaffolding he would have intimately known and remembered from his youth.

An example is depicted in 'The Lost Valley', which is portrayed as a new world of beauty that resembles both the Edenic one in Milton's *Paradise Lost* and Elysium where immortal Homeric heroes lived 'in the Isles of the Blest … for whom the life-giving Earth / Bears sweet fruit' (Hesiod; Lombardo 1993: 28). Milton paints his Paradise as a recognisable garden-estate landscape, filled with 'Flow'rs' which nature 'Pour'd forth profuse':

> Groves whose rich Trees wept odorous Gums and Balm,
> Others whose fruit burnisht with Golden Rind
> Hung amiable, *Hesperian* Fables true,
> If true, here only, and of delicious taste:
> Betwixt them Lawns, or level Downs, and Flocks
> Grazing the tender herb, were interpos'd,
> Or palmy hillock, or the flow'ry lap
> Of some irriguous Valley spread her store. ([*Paradise Lost*: IX. 248–55] in
>   Milton 2003)

Juxtaposed with 'The Lost Valley', Milton's Edenic 'valley' lends such materials as flowers, trees, and lawns to help Blackwood plant his own version. Visual and sensory attributes, nevertheless, are not the only facets that comprise Blackwood's mysteriously novel landscape. The setting in Blackwood's narrative provides Stephen with a refuge in which to seek shelter from the maelstrom ravaging his conscience because of his internal conflict over his and his brother Mark's relationship with a woman. In this seclusion, Stephen had '[n]ever before … experienced anything approaching the wonder and completeness of it. … It was a peace unchangeable – what some have called, perhaps, the Peace of God' (Blackwood 2014b: 3997), not to be found in the everyday world. In Milton's *Paradise Lost*, Satan describes the garden's potential as 'Heaven on Earth: for blissful Paradise / Of God the Garden was' [IV. 208–9]. However, unlike in the Garden of Eden, human inhabitants apart from Stephen but including his brother are dead while the trees are actively alive. Stephen has been allowed a vision of Elysium that brings no Edenic comfort although earthly beauty is aligned with spiritual harmony in this unplaced place.

When Gould describes the setting in 'The Transfer', she leaves no ambiguity as to what type of terrain she experiences: 'The haze of June lay over that *big garden* like a blanket; the wonderful flowers … hung motionless; the lawns, so soft and thick, cushioned all other sounds; only the limes and huge clumps of guelder roses hummed with bees' (Blackwood 2014c: 4471, emphasis added). In 'The Lost Valley', the eponymous enclave is tucked away in the tresses of endless vegetation – hidden, minute. Yet Gould in 'The Transfer' describes the garden as if it were the only world she ever knew. This interpretation is fitting because the epicentre of the story's action and climax is embedded in this lush space. And like 'The Lost Valley', Blackwood emphasises the paradisiacal nature of this garden through allusion; according to Sullivan, Blackwood prefers to 'suggest' rather than 'define' and appears to do so here (1978: 121). The garden embodies Edenic characteristics not through narrative explication but through character action. Only three characters can experience the full spectrum of the garden: Jamie, Gould and Uncle Frank. David Punter and Joshi highlight the interpersonal triangles in Blackwood's fiction characteristically among two males and a female (Punter 2013: 45–6; Joshi 2003: 110), as in 'The Lost Valley'. I would argue there is a case for interpreting these three individuals as allusions to the trio of the Fall (Adam, Eve and Satan), which is not in itself a Gothic association but in 'The Transfer' is threaded through the significance of familiarity – middle-class gardens, tea on the lawn and children playing – with uncanny and shocking effects.

To explore the story's triangle further, Jamie is portrayed as a perceptive child, innocent and dependent on his father; his sole actions in the narrative occur within the garden he visits. Gould is a clairvoyant young woman who shares Jamie's innocence in the narrative and whose main actions likewise remain confined within the garden. Uncle Frank, on the other hand, is described as a supernaturally antagonistic force who 'vampires' the vitality of others, according to Miss Gould, and tempts his victims with his 'Eastern eyes' (Blackwood 2014c: 4477). Sullivan reads 'The Transfer' as a vampire tale (1978: 112), but Uncle Frank is not a vampire in the sense of Bram Stoker's *Dracula* or John William Polidori's 'The Vampyre' (1819). Blackwood's tale concentrates on Jamie, Gould and their interaction with the garden. Uncle Frank only enters the plot immediately before his climactic contact with the grass patch. And when his characteristics and behaviour become evident, they stand in opposition to those of Jamie and Gould, who are innocent and united in the face of Uncle Frank's worldly evil as long as they are contained within the bounds of the garden. Uncle Frank, conversely, bears striking satanic features. He reflects a devilish image and actions: he is described as having a diabolically wide face, a dangerously persuasive demeanour, and lives off the bodies and lives of others, as if he is missing something himself. In the biblical Book of Revelation, and as depicted in Milton's version of the story, Satan is thrust out of heaven and loses all his status, thereafter depending on evil manipulation to gain any power over humankind. Like Satan, Uncle Frank suffers a relegation of sorts after the climactic event in 'The Transfer', for he loses any cultural status he previously held and utterly disappears from normal society. And, by incarnating evil, Uncle Frank simultaneously facilitates the Gothic aesthetic. As an antagonist similar to that of Horace Walpole's Manfred in *The Castle of Otranto* (1764), Uncle Frank uncovers a buried secret that resurfaces to plague him physically. All these components operate in the container of the narrative's garden, and in so doing, 'The Transfer' ultimately gestures towards an Edenic setting in which Adam, Eve and Satan confronted one another.

Although Blackwood's gardens in both tales attempt to resemble Eden in the Judaeo-Christian sense, they remain anomalous Edenic representations. When juxtaposed with the biblical garden in Genesis, the Edenic settings in 'The Lost Valley' and 'The Transfer' fail to constitute paradise. Perhaps that was never Blackwood's intention, since they show some parallels only. William Golding's *Lord of the Flies* (1954) also presents a paradisiacal setting that bears similitude to Eden. The island in Golding's novel has been viewed as an Edenic allegory (Whitley 1970: 11, Friedman 1997: 65), although it could also be a 'prison' rather than paradise (Reilly 1999: 186). Though likeness exists between the island and Eden in Genesis, Golding's version is no mirror image of the familiar peaceful story. Violence and death coexist on the island until they culminate with the murder of innocent Simon, followed by the buffetings of a raging tempest. While the island exhibits paradisiacal elements, Golding's depiction of an Edenic setting remains complicated.

Blackwood's Edenic landscapes in 'The Lost Valley' and 'The Transfer' are similarly complex. Though they are not replicas of the biblical Eden, they demonstrate equivalences. The Edenic landscape in 'The Lost Valley' is hidden after the beginning of the plot or becomes so after the story's climax. When Augustine describes the Edenic setting in *De Civitate Dei* (426 CE), he emphasises a spiritual (that is, hidden from view) rather than physical landscape (Augustine; Dods 2015: XIV. 10, 26). Blackwood's tales apparently adhere to this Augustinian depiction because initially, their Edenic landscapes are difficult to locate by material means. In 'The Lost Valley', for example, the valley is tethered to legend and may or may not exist: Professor Samarianz 'tells ... of a charming and exquisite legend of a "Lost Valley" that exists hereabouts' (Blackwood 2014b: 3972). Samarianz's status as a scholar in legends and mythology hints at the valley's true elusiveness, for he should have discovered its whereabouts long before the untrained Stephen ever did. But Stephen did not find the valley by himself, he did so only with spiritual help:

> The cool wind ... followed him down, urging him forwards with deliberate pressure, as though a thousand soft hands were laid upon his back. And there were spirits in the wind that day. He heard the.ir voices; and far below he traced by the motion of the tree-tops where they coiled upwards to him through miles of forest. (Blackwood 2014b: 3996)

Spirits guide Stephen towards the hidden Edenic setting in the narrative, which would typically affect a story's protagonist and characters by heightening their level of anxiety, yet they operate as guides in an act that ostensibly saves Stephen from becoming lost. They become familiars in unfamiliar landscapes. Stephen never accomplishes anything in the plot to warrant such encouraging intervention, so it becomes apparent that the uncanny in 'The Lost Valley' identifies a hidden, supernatural source of grace responsible for redeeming those who enter the Edenic landscape.

Supernatural guidance and the redemptive qualities of the Edenic setting also exist in 'The Transfer'. When Uncle Frank arrives for tea, he senses an uncanny presence and feels drawn towards the centre of the narrative's Edenic garden:

> 'Wasn't it char—?' and then broke off abruptly, stammered, drew breath, stood up, and looked uneasily about him. For a second there was a gaping pause. It was like the click which starts some huge machinery moving – that instant's pause before it actually starts. ... He pointed to the empty patch. Then, before any one could answer, he started across the lawn towards it, going every minute faster. (Blackwood 2014c: 4478)

Spiritually prompted and interrupted mid-speech, Uncle Frank follows the presence to the garden's centre, where he meets Jamie and Gould (who followed closely behind him). The only way he discovers the disturbed garden in the story depends on spiritual influence, for without it, the garden's ontological secret would remain hidden from the uninitiated. The supernatural force that is the garden intervenes to consume Uncle Frank's evil and save Jamie. Like Stephen, Jamie never achieves anything worthy of this supernatural intervention on his behalf other than all the small offerings of nourishment he provided the garden patch beforehand. Even so, Jamie receives grace through the uncanny Edenic garden in 'The Transfer'. 'Without the fullness of grace', writes Willis Jenkins, 'a Christian environmental ethic will falter. Without its environmental dimensions, the Christian story of salvation will falter' (2013: 18). Jenkins illuminates an extant symbiotic nexus between grace, the natural environment and soteriology. Blackwood appears to anticipate this ecotheological arrangement when his uncanny Edenic gardens in 'The Lost Valley' and 'The Transfer' exhibit an elusive landscape that fosters supernatural intervention through the administration of grace. This spiritually redemptive function in Blackwood's writing underlines the prominence he places on the Edenic garden in his fiction, yet he does so through the medium of uncanny, even distressing experiences, similar in effect to many of the Christian stories.

Blackwood's fictional narratives constitute an intersection of life and landscape on a higher supernatural plane where his interpretation of the physical environment operates. From a young age, Blackwood stole opportunities for solitude in the wilds, even if his only experience at the time limited itself to the grounds adjacent the family home. From Blackwood's reflections during his lengthy journey by train through the Canadian frontier, the physical setting exemplified a higher sense of life in his fictional worlds. As an author, Blackwood creates settings that defy common expectations; his landscapes are mystical. These liminal locations operate with their own set of rules that fail to adhere to those in the quotidian world. Through Fechner's influence, Blackwood interprets his physical settings as potential carriers of consciousness, and these cognisant landscapes in his narratives separate themselves – through their living and sentient qualities – from other literary settings. The Blackwoodian landscape becomes a space in which Todorov's concept of the fantastic marvellous, operating under the veil of the weird aesthetic, functions as the vehicle through which Blackwood presents a nuanced understanding of the physical environment. This unconventional concept ostensibly reaches its apex in moments where the Blackwoodian landscape experiences such inexplicable anthropomorphic qualities as active cooperation from vegetal agents, or hunger and sensual satisfaction caused by the literal fall and psychic death of a human.

The concepts of falling and dying in a garden are undeniably recognisable in a biblical context, something with which Blackwood was intimately familiar. A feature of Blackwood's life and work is that although he studied other spiritual texts over the course of his life, he never shunned Christianity or the Bible. His path always led to learning new concepts and synthesising them with what he found already familiar. Perhaps Sullivan is correct to call Blackwood 'didactic', since the latter's fiction ostensibly serves as the vehicle in which he delivers his synthesised spiritual knowledge (1978: 114). In an increasingly modernising industrial society, Blackwood seemingly felt the weight of responsibility to warn his generation against forsaking spiritual engagement with bliss or dread in entangled Edens.

WORKS CITED

Alighieri, Dante. 2001. *The Purgatorio* (1320), trans. by John Ciardi (New York: Signet Classic)

Ashley, Mike. 2001. *Algernon Blackwood: An Extraordinary Life* (New York: Carroll & Graf) ebook, no page numbers

Augustine. 2015. *De Civitate Dei* (426 CE), trans. by Marcus Dods (London: Catholic Way Publishing)

Blackwood, Algernon. 1923. *Episodes Before Thirty* (London: Cassell & Co.)

Blackwood, Algernon. 2014a. 'Pines' (1914), in *Ten Minute Stories* (Hastings: Delphi Publishing), ebook, pp. 4768–72

Blackwood, Algernon. 2014b. 'The Lost Valley' (1910), in *The Lost Valley and Other Stories* (Hastings: Delphi Publishing), ebook, pp. 3962–4015

Blackwood, Algernon. 2014c. 'The Transfer' (1912), in *Pan's Garden: A Volume of Nature Stories* (Hastings: Delphi Publishing), ebook, pp. 4470–81

Chang, Elizabeth Hope. 2019. *Novel Cultivations: Plants in British Literature of the Global Nineteenth Century* (Charlottesville and London: University of Virginia Press)

Colbron, Grace Isabel. 1915. 'Algernon Blackwood – An Appreciation', in *The Bookman* (New York: Dodd, Mead & Co.), ebook, pp. 618–21

Darwin, Charles. 1875. *Insectivorous Plants* (London: Murray)

Darwin, Charles. 1898. *The Power of Movement in Plants* (1880) (New York: D. Appleton)

Del Principe, David. 2014. 'Introduction: The EcoGothic in the Long Nineteenth Century', *Gothic Studies*, 16–1: 1–8

Fechner, Gustav Theodor. 1906. *Zend-Avesta: On the Things of Heaven and the Hereafter* (Leipzig: Leopold Voss)

Freud, Sigmund. 2003. *The Uncanny* (1919), trans. by David McLintock (London: Penguin)

Friedman, Lawrence S. 1997. 'A Christian Interpretation', in *Readings on Lord of the Flies*, ed. by Clarice Swisher (San Diego: Greenhaven Press), pp. 65–74

Golding, William. 2016. *Lord of the Flies* (1954) (New York: Penguin)

Hesiod. 1993. *Works and Days* (800 BCE), trans. by Stanley Lombardo (Indianapolis: Hackett Publishing)

James, William. 2012. *Pluralistic Universe* (1909), ed. by Felicia Urbanski et al. (Champaign: Gutenberg)

Jenkins, Willis. 2013. *Ecologies of Grace: Environmental Ethics and Christian Theology* (Oxford: Oxford University Press)

Joshi, S. T. 2003. *The Weird Tale.* (Holicong: Wildside Press)

Lovecraft, H. P. 1973. *Supernatural Horror in Literature* (1927) (New York: Dover)

Milton, John. 2003. *Paradise Lost* (1667), in *John Milton: Complete Poems and Major Prose*, ed. by Merritt Y. Hughes (Cambridge, MA: Hackett Publishing), pp. 173–469

Penzoldt, Peter. 1952. *The Supernatural in Fiction* (London: P. Nevill)

Punter, David. 2013. 'Algernon Blackwood: Nature and Spirit', in *Ecogothic*, ed. by Andrew Smith and William Hughes (Manchester: Manchester University Press), pp. 44–57

Radcliffe, Ann. 2004. *The Romance of the Forest* (1791) (Adelaide: University of Adelaide Press)

Reilly, Patrick. 1999. '*Lord of the Flies:* Beelzebub's Boys', in *Modern Critical Interpretations of Lord of the Flies*, ed. by Harold Bloom (Philadelphia: Chelsea House), pp. 169–208

Sullivan, Jack. 1978. *Elegant Nightmares: The English Ghost Story from Le Fanu to Blackwood* (Athens, OH: Ohio University Press)

Todorov, Tzvetan. 1975. *The Fantastic: A Structural Approach to a Literary Genre* (1970), trans. by Richard Howard (New York: Cornell University Press)

Whitley, John S. 1970. *Golding: Lord of the Flies* (London: Arnold)

5

'That which roars further out': Gardens and wilderness in 'The Man who Went too Far' by E. F. Benson and 'The Man whom the Trees Loved' by Algernon Blackwood

Ruth Heholt

This chapter looks at uneasy and disrupted gardens in the supernatural stories; 'The Man who Went too Far' by E. F. Benson and 'The Man whom the Trees Loved' by Algernon Blackwood. Both tales feature gardens that lie in the heart of the New Forest in Hampshire with the wilderness of the Forest at their borders, and each follows the fate of a man who 'goes too far' in his desire to become at one with nature. These stories are remarkably similar in theme and tone, and published in the same year, 1912; I am going to examine them as a coincidental pair. At the heart of the stories lies the garden – bordered, vivid, beautiful and supposedly safe. These are human-sized spaces of cultivation and civilisation. Attached to the houses, they are a continuation of the domestic space and should offer sanctuary, peace and security. However, we are in the land of the Gothic and therefore that which appears to be homely quickly becomes uncanny and *unheimlich*. The Forest that lies alongside the gardens is a wilderness space, and the boundaries of the gardens are there to keep it at bay. Yet Nature in both tales does not recognise or respect human attempts at demarcation between the wild and the civilised, the nonhuman and the human. Both Benson and Blackwood break down these artificial binaries, showing the *aliveness* of Nature, be it roaring 'further out' in the wild Forest, or subtly (and perhaps slyly) residing in the ordered flowerbeds of the garden. In both spaces the consequences of straying too far are fatal, and the self will become lost.

Nicholas Freeman claims that Blackwood is hailed as 'a forebear of modern paganism', and Benson has been cited as 'nature-worshipping, pantheistic' (2005: 26, 23). In both authors' world-views there is a slippage between the human and nature. In the introduction to *Material Ecocriticism* Serenella Iovino and Serpil Oppermann ask how the often-accepted perception of the difference between the human and the nonhuman can 'conciliate with the entanglements of more-than-human forces and substances, which, visibly or imperceptibly, merge with the life of our bodies and places?' (2014: 3). The answer given by both these stories is that it cannot, and the entanglements are real and material. In the face of the confident, progressive, rationalist period just before the outbreak of World War I, these tales betray a wavering in certainty, a look back to that which has not yet gone, and a fearful sense of crushing forces that will blindly overtake humanity. This reading of Gothic modernism chimes with Simon Hay's critique of the 'process of modernity as one of disenchantment' (2011: 159). Instead of rationalist and progressive, filled with the electric light that will supposedly dispel all ghosts, he reads this era and its relentless movement and restlessness as embodying 'the presence of the ghost' and evincing an 'increasing ghostliness' whereby it is the 'real' that is phantasmal (159). In Hay's discussion it is the 'now' of the modernist era that is haunted.

Part of the disenchantment of the era involved a nostalgic harking back to a simple and primitive past. Robert Dingley points to a popular 'Pan cult' (Dingley 1992) and Gary Varner says that gods like Pan 'represent the spirits of everything – including plants, animals, stones, trees, the winds and all other aspects of this "natural" world and the Otherworld' (2006: 11). Freeman says that common pantheistic themes in late nineteenth- and early twentieth-century fiction 'demonstrated the popularity of tentative "paganism" amongst bourgeois cultural dissidents' (2005: 22). Yet, these cults and movements had, for the most part, a positive view of the melding and merging of human and nonhuman.

Pantheistic influences up to the advent of World War I came with what Michael Bell calls 'a central paradox of Modernism: the most sophisticated achievement of the present is a return to, or a new appreciation of, the archaic' (1999: 20). Bell says that 'as a literary convention primitivism allows the civilized to inspect, or to indulge, itself through an imaginary opposite' (20). A celebration of the 'opposite' carried a critique of contemporary society. In the tales examined here, the 'imaginary opposite' is wildness and the New Forest. In our stories there is a turn back to wild Nature, a refusal of the technologically new, but the transmutation into nonhuman, merging with something bigger and older than the human, does not offer redemption; rejecting the modernist project leads to Gothic horror and an annihilation of self.

CULTIVATION AND WILDERNESS

That the modernist project has both a light and a dark side is not surprising and this dichotomous view seeps into the gardens in the two tales. The garden itself had a troubled relationship with modernism. This latter project was often associated with art practice and gardening itself was viewed as a part of this. Our two stories have different types of gardens. We are told several times throughout 'The Man whom the Trees Loved' that the residence of David and

8 'A couple pose seated in a shaded corner of a back garden in Cobham, Norfolk.
They are surrounded with climbing plants and a well-kept lawn' (c. 1910).
Photograph, collection no: 2014.001

Sophia Bittacy is a cottage, with Blackwood drawing attention to 'their tiny cottage and garden' (2012: 57). The garden becomes a social construction between the home as a building and the world beyond; 'an ideal of domesticity that can contain growth within the bounds of ongoing, stable, organic social relations' (Sayer 2000: 39). The 'cottage' garden sits between the twin impulses of modernism – the relentless pursuit of the new, and the nostalgic glance backwards to folklore and the natural-primitive. In this way the garden can be seen as an unstable space that disrupts both impulses. Yet, for the majority of gardeners, rural or suburban, gardens offer 'an opportunity for the maintenance of order and thereby security; through the traditional practices of gardening, order can be reasserted and a distance put between the gardener and the rest of the world' (106).

Linking it with a nostalgic nod back to the Arts and Crafts movement, Anne Helmreich says the 'cottage' garden 'lacks apparent order, with plants arranged in masses or drifts, but is nevertheless fecund and productive' (2002: 72). Near the beginning of the story, David Bittacy sits at his window, gazing at an idyllic picture of an enclosed garden at the height of the English summer: 'Outside the blackbirds whistled in the shrubberies across the lawn. He smelt the earth and trees and flowers, the perfume of mown grass, and the bits of open heathland far away in the heart of the woods. The summer wind stirred very faintly through the leaves' (Blackwood 2012: 9). Peace, solitude and civilisation reside here. There are shrubberies and a tended lawn. We see David and Sophia Bittacy contemplating the prospect together: 'they looked out of the window where, upon the lawn of their Hampshire cottage, a ragged Lebanon stood in solitary state' (7). This cedar tree, the only one in their garden, is the one we begin the story with – it has been painted by a great tree-artist, Sanderson, who has, we hear, managed to capture its essence. Bittacy ruminates about the picture:

> What I like about it … is the way he has made it live. All trees have it of course, but a cedar taught it to me first – the 'something' trees possess that make them know I'm there when I stand close and watch … I'd like to ask [the artist] how he saw so clearly that it stands between this cottage and the Forest – yet somehow more in sympathy with the mass of woods behind it – a sort of go-between … It stands there like a sentinel – protective rather. (Blackwood 2012: 7)

This garden is bordered by the great mass of the New Forest, as is also the garden in Benson's story, 'The Man who Went too Far'. The garden borders demarcate the domestic, cultivated and civilised human spaces on which, in both stories, the wild Forest is encroaching.

Helmreich asserts that 'The garden as England and England as garden rendered the nation into a stable homeland' (2002: 231). Yet, in order for an English cottage garden to be truly idyllic, it must have some semblance of the wild and the uncultivated. Actual cottage gardens were filled with vegetables, animals such as rabbits and chickens, and accumulated waste as well as colourful flowers; they were intended to keep the labourer literally in his place. 'The country was secure as long as the labourer returned home to tend his flowers (metaphorical and literal)', writes Sayer, 'The male labourer was domesticated through useful toil' (2000: 84). The idealised cottage-style garden exemplified the ethics of the Arts and Crafts movement which was opposed to 'the artificiality and cheap gaudiness attributed to industrial goods' (Helmreich 2002: 68). A cottage garden was at least supposed to *look* natural. The garden in 'The Man whom the Trees Loved', however, has strayed from this type. David Bittacy cannot look at the garden without contemplating the Forest beyond:

> He saw the great encircling mass of gloom that was the Forest, fringing their little lawn. It pressed up closer in the darkness. The prim garden with its formal beds of flowers seemed an impertinence almost – some little coloured insect that sought to settle on a sleeping monster – some gaudy fly that danced impudently down the edge of a great river that could engulf it with a toss of its smallest wave. That Forest with its thousand years of growth and its deep spreading being was some such slumbering monster. Their cottage and garden stood too near its running lip. (Blackwood 2012: 8)

In this garden there is no attempt at an imitation of nature, nothing of the 'wild' garden that one might expect in a picturesque cottage in Hampshire. David's wife Sophia fears the Forest and for her the *raison d'être* of the garden is to keep the wilderness at bay – to protect the home and turn attention away from the wild wood. Therefore there is no attempt at a 'wild' garden here; the formal, artificial, bourgeois and 'prim' aesthetic of this garden is deliberate and reasoned.

The wild garden was an aesthetic choice by this time, made popular in reaction to annual bedding schemes so familiar in the Victorian urban park. William Robinson, in 1870, had championed 'wild' gardens, although it is worth noting the subtitle of his book, *The Wild Garden: Our Groves and Shrubberies Made Beautiful by the Naturalization of Hardy Exotic Plants*. The woodland grove, argued Robinson, close to the house need not be neglected in favour of mixed flower borders; it might respond favourably to some domestic approaches. Robinson alludes to the benefits for both garden and woodland in this, naturalising both areas with spring bulbs, for example. These wilder parts of the garden would allow one to 'acknowledge that you had indeed caught the true meaning of nature in her disposition of vegetation, without sacrificing one jot of anything in your garden, but, on the other hand, adding the highest beauty to spots hitherto devoid of the slightest interest' (Robinson 1870: 24). This garden appears to reject the unifying potential of organised wildness, perhaps recognising that it is only an aesthetic harmony, and if permitted an inch, the encircling woods might demand a mile. The cottage and garden are 'too near' the 'slumbering monster' that is the Forest, but there is the (vain) hope that a sliver of cultivation and civilisation might keep it from invading.

Frank Halton's garden in 'The Man who Went too Far' is also shadowed by the Forest. At sunset on a glorious summer evening we are told:

> This house at the end of the village stood outside the shadow, and the lawn which sloped down to the river was still flecked with sunlight. Garden-beds of daz-zling colour lined its gravel walks, and down the middle of it ran a brick pergola, half-hidden in clusters of rambler-rose and purple with starry clematis. (Benson 2012: 122)

The banked-up and smothering planting is apparent here (the house too is covered in flowers) as it might be in a 'wild' or cottage garden. But there is more order, and human-made architectural elements have been introduced: gravel walks and a brick pergola. There is a terrace linking the house to the garden but the garden aesthetic here is not an attempt to keep Nature at bay: it is also connected to a fluid, volatile presence.

> The river Fawn which runs below [the wood], lay in sheets of sky-reflected blue, and wound its dreamy devious course round the edge of this wood, where a rough two-planked bridge crossed from the bottom of the garden of the last house in the village, and communicated by means of a little wicket gate with the wood itself. Then once out of the shadow of the wood the stream lay in flaming pools of the molten crimson of the sunset. (Benson 2012: 122)

The river lies between the garden and the Forest, forming both a barrier and a link. But where, in Blackwood's story, the cedar tree acts as 'sentinel' with its arms outstretched against the Forest, here the winding river is devious, unstable. There is a bridge from the garden over the river and a gate to communicate with the Forest and which allows access to the garden. This is a deliberate choice: Frank Halton has made a conscious decision to eradicate any possibility of a 'great gulf fixed' between himself as human and Nature and the nonhuman. In Blackwood's story the bridging of the gulf is less conscious: 'That gulf, of course, existed, but Sanderson [through his tree painting] had somehow bridged it' (2012: 41). And it is this 'bridging' of the perceived gulf; its eradication or obliteration, the realisation that it never existed at all, that is at the crux of both stories.

MERGING

In *Material Ecocriticism* Iovino and Oppermann question the 'basic assumption' that there is 'a chasm between the human and the nonhuman world in terms of agency' (2014: 2). The 'new materialist' view of nature, Diana Cole and Samantha Frost argue, involves an ethical claim for 'foregrounding material factors and reconfiguring our very understanding of matter [as] prerequisites for any plausible account of coexistence and its conditions in the twenty-first century' (2010: 2). This is the 'turn to the material' evident in the new environmental and ecocritical debates (2). Here, as David Abram asserts in *Becoming Animal*: 'After three and a half centuries spent charting and measuring material nature as though it were a pure exterior, we've at last begun to notice that the world we inhabit (from the ocean floor to the upper atmosphere) is alive' (quoted in Cole and Frost: 1). These scholarly texts, extolling a new approach to the material and the natural were published in the twenty-first century, and yet the sentiments, ethical concerns and approaches from the earlier stories resemble each other to a remarkable extent. As David Bittacy murmurs to himself in 'The Man whom the Trees Loved': 'It is rather a comforting thought ... that life is about us everywhere, and that there is really no dividing line between what we call organic and inorganic' (Blackwood 2012: 29). And for Frank Halton in 'The Man who Went too Far', the quest of his life is to seek out what he calls the 'final revelation': 'a complete blinding and stroke which will throw open to me, once and for all, the full knowledge, the full realisation and comprehension that I am one ... with life' (Benson 2012: 131). As Sanderson, the tree-painter, says in relation to the universe; 'We're puzzled by the gaps we cannot see across, but as a fact, I suppose there are no gaps at all' (Blackwood 2012: 29). In the two stories of the supernatural, all the boundaries are broken down and the merging, absorption or meshing of human life with the nonhuman is both the goal and the consequence of philosophies, actions and bodily feeling in Frank and David.

> Sanderson tells David that in the Great Forest may stand a rather splendid Entity that manifests through all the thousand individual trees – some huge collective life, quite as minutely and delicately organised as our own. It might merge and blend with you under certain conditions, so that we could understand it by *being* it, for a time at least. (Blackwood 2012: 31, emphasis in original)

It is this concept of 'being it' that resonates with both our protagonists. David is drawn into the Forest and he cares so deeply for the trees that they acknowledge him back. Sanderson speaks to David of the Forest trees: 'their love for you, their "awareness" of your presence involves the idea of winning you – across the border – into themselves – into their world of living. It means, in a way, taking you over' (27). The 'taking over' begins by naming and through language. As Sanderson and David continue their strange conversation, prolonged over several days, about the life of trees, the fact that they are even speaking of such things brings them to pass. '[T]he talk had somehow brought the whole of vegetable kingdom nearer to that of man. Some link had been established between the two. It was not wise, with that great Forest listening at their very doors, to speak so plainly. The Forest edged up closer while they did so' (24–5).

It is speech which has awakened the trees and which forges the link. As Iovino and Oppermann suggest,

> the world's material phenomena are a vast network of agencies, which can be 'read' and interpreted as forming narratives, stories … All matter is 'storied matter'. It is a material 'mesh' of meanings, properties, and processes, in which human and nonhuman players are interlocked in networks that produce undeniable signifying practices. (Iovino and Oppermann 2010: 1–2)

This 'signifying practice' forms an important part of the process of becoming for David Bittacy. The mysteries and secrets of the true nature of matter and life are *spoken*, and there is a suggestion that they are so powerful that silence might be wiser.

In 'The Man who Went too Far', Frank is attempting a conscious 'becoming'. He tells his friend Darcy: 'When a man's body dies, it passes into trees and flowers. Well, that is what I have been trying to do with my soul before death' (Benson 2012: 129). Frank, too, names the mysteries he has been uncovering and sets out to describe to Darcy his great project. He says when he left London:

> I intended to devote my life to the cultivation of joy, and, by continuous and unsparing effort, to be happy. Among people, and in constant intercourse with others, I did not find it possible; there were too many distractions in towns and work-rooms, and also too much suffering. So I … went straight to Nature, to trees, birds, animals, to all those things which quite clearly pursue one aim only, which blindly follow the great native instinct to be happy without any care at all for morality, or human law or divine law. … I sat down here in this New Forest, sat down fair and square, and looked. (Benson 2012: 127)

Frank practises stillness, observation and openness. Then, one day he hears a flute playing. It came from the reeds and the sky and from the trees: 'It was everywhere, it was the sound of life. It was … as the Greeks would have said, it was Pan playing on his pipes, the voice of Nature. It was the life-melody, the world-melody' (129–30). Frank moves away from a distanced observation of Nature and begins to respond affectively to it; the 'affective turn' in contemporary culture is discussed, for example, in cultural geography (Clough and Halley 2007). In this schema, the landscape is not 'over there' – not distanced, not representable, instead it is lived, breathed and the body is immersed. In this manner of contemplating the landscape, 'rather than constituting fixed, static, material entities whose character is primary visual, non-representational approaches see landscape as a sort of performance that is enacted much as is music or theatre' (Oakes and Price 2008: 151). As Frank hears the music, so he is implicated in it; immersed in the wonder of what he is experiencing. As he begins to merge with Nature, Frank's body becomes young and vigorous, expressing his quest in an embodied manner. When we first see Frank, he dives into the river Fawn that acts as both barrier and link between his garden and the Forest beyond. As he floats on his back:

> His eyes were shut, and between half-parted lips he talked gently to himself ... 'I am one with it,' he said to himself, 'the river and I, I and the river. The coolness and splash of it is I, and the water-herbs that wave in it are I also. And my strength and my limbs are not mine but the river's. It is all one, all one, dear Fawn.' (Benson 2012: 123–4)

This is the blending, the becoming, the 'being' that David Bittacy is also destined to experience. Yet there is a difference. Frank's is a conscious enterprise while in 'The Man whom the Trees Loved' David has unconsciously given the Forest 'special invitation' (Blackwood 2012: 57) to come in and, at least to begin with, he fights it for Sophia's sake.

In 'The Man whom the Trees Loved' it is the solitary cedar tree on the lawn of the garden that aids Sophia in her fight to keep David in the human realm and holds the Forest back. Sanderson tells David, 'That cedar will protect you here, though, because you both have humanised it by thinking lovingly of its presence. The other can't get past it' (127–8). The 'other' is the wild Forest. The cedar is more associated with the human – it is in the garden, standing tall between the house and the Forest. However, as Sanderson and David speak more of the mysteries of the links between the Great Vegetable Kingdom and the human, Sophie Bittacy becomes more and more aware of the Forest shifting and moving towards the house:

> It seemed to her that what she saw came from the enveloping forest just beyond their little garden. It emerged in a sort of secret way, moving towards them as with a purpose, stealthily, difficultly. Then something stopped it. It could not advance beyond the cedar. The cedar – this impression remained with her afterwards too – prevented, kept it back. (Blackwood 2012: 35–6)

However, the impression is also that this protection cannot hold and after a great storm, the cedar tree is damaged and two of its limbs are torn away. Sophia sees with fear that '[f]ar more of the Forest was now visible than before; it peered through the breach of the broken-down defences' (48). After this event, for David Bittacy, 'life was somehow becoming linked so intimately with trees' (52) that he is melding with the trees, wandering further and deeper into the Forest:

> From morning to night he wandered in the Forest ... his mind was charged with trees – their foliage, growth, development; their wonder, beauty strength; their loneliness in isolation, their power in a herded mass ... He spoke all day of their sensations: how they drank the fading sunshine, dreamed in the moonlight, thrilled to the kiss of stars. (Blackwood 2012: 64–6)

David has an affective response to the trees. He *feels* them rather than observes them; and as he moves through the wood the man's body changes and the

9 'The Man whom the Trees Loved', frontispiece to Algernon Blackwood. 1912. *Pan's Garden: A Volume of Nature Stories* (London: Macmillan). Drawing, W. Graham Robertson (1866–1948)

Forest bends itself around him. Sophia, terribly worried, follows him into the wood:

> [S]he saw the figure of her husband moving among the trees – a man like a tree, walking ... She saw him go away from her, go of his own accord and willingly beyond her; she saw the branches drop about his steps and hide him. His figure faded out among the speckled shade and sunlight. The trees covered him. The tide just took him, all unresisting and content to go. Upon the bosom of the green sea he floated away beyond her reach of vision. (Blackwood 2012: 79)

Blackwood has great sympathy for Sophia, but her vision (physical, spiritual and metaphorical) is bounded by the human and the bourgeois, as materialised in the trim garden, and cannot keep up with David in the 'rushing splendour' of his new state (65). Frank in 'The Man who Went too Far' is also in a state of ecstasy; Darcy sees this and 'for all his matter-of-fact common sense could have sworn that his companion's face shone, was luminous in itself' (Benson 2012: 129). While Sophia and Darcy remain human, David and Frank are transcending humankind. Yet there is a danger of self-annihilation: Nature has taken over and the human has become de-centred. There is something greater than the human, something larger and more expansive, but also something older. Benson, describing the village of which Frank's house is the last – bordering the Forest – says that for all that humans have learned

> to defy [Nature's] most violent storms in its well-established houses, to bridle her torrents and make them light its streets, to tunnel her mountains and plough her seas, the inhabitants of St Faith's will not willingly venture into the forest after dark. For in spite of the silence and loneliness of the hooded night it seems that a man is not sure in what company he may suddenly find himself. (Benson 2012: 2)

There is danger here; the wilderness spaces are not controllable or civilised. And this is where the garden should sit – as marker, boundary and clear demarcation between the nonhuman wilderness and the human cultivated, domestic spaces. As Mark Francis and Randolph T. Hester claim, 'The garden has been viewed philosophically as the balancing point between human control on the one hand and wild nature on the other. The garden has represented safety from the threat of wild nature or escape from barbarian outsiders. The garden has been nature-under-control' (1992: 2).

THE FOREIGN AND THE OTHER

The gardens in our tales fail: Nature is not under control. One reason is the setting. David Bittacy has chosen to live in the New Forest because, 'in the little island [England] there is nothing that suggests the woods of wilder countries so nearly as the New Forest. It has the genuine air and mystery, the depth and splendour, the loneliness and here and there the strong, untamable [sic] quality of old-time forests' (Blackwood 2012: 58). Despite the beauty and splendour of the Forest, this smacks of the foreign: 'wilder countries', the 'untameable' and the too old. David Bittacy has spent time working with trees in the East, in India and in Canada, and 'he had kept alive a sense of beauty that hardly belonged to his type, and was unusual for its vitality'; 'Few divined in him the secretly tenacious love of nature that had been fostered by years spent in the forests and jungles of the eastern world' (4).

David is not quite English enough. His ancestry is suspect and he has rambled too long in the forests of India. As Sanderson tells him, 'Trees love you, that's the fact ... Your service to them all those years abroad has made them know you ... made them *aware of your presence*' (25–6, emphasis in original). The Bittacys' cottage garden should have 'offered a sense of national identity, particularly for those returning home or imagining England from overseas' (Helmreich 2002: 89). However, the garden is bordered by the wild Forest, reminiscent of those of more exotic countries, and a sense of the East has been brought into this garden. Sayer notes, though, the collusion between gardeners and the exotic, even in a desire for an English sense of security: 'Gardening and gardeners are far from being "innocent" ... one can see in process ... a naturalising of the colonial language of the "exotic" and "alien", the "temperate" and "native" into gardening discourse' (Sayer 2000: 82). Robinson's 'wild' gardening presents a prime example, 'naturalising' plants found in the Americas, South Africa, Southern Europe and the Alps, resulting in an 'English' garden.

In Benson's story Frank's practice too is un-English: 'he confessed to what others would call paganism; it was sufficient for him that there existed a principle of life. Some of it existed in all human beings, just as it existed in trees and animals' (Benson 2012: 133). His is a pagan world-view and when speaking to Darcy he goes so far as to reject Christianity verbally. While bathing in the river Frank called on the 'dear Fawn' (123–4). The Fawn that he addresses is not the river itself, but the entity that he eventually calls into the garden: the Greek god Pan. In Benson's story Pan stalks the woods of the New Forest and in Blackwood's the trees of England have communed with the trees of India. Sanderson says:

> There is communion among trees all the world over ... The winds, you see – the great, swift carriers! They have their ancient rights of way about the world. An easterly wind, for instance, carrying on stage by stage as it were – linking dropped messages and meanings from land to land like the birds – an easterly wind. (Blackwood 2012: 28)

There is no real 'east' or 'west', but a flow and a movement. The boundaries of England have been transgressed.

There is different emphasis in the stories, but the foreign-alien is present in both. In each story, the New Forest therefore becomes an othered, uncanny, outlandish space. In the ecocritical schema offered by our two tales it is not surprising that the gardens collapse and cease to signify the English cottage garden. Blackwood tells us of the trees in the gardens of the village on the edge of the Forest: 'They longed and prayed to enter the great Peace of the Forest yonder, but they could not move. They knew, moreover, that the Forest with its august, deep splendour despised and pitied them. They were a thing of artificial gardens, and belonged to beds of flowers all forced to grow one way' (10–11). The gardens themselves are spaces of unease and dislocation: sites of despair and longing. However, where the Forest is seen as the unruly, wild and atavistic place, in the end it is the gardens that prove to be the most uncanny and Gothic spaces of all.

David Bittacy is lost to the Forest. In the final lines of the story, the cedar tree has been torn to the ground by the wind. Sophia wakes and looks out of the window:

> Only the gaunt and crippled trunk of it remained. The single giant bough that had been left to it lay dark upon the grass, sucked endways towards the Forest by a great wind eddy. It lay there like a mass of drift-wood from a wreck … remnant of some friendly splendid vessel that once sheltered men. And in the distance she heard the roaring of the Forest further out. Her husband's voice was in it. (Benson 2012: 98–9)

David has become at one with the Forest, left the garden and the human, merging with the wild and nonhuman Forest in a process David Punter has called 'becoming-forest' (2013: 47). Punter claims that David 'becomes one with the trees, becomes forest, but in the process necessarily dehumanizes' (47). I prefer to think of David becoming more-than-human or perhaps posthuman rather than unhuman; uncanny in the Forest as well as the garden. And while there is horror, particularly for Sophia, there is also the resonating splendour of David's mutation.

Frank's fate is somewhat different. At the start of the story our narrator tells us he is attempting to 'piece together' a story of:

> a young artist who died here not long ago, a young man, or so he struck the beholder, of great personal beauty. … His ghost they will tell you 'walks' constantly by the stream and through the woods which he loved so, and in especial haunts a certain house, the last of the village, where he lived, and its garden in which he was done to death. (Benson 2012: 122)

From the start the garden is associated with death, and in the selfishness of his actions, of attempting 'too much', of 'going too far', Frank has brought his doom upon himself. In Benson's story David becomes absorbed by the Forest through love. Frank, though, turns his face away from love and pity, suffering and pain because 'that sort of thing, pain, anger, anything unlovely, throws me back, retards the coming of the great hour!' (134). Frank is attempting a blinkered, linear journey and his friend Darcy realises he has missed something vital in his quest for a joyous merging with Nature:

> All Nature from highest to lowest is full, crammed full of suffering; every living organism in Nature preys on another, yet in your aim to get close to, to be one with Nature, you leave suffering altogether out; you run from it, you refuse to recognise it. ... Cannot you guess then when the final revelation will be? ... [I]t will be the revelation of horror, suffering, death, pain in all its hideous forms. (Benson 2012: 137–8)

Frank has been refusing the darkness, intent only on seeing the light. But he has invited the Great Goat into his garden.

As we have seen, Frank's is a formal garden which is intended to be 'enclosed, ordered, peaceful, civilized ... a symbol of a desired sense of Englishness' (Helmreich 2002: 92). Frank's own garden is at odds with his philosophy – the non-Christian, non-Englishness of his pursuit and desires. At the end of the story Darcy wakes suddenly:

> as he recovered himself from the panic-land which lies between sleeping and waking, there was silence, except for the steady hissing of rain on the shrubs outside his window. But suddenly that silence was shattered and shredded into fragments by a scream from somewhere close at hand outside in the black garden, a scream of supreme and despairing terror. Again and again it shrilled up, and then a babble of awful words was interjected; a quivering sobbing voice that he knew said: 'My God, oh, my God; oh, Christ!' (Benson 2012: 138)

In the end, Frank is forced to call upon a Christian god. Darcy rushes into the garden and races towards the hammock where Frank liked to sleep:

> A gleam of white shirt was there, as if a man were sitting up in it, but across that there was an obscure dark shadow ... He was now only some few yards away, when suddenly the black shadow seemed to jump into the air, then came down with tappings of hard hoofs on the brick path that ran down the pergola, and with frolicsome skippings galloped off into the bushes. (Benson 2012: 138)

The great god Pan has invaded the English garden and killed Frank. He skips off through the formal garden which is now filled with his smell that suggestively reminds Darcy of 'a certain chalet ... in the Alps' (138). Garden, rather than forest, has become the Gothic space; Frank's body itself is marked 'by the hoofs of some monstrous goat that had leaped and stamped upon him' (139).

CONCLUSION

In both stories nature-nature has 'won'. The humans have gone too far and their gardens cannot protect them from the wilderness, material and metaphorical.

Indeed, for both Benson and Blackwood, the gardens are always-already a part of the wildness that roars further out. In light of the most recent thinking about the life of trees, Blackwood's tale is particularly prescient. Sanderson says he has noticed how trees 'choose their companions ... beeches for instance, allow no life too near them – birds or squirrels in their boughs, nor any growth beneath? ... And how pines like bilberry bushes at their feet and sometimes little oaks – all trees making a clear, deliberate choice' (Blackwood 2012: 24). Science has now proved the communication between trees and the choices they can make to help and nurture some nearby trees, stifle the growth of not-favoured trees and saplings by restricting light, or pass nutrients on to each other through their root systems (Simard 2016). Yet even without this revelation, both Benson and Blackwood present an ecocritical view of Nature and narrative. Jeffrey Theis says that 'the forest often is a spatially disruptive force that challenges a culture's preconceived notions of itself and nature. These inversions and this sense of the "topsy-turvy" invade, or perhaps pervade, more than just the sense of "nature"' (2010: xii). In a recent book that explores (in part) plant horror, Elizabeth Hope Chang argues that, 'Blackwood and weird fiction propose an iteration of the posthuman that is also the more-than-human; this revision fits well in our current moment with recent explanations of nonhuman studies, object-oriented ontologies, and other anthropo-decenterings' (2019: 178). Blackwood's story certainly fits with the notion of the posthuman, while the nonhuman in Benson's story destroys and overtakes the human as it destroys Frank. Chang cites what she calls tales of 'plant carnivory and plant amalgamation' but she says that they

> should not be read exclusively in a category with other 'monster' stories of vampires and mummies that proliferated at the end of the nineteenth century. They should equally importantly be read as examples of the growing canon of environmental literature, in which plant life gained a history, a coherent range of cause and effect and a particular scale of engagement. All these served a perpetual investigation of intentionality as a revelatory condition of mind, and depended on a concern (however sensationalized) for that discernible conceptual quality across the foreign and colonized worlds and beyond the bounds of the mobile human/animal body. (Chang 2019: 179)

Both Blackwood's and Benson's stories interrogate the boundaries of the 'foreign and the colonized', here in the case of the garden and the wilderness, and this is looked at via a questioning of the human/animal body, but also the human/ plant body. The concept of the human body itself is being deconstructed and blown apart.

The over-cultivated gardens in our stories are too near the 'slumbering monster' (Blackwood 2012: 8), but in 1912 England itself was lying too close to another monster. On the cusp of World War I, the fact that the garden space, which has so often been seen as a metaphor for England, has been invaded is not so much a case of 'reverse colonization' (Arata 1990) but more of a forewarning of the relentless forces abroad that were gathering and which would turn the world upside down and return so many young bodies back to the ground beneath our feet.

WORKS CITED

Arata, Stephen D. 1990. 'The Occidental Tourist: *Dracula* and the Anxiety of Reverse Colonization', *Victorian Studies* 33. 4: 621–45

Bell, Michael. 1999. 'The Metaphysics of Modernism', in *The Cambridge Companion to Modernism*, ed. by Michael Levenson (Cambridge: Cambridge University Press), pp. 9–32

Benson, E. F. 2012. 'The Man who Went too Far' (1912), in *Night Terrors: The Ghost Stories of E. F. Benson* (Ware: Wordsworth Editions), pp. 121–40

Blackwood, Algernon. 2012. 'The Man whom the Trees Loved' (1912), in *Pan's Garden: A Volume of Nature Stories* (London: Forgotten Books), pp. 3–104

Chang, Elizabeth Hope. 2019. *Novel Cultivations: Plants in British Literature of the Global Nineteenth Century* (Charlottesville and London: University of Virginia Press)

Clough, Patricia and Jean Halley. 2007. *The Affective Turn: Theorizing the Social* (Durham, NC: Duke University Press)

Cole, Diana and Samantha Frost (eds). 2010. *New Materialisms: Ontology, Agency and Politics* (Durham, NC: Duke University Press)

Dingley, Robert. 1992. 'Meaning Everything: The Image of Pan at the Turn of the Century', in *Twentieth-Century Fantasist: Essays on Culture, Society and Belief in Twentieth-Century Mythopoeic Literature*, ed. by Kath Filmer (New York: St Martin's Press), pp. 47–59

Francis, Mark and Randolph T. Hester (eds). 1992. *The Meaning of Gardens: Idea, Place and Action* (Cambridge, MA: MIT Press)

Freeman, Nicholas. 2005. '"Nothing of the Wild Wood"? Pan, Paganism and Spiritual Confusion in E. F. Benson's "The Man who Went too Far"', *Literature and Theology*, 19. 1: 22–33

Hay, Simon. 2011. *A History of the Modern British Ghost Story* (New York: Palgrave Macmillan)

Helmreich, Anne. 2002. *The English Garden and National Identity: Competing Styles of Garden Design, 1870–1914* (Cambridge: Cambridge University Press)

Iovino, Serenella and Serpil Oppermann. 2014. 'Introduction', in *Material Ecocriticism*, ed. by Serenella Iovino and Serpil Oppermann (Bloomington: Indiana University Press), pp. 1–17

Oakes, Timothy and Patricia Price. 2008. *The Cultural Geography Reader* (London: Routledge)

Punter, David. 2013. 'Algernon Blackwood: Nature and Spirit', in *Ecogothic*, ed. by Andrew Smith and William Hughes (Manchester: Manchester University Press), pp. 44–57

Robinson, William. 1870. *The Wild Garden; or, Our Groves and Shrubberies Made Beautiful by the Naturalization of Hardy Exotic Plants* (London: John Murray)

Sayer, Karen. 2000. *Country Cottages: A Cultural History* (Manchester: Manchester University Press)

Simard, Suzanne. 2016. 'How Trees Talk to Each Other', TEDSummit, June, www.ted.com/talks/suzanne_simard_how_trees_talk_to_each_other [accessed 1 June 2020]

Theis, Jeffrey S. 2010. *Writing the Forest in Early Modern England: A Sylvan Pastoral Nation* (Pittsburgh: Duquesne University Press)

Varner, Gary R., 2006. *Mythic Forest, the Green Man and the Spirit of Nature: The Re-Emergence of the Spirit of Nature from Ancient Times into Modern Society* (New York: Algora Publishing)

6

Darwin's plants and Darwin's gardens: Sex, sensation and natural selection

Jonathan Smith

Reminiscing about his many visits over the years to the home of his dear friend and scientific colleague Charles Darwin, Joseph Hooker, Britain's leading botanist for much of the second half of the nineteenth century, noted that a regular feature of those visits was joining Darwin on his noontime walk: 'away we trudged through the garden,' recalled Hooker, 'where there was always some experiment to visit' (F. Darwin 1887: II. 27). Hooker's description – despite the begrudging 'trudge' – captures nicely the multiple roles that the garden behind Darwin's home in the Kentish countryside played in Darwin's domestic life.

It was, simultaneously, a place of relaxation, of exercise, of thinking and, more unusually, of experiment. For even before the publication of *On the Origin of Species* (1859), Darwin had begun to turn his thinking, and much of his experimental life, to plants and flowers, and over the course of the ensuing two decades he managed to transform botany. In the flowerbeds of his garden and especially in the hothouses he had constructed on the far side of it, he worked at some of the botanical world's strangest, but also some of its most familiar, plants: orchids, insectivorous species, climbers and twiners, cowslips, loosestrife and flax. Darwin used natural selection to solve long-standing botanical problems, but the overall cultural impact of his botanical work was to make plants both even stranger and more like us. For Darwin showed that plants moved constantly and ubiquitously, that some captured and digested 'prey', and that they deployed a wide array of enticements and mechanisms for securing the services of insects in cross-fertilisation. Darwin's garden and its adjacent hothouses were both sites of recreation and arenas in which to observe natural selection. They were places to admire plants as well as to manipulate, control and even torture them. If nature gave up many of her secrets to Darwin's patient methods, the cultural

10 'The House of Charles Darwin (Down House) in Kent'. Wood engraving,
J. R. Brown (active 1874–90)

and literary impacts of his botanical discoveries could be as discomforting as
they were astonishing. The literary analogue of Darwin's botanical work of the
1860s and 1870s was the sensation fiction that flourished in those same decades,
and the literary offspring of Darwin's botanical work were the late-century tales
of monstrous and man-eating plants, the ancestors of which still walk among
us today.

Since the publication of Gillian Beer's *Darwin Plots* (1983) and George Levine's
Darwin and the Novelists (1988), Darwin's work has been closely connected
with the high Victorian realism of novelists like George Eliot, Thomas Hardy,
George Meredith and Anthony Trollope. Attention to the details of the everyday
world and to the cumulative effects of small changes over time made *On the
Origin of Species* and novels like *Middlemarch* reflective of a similar methodology
and world-view. Yet it is sensation fiction, the hybrid form that exploded in
popularity at almost the moment *Origin* was published, that most closely
approximates Darwin's project. Sensation fiction seemed to contemporaries to
have burst on the scene with Wilkie Collins's serialised best-selling thriller, *The
Woman in White*, in 1859–60. Other wildly popular works, like Ellen Wood's
East Lynne (1861) and Mary Braddon's *Lady Audley's Secret* (1862), followed
quickly on Collins's heels, and soon sensation was the rage. While recent
scholarship has seen the emergence of sensation fiction as more gradual, and
has come to appreciate the ways even realist writers like Eliot appropriated the
sensational into their plots, sensation fiction was identified by Victorian commentators and reviewers as something new and distinctive. Sensation fiction
took the trappings of Gothic romance and domesticated them. The violence
and deviant sexuality of the Gothic – the murders and threats and incarcerations,
the bigamy and incest and illicit affairs – were set not in medieval castles in

southern Europe but in the comfortable middle- and upper-class drawing-rooms of modern England, with plot lines ripped from headlines about real-life scandal and crime.

In sensation fiction, gardens tended to be both familiar and domestic on the one hand, vaguely ominous and foreboding on the other. In Braddon's *Lady Audley's Secret*, the opening description of Audley Court's gardens, with its avenue of umbrageous lime trees, captures this duality, and the genre's Gothic roots, vividly: 'it seemed a chosen place for secret meetings or for stolen interviews; a place in which a conspiracy might have been planned, or a lover's vow registered with equal safety; and yet it was scarcely twenty paces from the house' (1862: I. 7). Just beyond this avenue stands the old well into which, we will later discover, the bigamous title character, having previously feigned her own demise, pushes her first husband, murdering him when he returns to England and recognises her. If, as Lisa Kröger (2013) has shown, the forest is the overlooked third space of eighteenth-century Gothic novels, sensation fiction's domestication of the Gothic made the garden a liminal space, partly an extension of the domestic world of the home and partly a wild space that stands in for the forest. Kröger sees nature in the Gothic tradition as either a prelapsarian Eden (as in the works of Ann Radcliffe) or a perverted one (as in Matthew Lewis), depending on whether the violence and lurid sexuality of the castle or abbey is separated from it or encroaches upon it.

In Wilkie Collins's early novel, *Basil* (1852), we see a different variation on the garden's dual nature. The garden of the title character's family home in London is 'a close-shut dungeon for nature, where stunted trees and drooping flowers seemed visibly pining for the free air and sunlight of the country, in their sooty atmosphere, amid their prison of high brick walls. But the place gave room for the air to blow in it, and distanced the tumult of the busy streets' (Collins 1852: I. 146). The Gothic prison and dungeon that is the garden nonetheless also affords a breeze and muffles the noise of the urban streets. The house to which it is attached, presided over by Basil's proud and emotionally distant father, is sexually repressive and violent only in the father's verbal sternness, but it, too, is prison-like for Basil, whose desire to flee from it leads him into a secret marriage with an unfaithful wife and the attempted murder of her lover.

The connection of Darwinism to realism pioneered by Beer and Levine has become so well established that it has perhaps obscured just how sensational Darwin's major theoretical works were. The books that comprised the fleshing-out of the 'Abstract' (Darwin 1859: 1) of *On the Origin of Species – The Variation of Animals and Plants Under Domestication* (1867), *The Descent of Man, and Selection in Relation to Sex* (1871) and *The Expression of the Emotions in Man and Animals* (1872) – were inherently shocking, bringing into alignment all that supposedly separated humanity from animals. *Variation* was about the breeding of animals and plants, and Darwin offered in it his own theory of how sexual reproduction enabled the slight variations on which natural selection worked to be passed down to offspring. *Descent* was far more ambitious than merely arguing for humanity's physical evolution from animals – that was old news by 1871. Rather, Darwin focused on explaining the evolution of our mental abilities, our moral sense and our sense of beauty. He celebrated the 'heroic' little monkey who had saved his human keeper at London's Zoological Gardens from the attack of a 'great and dreaded baboon' (Darwin 1871: I. 87) and decried the immorality of human 'savages'. With his theory of sexual selection, Darwin explained how a species could evolve through mate-selection and reproduction. In many parts of the animal world, the struggle for a mate was as violent and ruthless as was the struggle for survival. 'The season of love is that of battle', Darwin wrote (II. 48). Elsewhere, particularly among birds, the selector was the female, and the competition between males often non-violent but equally intense: battles of preening display, musical performance and even architectural design. Darwin's treatment of sexuality among animals and humans, as Gowan Dawson (2007) has shown, was seen by many critics as culturally and religiously dangerous, *Descent* lumped together with the poetry of Swinburne, the eroticism of Pre-Raphaelite art and the pamphleteering of advocates for free love as a threat to moral decency and the social order. *Expression of the Emotions*, spun off from *Descent*, argued similarly that human emotions and their expression were shared by and inherited from animals, and the specific emotions Darwin analysed read like an inventory of the high-pitched, even melodramatic, feelings that helped give sensation fiction its name: hatred and anger, contempt, disgust, surprise, astonishment, fear, horror and – at the end of the catalogue, in a chapter to itself – the modesty and shame of the blushing girl.

It was in Darwin's botanical writings, though, that the connections with sensation fiction are most clearly visible. Those writings similarly overflowed with sex and violence, both exotic and domestic, particularly in his accounts of the botanical experiments that fascinated him. Darwin's very first book after *Origin* was *The Various Contrivances by which British and Foreign Orchids are Fertilised by Insects* (1862). It was followed by a long essay *On the Movements and Habits of Climbing Plants*, published in the *Journal of the Linnean Society* in 1865 but with a second edition in book form a decade later. *Insectivorous Plants* appeared in 1875, *The Effects of Cross and Self Fertilisation in the Vegetable Kingdom* in 1876, *The Different Forms of Flowers on Plants of the Same Species* in 1877 and *The Power of Movement in Plants* in 1880. As their titles suggest, Darwin's botanical interests focused on fertilisation, movement and digestion. If sensation fiction incorporated the trappings of the Gothic into domestic realism, Darwin's botanical books provided shocking and uncanny accounts of plant behaviour that made plants seem animal-like, even conscious, but these accounts were delivered via careful, detailed descriptions of familiar domestic species. If crime, violence and sexual transgression were at the heart of sensation fiction's plots, Darwin's plant researches were full of their botanical counterparts: the lures and traps set by orchids and insectivorous species to secure food and sex, the array of sexual arrangements and reproductive possibilities offered by heterostyled dimorphic and trimorphic plants, the little shop of horrors in which insectivorous plants imprisoned, drowned, crushed and dissolved their victims. And if sensation fiction induced the same physiological response in its readers – fear, anxiety, nervous excitement – that it depicted in its characters, Darwin's botany did much the same, the accounts of his experiments sounding at times like a catalogue of torture methods or a Kama Sutra of botanical sexuality.

In his depictions of botanical sex and violence, crimes and torture, Darwin brought the exotic home. His paradigmatic insectivorous species was *Drosera rotundifolia*, the common sundew of English heaths and marshes. *Different Forms* featured such familiar English plants as the primrose, cowslip, flax and loosestrife. It was not a species from the tropics with which Darwin opened *Orchids*, but *Orchis mascula*, the early purple orchid, which grew wild in the meadows near his house in the Kentish countryside. *Climbing Plants* opened with an even more famous Kentish denizen, the hop.

Darwin and his wife, Emma, were themselves readers of sensation fiction. As Darwin recalled in the autobiographical reflections written towards the end of his life, novels 'have been for years a wonderful relief and pleasure to me' (Barlow 1958: 138). He, Emma and the children would gather in the evening to read aloud, and Emma read to him when he was ill. Darwin preferred novels that were 'works of imagination, though not of a very high order' (138), with happy endings and pretty, lovable heroines – a description that accords with much of the sensation genre. And indeed, we know from the family correspondence and Emma's diaries that the Darwins read works by leading sensationalists like Collins, Braddon and Wood, as well as a host of their less-remembered contemporaries. They read Collins's *The Woman in White* to their children in 1861, not long after it appeared in volume form. The Darwins' letters of the 1860s and 1870s sometimes lament the low quality of the novels they are reading and even express determination not to read so much 'trash', an epithet frequently hurled against sensation fiction by its critics. 'Good Heavens the lot of trashy novels, which I have heard is astounding' (Darwin Correspondence Project (hereafter DCP): Letter 4415), exclaimed Charles to the American botanist Asa Gray in an 1864 letter that also speaks of climbing plants and loosestrife crosses. Darwin's botanical correspondence with both Gray and Hooker during the 1860s in particular frequently veers from the sensational results of Darwin's latest plant experiments to assessments of the latest sensation fiction.

At root, Darwin used natural selection to solve some botanical puzzles and to explain how common characteristics and behaviours in plants had arisen.

Cross-fertilisation, he showed, led on average to the production of more seeds, and in turn to more and more vigorous offspring, than self-fertilisation, and the evolutionary dance between flowers and insects was both cause and effect. The striking structures, colours and markings of orchids attracted insects and led them to the nectary in just the right way to secure cross-fertilisation. The different sexual forms of certain species, their stamens and pistils set at varying heights, functioned almost as separate sexes, the spectrum of different sexual combinations leading to differing levels of fertility. Plant movement, he argued, was virtually ubiquitous, a feature of roots and leaves as well as stems, and hardly confined to species that climb or twine, or whose leaves 'sleep'. Plants were not stationary, and many species had evolved highly specialised ways to seek out and obtain the sunlight they needed. Insectivorous species act almost as animal predators, luring insect 'prey' into gluey traps and cages, spiky pits and slippery pools, where they are dissolved and digested. It was, he argued, a kind of botanical dietary supplement, an evolutionary adaptation to living in habitats with nitrogen-poor soils.

Darwin was hailed by his contemporaries for having effected a revolution in botany, and his botanical writings captured the public imagination. In seconding the nomination of Darwin for the 1864 Copley Medal, the Royal Society's highest honour, Hugh Falconer cited *Orchids* and the recently published papers that would become *Different Forms of Flowers* as 'of the highest order of importance. They open a new mine of observation, upon a field which had been barely struck upon before' (DCP: Letter 4644). In his presidential address to the British Association for the Advancement of Science in 1868, Hooker called Darwin's fertilisation studies 'the greatest botanical discoveries made during the last ten years' (*Report* 1868: lxvi). Victorian periodicals were peppered with articles on Darwin's discoveries, particularly about orchids and insectivorous plants. The writer and novelist Grant Allen, by far the most prolific of Darwin's botanical popularisers, used and extended Darwin's work on the role of insects in plant fertilisation to argue that insects, too, had an aesthetic sense, as part of his promotion of a physiological or evolutionary aesthetics. The authors of popular botanical books, like J. E. Taylor in *The Sagacity and Morality of Plants* (1884) and M. C. Cooke in *Freaks and Marvels of Plant Life* (1882), devoted extended attention to Darwin. *Punch* got in on the act as well, finding comic fodder in both insectivorous species (in 'Flowers of the Future' (1874: 255), a young man gives his beloved a bouquet of such plants to carry to a dinner party only to watch helplessly as the hungry flowers attack the platters of meat) and in climbing plants, with a 'suggested illustration' (Sambourne 1875: 242) for that work featuring Darwin as ape sitting in an ivy-entwined tree.

While *Origin*, *Descent* and *Expression* blurred the boundary between humans and animals, making possible our own notion of the nonhuman animal, far less appreciated is the extent to which Darwin also blurred what had been thought to be the firm boundary between animals and plants. Darwin later confessed in his autobiographical recollections that it 'always pleased me to exalt plants in the scale of organised beings' (Barlow 1958: 135). Whether that exaltation of plants induced delight or discomfort tended to depend on whether the beholder was an evolutionist. In 'On the Border Territory Between the Animal and the Vegetable Kingdoms' for *Macmillan's Magazine*, Darwin's friend and ally T. H. Huxley (1876) declared that the old distinctions between these two kingdoms had been completely broken down, with the differences between plants and animals a matter of degree rather than kind. In the *Cornhill*, Andrew Wilson (1878), another Darwinian, also answered with a Huxleyan negative the question of his title, 'Can we Separate Animals from Plants?'. Opponents, for their part, understood that this boundary-blurring served the interests of evolutionists, and they knew the public fascination with these surprising discoveries was affording the Darwinians another platform for popularising natural selection. Reviewing Darwin's *Power of Movement in Plants* for the *Edinburgh Review*, the popular textbook author R. J. Mann complained that analogies between plant movement and animal locomotion, 'especially dear to the hearts of evolutionists' (1881: 506), should not be allowed to obscure the crucial distinction that the latter is volitional while the former is not. In *Proserpina*, his own book on flowers that began appearing in 1875, the art and social critic John Ruskin simply lamented that examinations of 'every sort of plant that looked or behaved like an animal, and every sort of animal that looked or behaved like a plant' had merely resulted in the useless conclusion that 'nobody could say either what a plant was, or what a person was' (1903–11: XXV. 507–8).

Sensation fiction, like the Gothic before it, came in for criticism from conservative commentators for its dangerous depictions of immoral and criminal behaviour. Ruskin regarded Darwin's botanical work in a similar way, declaring in *Proserpina* that he would have 'nothing whatever to do' with 'the recent phrenzy for the investigation of digestive and reproductive operations in plants', and lamenting the 'ill-taught curiosity' that seeks to explain 'every possible spur, spike, jag, sting, rent, blotch, flaw, freckle, filth, or venom, which can be detected in the construction, or distilled from the dissolution, of vegetable organism' (XXV. 390–1). The *Athenaeum*, reviewing *Insectivorous Plants*, regarded the term 'insectivorous' as unscientific and needlessly sensational, and accused Darwin of catering to the tastes of a public that was itself now 'fed' on an 'unwholesome, frothy literary diet' of sensation ('Review' 1875: 88). Others, while less censorious, nonetheless expressed anxiety at the prospect of what some writers called – out-sensationalising Darwin – 'carnivorous' plants. T. S. Miller (2012) credits Darwin's work on insectivorous species and plant movement with the proliferation of 'monster plants' in the speculative fiction of the century's last quarter, and as Jim Endersby (2016a, 2016b) has shown, Darwin's work on orchids and insectivorous species were mashed up in the same period in a surprising number of stories about man-eating orchids, a reflection of the way various forms of cultural unease were tapped by Darwin's demonstration of plants' deceptive and cruel behaviour. Such fiction had its inspiration in Darwin's own botanical writings, but also in the reviews and popularisations that originally brought those writings to wider public attention. For Taylor in *The Sagacity and Morality of Plants*, insectivorous species offered a parable of the dangers of the 'fast life' (1884: 273) so often depicted in sensation novels, while climbers and twiners were 'vegetable Thugs' (237) – crafty, weak-stemmed, ambitious foreigners pulling themselves upwards on the trunks of trees they eventually strangled.

In the fraught responses to and appropriations of Darwin's botanical boundary-blurring we can see that Darwin was significantly responsible for making plants and flowers uncanny, sources of horror as well as attraction. The Romantics had been drawn to the mimosa, the 'sensitive plant' whose leaves folded inwards when touched or disturbed, but the late Victorians were fascinated and repelled by the sundew's ability to attract, ensnare and consume its victims, and by the orchid's turning bees and butterflies into unwitting pandars. In her introduction to *Plant Horror*, Dawn Keetley (2016) offers six theses on what makes plants horrifying; many of these involve various ways that plants can upend our long-standing assumptions about them: that plants are not utterly different from humans and other animals (nor humans and other animals from them); that plants are not mere 'background', invisible and harmless; and that plants do move and devote themselves relentlessly to growth and reproduction. As the above makes clear, it was Darwin's botanical writings and their popularisation that initiated, advanced or heightened these realisations.

What troubled Ruskin and other commentators delighted Darwin. That delight is palpable with the sundew, particularly the fact that it could be said to digest the insects it captured and in the sensitiveness and movements of the leaves and tentacles. 'The experiments proving that the leaves are capable of true digestion', he wrote in *Insectivorous Plants*, are 'the most interesting of all my observations on *Drosera*, as no such power was before distinctly known to exist in the vegetable kingdom' (Darwin 1875: 268). That minute quantities of some substances, and the faintest pressure of a bit of hair, could cause 'conspicuous movement' in another part of the leaf, left Darwin 'astonished': 'this extreme sensitiveness', he marvelled, 'exceed[s] that of the most delicate part of the human body' (272). So astonished was he by the plant's sensitivity that he initially did not fully trust his own results, determining to delay publication for another year so that he could run his experiments again. In his letters, Darwin spoke of these phenomena even more colourfully. 'By Jove I sometimes think Drosera is a disguised animal!' he wrote to Hooker (DCP: Letter 3008). Good-naturedly chastising Asa Gray for his failure to appreciate 'my beloved Drosera', Darwin called the sundew 'a most sagacious animal' (DCP: Letter

4262). When he resumed work on *Drosera* in 1872, Darwin likened his own non-electrical experiments on the plant to Luigi Galvani's famous experiments on frogs, reporting to Gray:

> The point which has interested me most is tracing the *nerves*!!! which follow the vascular bundles. By a prick with a sharp lancet at a certain point, I can paralyse 1/2 the leaf, so that a stimulus to the other half causes no movement. It is just like dividing the spinal marrow of a Frog: – no stimulus can be sent from the Brain or anterior part of spine to the hind legs; but if these latter are stimulated, they move by reflex actions. (DCP: Letter 8568)

Not only did the sundew eat and move, but it also seemed to have a nervous system that communicated motor impulses through the leaf and tentacles, and initiated the release of digestive fluids.

At the same time, Darwin subjected insectivorous plants and those on which he conducted experiments on movement to all manner of violence he would never have inflicted on a sagacious animal. The triple exclamation points expressing amazement that the sundew has nerves are quickly followed by the news that he can 'paralyse' the leaf with the prick of a sharp lancet. Darwin poked and prodded 'his' *Drosera*, submerged it in hot water, dosed it with chloroform vapour and subjected it to poisons ranging from curare to cobra venom. He tested its appetite for everything from raw beef and cooked egg white to his own mucus and urine. Popularisers often drew attention to the way Darwin's work on insectivorous species made Gothic tales of horror literally true, but Darwin himself also invited such meldings, as in his recruitment of J. Burdon Sanderson, Professor of Physiology at University College London, to conduct a series of Frankenstein-like experiments on insectivorous species by attaching electrodes to the leaves and inducing movement in them with pulses of current, experiments Sanderson then described to a popular audience at the Royal Institution in 1874. In investigating the sensitivity and movement of plants, Darwin severed the tips of roots, which he regarded as analogous to the brain of animals, to see if they could find their way downwards again. Seedlings and leaves of various species he whacked with sticks, scratched with needles, subjected to drops of nitric acid, exposed to the heat of a summer sun, glued to stakes and doused with streams of water from a syringe. In his testimony to the Royal Commission investigating the practice of subjecting live animals to scientific experiments in 1875, Darwin defended the necessity of vivisection but abhorred its use without anaesthesia if anaesthesia was available; his plant experiments show that any analogy between plants and animals had its limits, even for him.

Darwin was similarly enthused with plant sexuality. He delighted in mimicking the action of an insect's proboscis with a needle or pencil tip to reveal the various structures and mechanisms by which the insect was dusted with pollen in just the right way at just the right spot to ensure cross-fertilisation. The title of his original 1862 paper on the cowslip and oxlip referred to the 'remarkable sexual relations' of their two sexual forms (Darwin 1862). Of the astonishing eighteen different reproductive combinations offered by loosestrife, with its three sexual forms, Darwin noted that 'these plants offer a more remarkable case than can be found in any other plant or animal' (Darwin 1877: 137). Loosestrife sexuality, he memorably summarised, consisted of 'a triple union between three hermaphrodites, – each hermaphrodite being in its female organ quite distinct from the other two hermaphrodites and partially distinct in its male organs, and each furnished with two sets of males' (138). As his use of 'union' (and in his letters, 'marriage' and 'alliance' as well (DCP: Letters 3753 and 4262)) suggests, however, Darwin cast this queer (in both the Victorian and modern senses of that term) arrangement largely in the discourse of Anglican marriage, with 'legitimate' crosses restricted to the six fully fertile ones between different forms, while the twelve 'illegitimate' crosses involved wholly or partly the same form. As with orchids, Darwin's pleasure in the sex lives of plants lay in the emergence – and evolutionary advantages – of sexual dimorphism.

If *On the Origin of Species* contributed to a shift in the perception of 'wild' nature as a place red in tooth and claw, it enabled gardens to be seen as refuges from the violence and competition that elsewhere defined the 'state of nature' (Darwin 1859: 4) even as it highlighted the labour involved in keeping those tendencies within bounds. Darwin acknowledged how easy it was to 'admit in words the truth of the universal struggle for life', but how difficult 'constantly to bear this conclusion in mind': 'We behold the face of nature bright with gladness', he wrote, but 'we do not see, or we forget, that the birds which are idly singing round us mostly live on insects or seeds, and are thus constantly destroying life; or we forget how largely these songsters, or their eggs, or their nestlings, are destroyed by birds and beasts of prey' (62). How much more difficult to keep the struggle for life in mind in the garden, that traditional site of beauty and repose. Yet for Darwin, gardens were in many respects a place for research and experiment. This is certainly true of botanical gardens, chiefly the Royal Botanic Gardens at Kew but also others around Britain and around the world where friendly directors and assistant directors were often happy to assist Darwin from afar. In his botanical work he was particularly dependent on Hooker, the assistant director and then, from 1865, the director, and on Daniel Oliver, from 1864 the keeper of the herbarium and library, as sounding boards as well as for specimens, botanical information and observations.

The gardens on which Darwin most depended, though, were his own. He carried out most of his botanical researches at his home at Down. Across the lawn adjacent to the house was a long kitchen garden, a corner of which Darwin appropriated for experiments on flowers. He put up a greenhouse in 1855–56 along one of the kitchen garden's walls and then, in 1863 and 1864, as his botanical investigations began to take up more and more of his attention,

THE GREENHOUSE IN WHICH MR. DARWIN'S EXPERIMENTS
AND OBSERVATIONS WERE MADE.

11 'Down House Hothouse'. Engraving from *Century Illustrated Monthly Magazine*,
25. 3 (1883): 423

adjacent hothouses, creating a greenhouse complex with four sections, each at a different temperature. Beyond the kitchen garden were an orchard, a woodland and meadows. Often, plants moved inside, into pots on the window sills in Darwin's study. In all these spaces and habitats, Darwin enlisted his children's assistance in observing and counting. His botanical realm, then, was simultaneously professional and domestic, laboratory and field site. The hothouses enabled Darwin to conduct his own observations and experiments on tropical plants rather than depending on others', but they also allowed for the exertion of more control over the specimens, especially when fertilisation needed to be limited or insectivorous specimens needed to be starved. The hothouses were places of experiment rather than recreation, and while pleasure was to be had there, the horticulture conducted in them was not that of the Victorian orchid-collector, and since the house had no conservatory, the plants destined to travel indoors were bound for Darwin's study and more intimate observation.

Yet, the gardens and adjacent orchard were also places to observe natural selection in action. In 1857, working on *Origin* (1859), Darwin had a tiny plot in his orchard cleared of perennials and from early March to the beginning of August marked and counted each seedling and charted its fate, 'to see at what time of life they suffer most' (DCP: Letter 2067). This 'weed garden', as he called it, documented the struggle for existence, with just sixty-two of its 357 seedlings surviving to the height of summer. These observations dramatised the struggle for existence for Darwin, enabling him to 'see a little clearer how the fight goes on' (DCP: Letter 2101). By early June, fifteen of sixteen types of seeds sown in his meadows had germinated, but they were dying off so rapidly, he wrote to Hooker, that he doubted if more than one would flower (DCP: Letter 2101). Years later, in 1874, the struggle for existence well established, Darwin was still observing and commenting on its presence in his garden, noting to the Cambridge ornithologist Alfred Newton in late winter that mistle thrushes 'compete in my garden with thrushes & blackbirds for yew-berries' (DCP: Letter 9359). For Darwin, both the garden and the transitional spaces beyond it were at a certain level spaces where natural selection operated – and its effects could be observed – just as readily as in a Brazilian rain forest or on an Andean peak. The image of the garden gone to seed was a vivid one for the Victorians; Swinburne's 'Forsaken Garden' (1878) and the Prolegomena to Huxley's *Evolution and Ethics* (1894) come to mind. But even the actively maintained garden visible from his study window was for Darwin a place of struggle and death.

Another early Braddon novel, *The Doctor's Wife* (1864), brings together sensation, gardens and Darwinian plants in explicit ways. Braddon's heroine, Isabel Sleaford, is introduced lounging in a garden chair at her father's suburban villa, reading one of the novels whose romance and excitements contrast unfavourably with her mundane existence. In this reworking of Gustave Flaubert's

Madame Bovary (1856), which had not yet been translated into English, Isabel is introduced to George Gilbert, a country doctor, by her family's boarder, a 'sensation author' (Braddon 1864: I. 16) named Sigismund Smith, who writes penny dreadfuls but aspires to more serious work and warns Isabel about her taste in fiction. The garden at Mr Sleaford's villa is 'neglected' and 'untidy', a place where 'bright garden-flowers' and 'rare orchids' grow among the weeds, and where the roses are 'choked with wild convolvulus tendrils, that wound about the branches like weedy serpents' and the arbour is 'half-smothered by the vulgar luxuriance of wild hops' (I. 34, 42–3, 86). The presence of orchids and climbing plants is probably not a deliberate reference to Darwin's botanical work, but they do reflect the Darwinian melding of the domestic and the exotic, the literally creepy ways of 'vulgar' and 'wild' climbers that 'choke' and 'smother' the elements of civilisation and order. As with the dungeon-like garden in *Basil*, this Gothic language of choking and smothering is misleading – no one is murdered in *The Doctor's Wife* – but it points simultaneously to Isabel's dissatisfied idleness and to her obliviousness about the 'weedy serpents' lurking in her Eden.

The novel returns repeatedly to this scene of Isabel reading in the garden; the narrator, Sigismund Smith, George Gilbert and Isabel herself all recall it at various points. So, too, does the novel return repeatedly to the sensational plots of Sigismund's stories, actual or contemplated, and to their production. Indeed, gardens and flowers mark other characters as much as they do Isabel and her family. In the garden at George Gilbert's family home, 'the useful element very much preponderated over the ornamental' (I. 118); like the Sleafords' garden, it is 'old-fashioned' and weedy. Tended by the loyal and loving but rather lazy family retainer, William Jeffson, it manages to achieve a balance between natural selection and cultivation, the snails eaten by the toads and the weeds left to grow amongst the fruit and vegetables: 'The harmony of the universe asserted itself in that Midlandshire garden, unchecked by any presumptuous interference from Mr. Jeffson', yet 'Mr. Gilbert had more fruit and vegetables than he could eat, or cared to give away' (I. 118–19). The gardens of the kindly, philanthropic Charles Raymond, in contrast, are 'trimly kept' by an 'indefatigable' gardener (I. 150). Raymond hires Isabel as governess after her family's fall in fortunes, and it is in his gardens that George Gilbert sees her again. Isabel soon marries Gilbert but, like Emma Bovary, finds both her husband and provincial life rather dull. The attractions of Roland Lansdell, the Byronic neighbouring squire, are signalled by the hothouse flowers and fruits he sends to the doctor's wife and her husband; to Isabel they represent the fashionable world of London for which she pines, 'in which existence is a perpetual whirlpool of balls and dinner-parties and hothouse flowers and despair' (I. 272). In the end, Isabel's affair with Lansdell remains unconsummated, and she breaks it off when he proposes that she run away with him as his mistress. Isabel not only avoids Emma Bovary's suicidal fate, but inherits the estates of both Lansdell and her husband, her maturation marked by the model cottages and allotment gardens she establishes for Lansdell's tenants.

In her analysis of *The Doctor's Wife*'s gardens, Narin Hassan astutely situates Braddon's botanical imagery in relation to mid-nineteenth-century social and cultural change. The gardens are 'a hybrid site of exchange referencing industry, artificiality, imitation, and the mutability of class and gender boundaries' (Hassan 2005: 69). I want, however, simply to note that these symbolic meanings and functions of the garden were also shaped by shifting views of many of the plants within them, and those shifting views in turn were shaped by Darwin's botanical studies. And at Down House, as in the spaces and plots of sensation fiction, violence and sexuality were always present, for violence and sex lay at the heart of natural selection and were what Darwin's plant work was bent on unearthing. It should come as no surprise, then, that the botanical murders, conspiracies and trysts transpiring in Darwin's gardens and hothouses, many of them witnessed or even presided over by Darwin himself, provoked similar anxieties, fears and fascination for his contemporaries as those induced by the reading of Braddon and Collins.

WORKS CITED

Barlow, Nora (ed.). 1958. *The Autobiography of Charles Darwin 1809–1882* (London: Collins)

Braddon, M. E. 1862. *Lady Audley's Secret*, 3 vols (London: Tinsley)

Braddon, M. E. 1864. *The Doctor's Wife*, 3 vols (London: Maxwell)

Collins, W. Wilkie. 1852. *Basil: A Story of Modern Life*, 3 vols (London: Richard Bentley)

Cooke, M. C. 1882. *Freaks and Marvels of Plant Life* (London: Society for Promoting Christian Knowledge)

Darwin, Charles. 1859. *On the Origin of Species* (London: Murray)

Darwin, Charles. 1862. 'On the Two Forms, or Dimorphic Condition, in the Species of Primula, and on their remarkable Sexual Relations', *Journal of the Proceedings of the Linnean Society of London (Botany)*, 6: 77–96

Darwin, Charles. 1871. *The Descent of Man, and Selection in Relation to Sex*, 2 vols (London: Murray)

Darwin, Charles. 1875. *Insectivorous Plants* (London: Murray)

Darwin, Charles. 1877. *The Different Forms of Flowers on Plants of the Same Species* (London: Murray)

Darwin, Francis (ed.). 1887. *The Life and Letters of Charles Darwin*, 3 vols (London: Murray)

Dawson, Gowan. 2007. *Darwin, Literature and Victorian Respectability* (Cambridge: Cambridge University Press)

Endersby, Jim. 2016a. 'Deceived by Orchids: Sex, Science, Fiction and Darwin', *British Journal for the History of Science*, 49: 205–29

Endersby, Jim. 2016b. *Orchid: A Cultural History* (Chicago and London: University of Chicago Press)

'Flowers of the Future', *Punch*, 67 (19 December 1874): 255

Hassan, Narin. 2005. '"Hothouse Flowers and Despair": Reading the Victorian Garden in M. E. Braddon's *The Doctor's Wife*', *Mosaic*, 38. 4: 67–81

Huxley, T. H. 1876. 'On the Border Territory Between the Animal and the Vegetable Kingdoms', *Macmillan's Magazine*, 33: 373–84

Keetley, Dawn. 2016. 'Introduction: Six Theses on Plant Horror; or, Why Are Plants Horrifying?', in *Plant Horror: Approaches to the Monstrous Vegetal in Fiction and Film*, ed. by Dawn Keetley and Angela Tenga (London: Palgrave Macmillan), pp. 1–30

Kröger, Lisa. 2013. 'Panic, Paranoia and Pathos: Ecocriticism in the Eighteenth-Century Gothic Novel', in *EcoGothic*, ed. by Andrew Smith and William Hughes (Manchester: Manchester University Press), pp. 15–27

[Mann, R. J.] 1881. 'Darwin on the Movements of Plants', *Edinburgh Review*, 153: 497–514

Miller, T. S. 2012. 'Lives of the Monster Plants: The Revenge of the Vegetable in the Age of Animal Studies', *Journal of the Fantastic in the Arts*, 23: 460–79

Report of the 38th Meeting of the British Association for the Advancement of Science (London: Murray, 1868)

'Review of *Insectivorous Plants*, by Charles Darwin', *Athenaeum* (17 July 1875): 88–9.

Ruskin, John. 1903–11. *The Works of John Ruskin*, ed. by E. T. Cook and Alexander Wedderburn, 39 vols (London: George Allen)

Sambourne, Linley. 1875. 'Suggested Illustration for "Dr. Darwin's Movements and Habits of Climbing Plants"', *Punch*, 69 (11 December): 242

Taylor, J. E. 1884. *The Sagacity and Morality of Plants* (London: Chatto and Windus)

W[ilson], A[ndrew]. 1878. 'Can we Separate Animals from Plants?', *Cornhill*, 37: 336–50

Archive sources

Darwin Correspondence Project. Letter 2067, Charles Darwin to Joseph Hooker, 21 March 1857, www.darwinproject.ac.uk/DCP-LETT-2067 [accessed 8 May 2019]

Darwin Correspondence Project. Letter 2101, Charles Darwin to Joseph Hooker, 3 June 1857, www.darwinproject.ac.uk/DCP-LETT-2101 [accessed 8 May 2019]

Darwin Correspondence Project. Letter 3008, Charles Darwin to Joseph Hooker, 4 December 1860, www.darwinproject.ac.uk/DCP-LETT-3008 [accessed 8 May 2019]

Darwin Correspondence Project. Letter 3753, Charles Darwin to Joseph Hooker, 6 October 1862, www.darwinproject.ac.uk/DCP-LETT-3753 [accessed 8 May 2019]

Darwin Correspondence Project. Letter 4262, Charles Darwin to Asa Gray, 4 August 1863, www.darwinproject.ac.uk/DCP-LETT-4262 [accessed 7 May 2019]

Darwin Correspondence Project. Letter 4415, Charles Darwin to Asa Gray, 25 February 1864, www.darwinproject.ac.uk/DCP-LETT-4415 [accessed 7 May 2019]

Darwin Correspondence Project. Letter 4644, Hugh Falconer to William Sharpey, 25 October 1864, www.darwinproject.ac.uk/DCP-LETT-4644 [accessed 7 May 2019]

Darwin Correspondence Project. Letter 8568, Charles Darwin to Asa Gray, 22 October 1872, www.darwinproject.ac.uk/DCP-LETT-8568 [accessed 8 May 2019]

Darwin Correspondence Project. Letter 9359, Charles Darwin to Alfred Newton, 14 March 1874, www.darwinproject.ac.uk/DCP-LETT-9359 [accessed 8 May 2019]

7

'Tentacular thinking' and the 'abcanny' in Hawthorne's Gothic gardens of masculine egotism

Shelley Saguaro

As the writer of often whimsical 'story-books', of Romances set in 'a neutral territory, somewhere between the real world and faery-land' (Hawthorne 1981: 66), Nathaniel Hawthorne also focused on 'all the ghastliness which the Gothic mind loves to associate with the idea of death' (1961: 26). Writing in mid-nineteenth-century America, Hawthorne chose various locations at home and abroad for his richly ambiguous tales and novels. The focus here is on three of Hawthorne's well-known 'Gothic' texts. The short story 'Rappaccini's Daughter' (1844; Hawthorne 1987, hereafter RD) and the novel, *The Marble Faun: or the Romance of Monte Beni* (1859; Hawthorne 1961, hereafter MF), are both located in Italy, in sixteenth-century Padua and nineteenth-century Rome, respectively. *The Blithedale Romance* (1854; Hawthorne 1996, hereafter BR) is a novel set in rural Massachusetts, and Blithedale, an experimental communal farm, is modelled on the utopian community Brook Farm, with which Hawthorne was familiar. These texts, although distinctive in their own right and written over a fifteen-year period, bear some traits and tropes in common, including repeated reference to the Gothic tradition. Also in common are 'fallen' young women, the daughters of abusive men and absent mothers; allegorical flora and fauna; the investigation of the conventional oppositions of good versus evil, masculine versus feminine, nature versus artifice.

Each text uses gardens and outdoor settings, from the sun-drenched Renaissance parks and gardens of Italy to the often-inclement pioneering farmlands of Massachusetts, as the venues for dramas with diabolical aspects and subversive meanings. As D. H. Lawrence so famously put it, Hawthorne was careful to send his meanings 'out in disguise' (1981: 89). Complex entanglements, whether relational, botanical, ideological or narratological, are a prominent theme throughout. Like the 'entanglement of a shrub that wreaths its tendrils over a hidden entrance' (RD: 403) in 'Rappaccini's Daughter' or the 'luxuriant' wild grape vine, in *The Blithedale Romance*, that had 'twined and twisted itself up into the tree', 'wreathing the entanglement of its tendrils around almost every bough' (BR: 110), human relations are also repeatedly described as 'knots', 'intricacy', 'entanglements', with either sustained ensnarement or bonds being 'violently broken' (156). Women, primarily, suffer from the consequences of 'a life hopelessly entangled with a villain's' (202) and are allegorised as subject to distorted growth, thwarted vigour and various other impoverishments. For example, in *The Blithedale Romance*, from the drowned Zenobia's pierced and broken heart grows a 'tuft of ranker vegetation ... a crop of weeds' (216), whereas Priscilla, in the same text, is seen as reminiscent of a plant 'doing its best to vegetate among the bricks of an enclosed court, where there is scanty soil, and never any sunshine' (73). Zenobia throughout is emblematised by the exotic hothouse bloom with which she adorns herself in a community otherwise devoted to outdoor toil and regimented cultivation of cabbages: 'the enlightened culture of the soil' (82) rather than luxuriant hothouse fripperies or, indeed, wayward entanglements.

Such allegories are, perhaps, not so surprising, but new readings are afforded by digging deeper into Hawthorne's radical thought with ecocritical and posthuman theoretical tools. Here I argue that the apparently superficial symbolism of luxuriant or thwarted plants and entangled gardens represents more complex ideological challenges than are generally acknowledged or than pertain simply to Hawthorne's (and America's) Puritan heritage or the search for a new Eden. By bringing Donna Haraway's recent theoretical work on what she names as the 'Chthulucene' to bear on Hawthorne's elusive, ambiguous, nineteenth-century tales, correlations can be found between their respective concerns and the manner in which these are addressed. Attention to ambiguity and entanglement is, for both Hawthorne and Haraway, a *method* as well as the subject matter. The now urgently required 'tentacular thinking' (Haraway 2016b), tentative, connected, interlaced, is anticipated by Hawthorne's own poetics, just as Haraway's commitment to 'chthonic ones', to the various monstrous, entangled and curious beings, often 'replete with tentacles, feelers ... and very unruly hair' (2016b: 2), for example, is not unfamiliar in Hawthorne's depictions, as we shall consider.

Haraway is well known for her transdisciplinary theoretical work and has recently turned her attention to the three prevailing epochs to which the planet's inhabitants are in thrall and which have brought us to a critical juncture: 'Anthropocene, Capitalocene, Chthulucene' (2016a: 31). The Anthropocene, now so widely discussed as our current geological epoch, is successor to and companion of the Capitalocene, which rose to predominance in the West in the nineteenth century. With America as its flagbearer and, arguably, its founder, the Capitalocene is the era of capital investment, the growth of material wealth, private ownership of property, persistent development and perpetual competition. It privileges wealth, status, caste or class, and men – hence the commonly used attribution 'patriarchal capitalism':

> No wonder the world's great monotheisms in both religious and secular guises have tried again and again to exterminate the chthonic ones. The scandals of times called the Anthropocene and the Capitalocene are the latest and most dangerous of the exterminating forces. Living-with and dying-with each other potently in the Chthulucene can be a fierce reply to the dictates of both Anthropos and Capital. (Haraway 2016a: 2)

The Chthulucene, however, is anything but nostalgic, or natural, or 'pure', in the conservative, controlling and human-extolling ways that monotheism has construed these categories. 'Flourishing' in the Chthulucene, states Haraway, 'will be cultivated as a multispecies response-ability' (55): 'The chthonic powers of Terra infuse its tissues everywhere, despite the civilizing efforts of the agents of sky gods to astralize them and set up chief Singletons and their tame committees' (32). The 'sky gods' and 'chief Singletons' are Haraway's terms for those figureheads and champions of the 'civilizing efforts' manifest in the binaries of patriarchal monotheism, anthropocentrism, capitalism, unchecked growth and the single-minded exploitation of the planet's resources. They are the proponents of human stardom, as befits a perceived natural order that puts mankind in charge and elevates the privileged within that category no matter what the collateral cost. Despite their apparent power and long-standing rhetoric, however, Haraway is at pains to show that their reign is arbitrary, short-sighted and ultimately doomed. Thus it is, in this time of trouble for the whole planet, that she champions instead, not fatalism, but the messy, repressed, disordered or disregarded biotic and abiotic beings of the earth, the 'chthonic creatures of Terra'.

Such a 'rich wallow of multispecies muddles' (31) includes genetically modified 'frankenplants' (Pollan 1998) and myriad other biotech and transgenic entities. Multispeciesism and hybridism have a lineage in myth, an established practice in horticulture and now, crucially, a central place in Chthulucenic 'multispecies stories and practices' (Haraway 2016a: 55). Returning to Hawthorne is also to find foreshadowed in his work, not just the Gothic *uncanny*, with its repressed dreads of the strangely familiar, including the dark interiors of human bodies (as in Freud) or its exploitation of 'the repugnance of death and skulls' (MF: 26) but the Chthulucenic *abcanny*. The 'abcanny', explains New Weird author and proponent of tentacularity, China Miéville, in an online essay, 'M. R. James and the Quantum Vampire', is 'the eruption of the utterly unknown and unthinkable' (Miéville 2011), as befits a posthuman, digital, chimerical era, and which announces a Gothic sensibility not of repressed human darkness but of yet unthought-of futures that topple the predominance of the natural and the human.

12 Padua Botanical Garden (Orto dei Semplici), with Saint Anthony Basilica (1545).
Unknown, reprinted in Roberto De Visiani. *1842. L'Orto botanico di Padova
nell'anno 1842* (Padua)

THE GARDEN WAS NEVER PURE OR NATURAL ...

Hawthorne's tale 'Rappaccini's Daughter' has its setting in a famed botanical garden at the University of Padua in Italy. Padua is home to one of the world's oldest, if not the oldest, botanic garden, the Horta Botanico, established in the sixteenth century, which is also the likely time-frame of the story. Gardener and garden historian Susan Rutherford notes that of the botanical collections first established in Europe in the sixteenth century, to study medicinal plants and imported rarities, Padua 'was and remains outstanding' (2015: 11):

> The first true botanic gardens were scientific university institutions set up in the 1540s, early in the European Renaissance, in the quest for experimental data. The earliest ones, known then as physic gardens, were founded in the northern Italian states by established universities at the heart of new ideas of scientific enquiry, to grow medicinal plants for identification and study by medical students. This scientific study of medicinal drugs and their sources, preparation and use was known as *materia medica*, when botany was merely ancillary to medicine. (Rutherford 2015: 9)

In the story's terms, scientific knowledge and human hubris is represented by 'the famous Doctor' (RD: 388) and 'his insane zeal for science' (412). The story is one of Hawthorne's best known and, beyond its literary merits, it is found in collections that focus on stories of weird, monstrous, poisonous and murderously tentacled plants, such as Chad Arment's *Flora Curiosa: Cryptobotany, Mysterious Fungi, Sentient Trees and Deadly Plants in Classic Science Fiction and Fantasy* (2013). Dr Rappaccini's garden is replete with hybridised and exotic plants of his own creation, some creeping 'serpent-like along the ground' (RD: 390) and others that 'climbed on high' in a shrouded 'drapery of hanging foliage' (390). Most prominent, and most poisonous of all the weird plants that are cultivated there, is the strange centre-piece, a 'resplendent' purple-blossomed shrub. A kindred exotic is the doctor's daughter, Beatrice, with 'the Oriental sunshine of her beauty' (403) and 'a voice as rich as a tropical sunset … of purple or crimson' (391) and 'arrayed with … a bloom so deep and vivid that one shade more would be too much' (391). It is she who nurtures the purple-blossomed shrub, embracing and addressing it as 'sister' (416). However, nothing else can seem to endure the exhalations or touch of either maiden or plant; her breath alone can kill the insects or small reptiles that approach and wither immediately the mundane florist's bouquet of flowers with which suitor Giovanni seeks to woo her. One drop of the plant's sap also has fatal consequences for any being other than Beatrice. Beatrice appears as the doomed prisoner of her father's scientific fanaticism and the victim of her harshly judgemental lover, who equates toxicity with evil, and who attempts to administer an antidote, 'distilled of blessed herbs' (419), only to kill her. The moral of the tale appears to be straightforward: 'And thus the poor victim of man's ingenuity and of thwarted nature, and of the fatality that attends all such efforts of perverted wisdom, perished there, at the feet of her father and Giovanni' (420). A recent summary of the tale found in *Orchid: A Cultural History* (2016), for instance, is indicative of the line usually taken:

> It's an intriguing, rather Gothic story, that blends the girl and the flower back into a single, sinister image of untouchable toxicity, but it is striking that the girl is depicted as having no more agency or willpower than the flowers do. She may be (very literally) a *femme fatale*, but she's no seductress, merely the passive recipient of her father's obsession and the young man's fascination. (Endersby 2016: 136)

However, the story also demonstrates aspects that are less obvious than at first assumed.

Without doubt, the reader cannot help but abhor the sinister, hyper-vigilant and spectral presence of Beatrice's father as he is depicted, both as a father and as a gardener:

> Nothing could exceed the intentness with which this scientific gardener examined every shrub … as if he was looking into their inmost nature, making observations in regard to their creative essence … Nevertheless, in spite of this deep intelligence on his part, there was no approach to intimacy between himself and these vegetable

existences. On the contrary, he avoided their actual touch, or the direct inhaling of their odors ... the man's demeanor was that of one walking among malignant influences, such as savage beasts, or deadly snakes, or evil spirits. (RD: 390)

Although his daughter has been instructed in his methods so that reputedly 'she is already qualified to fill a professor's chair' (395), her manner among the plants is one of intimacy and kinship.

An aspect often overlooked in readings of 'Rappaccini's Daughter' is the role of Professor Pietro Baglioni, who sits in (perhaps, jealous) judgement of Rappaccini and actively counsels the young Giovanni against him. It is, however, the antidote he provides that actually kills Beatrice; Giovanni's own denunciation of her with 'blighting words' such as 'hateful', 'ugly', 'loathsome and deadly' and 'a world's wonder of hideous monstrosity' also play their part. Rappaccini, who is a surrogate god in this scenario, has inoculated Giovanni with the poison that affects his daughter, but Giovanni is determined that he and Beatrice must be 'purified from evil' – with tragic consequences. Giovanni, Baglioni and Rappaccini all collude in this debacle which we might, through Haraway, read as a moral tale for the Chthulucene. These Capitalocenic 'sky gods', the professors, compete and hubristically create their 'monsters', but they finally lose the control they assume is unending and theirs by right. Beatrice is, not unfamiliarly, the focus for and pawn in all their respective projections of duty, beauty, purity and monstrosity. However, more attention should be paid to Beatrice's pleas; of her maligned sister-plant, for which she proclaims her deep love ('it has qualities that you little dream of') (416); and for herself she explains: 'though my body be nourished with poison, my spirit is God's creature, and craves love as its daily food' (418).

How might we now approach both Beatrice's monstrosity and her toxic, 'unnatural', genetically engineered sister-plant? Rather than merely see Beatrice as Victim and the plant as Taboo (evil, artificial, unnatural), is there a way to reread the story, tentacularly, which does not let Dr Rappaccini 'off the hook' but which recuperates his intellectual and biological offspring?

WHAT MAKES A MONSTER?

Beatrice is but one of Hawthorne's many heroines who, despite their beauty and competence, find themselves ambiguously positioned in the societies in which they live. Their independence (in part thrust upon them) is, on the one hand, admirable, but it also creates isolation and despair, in line with Hawthorne's overriding view that isolation from one's fellow beings – whether by egotism or abjection – is the worst situation and the greatest evil. Hester, in *The Scarlet Letter*, is ostracised for the sin of adultery as if she alone were responsible; Zenobia, in *The Blithedale Romance*, a writer and women's rights advocate, has a 'past' that taints and haunts, and so, rejected by suitor Hollingsworth in favour of the more compliant, clinging Priscilla, she kills herself.

Typically, these women are described as being 'exotic' – that is, outside Western feminine norms: Beatrice, in 'Rappaccini's Daughter', possesses a near-surfeit of Oriental beauty and looks 'redundant with life, health and energy' (RD: 391). Zenobia is 'just on the hither verge of her richest maturity', 'remarkably beautiful', with a 'fine intellect' and overflowing with 'bloom, health and vigor' (BR: 48) although, from a 'fastidious' perspective, she is 'deficient in softness and delicacy' (48). In *The Marble Faun*, Miriam, also beautiful, and whose origins are mysterious (Jewish, perhaps, or possibly with 'one burning drop of African blood' (MF: 25)), is described as having an 'ambiguity' about her, which 'operated unfavorably as regarded her reception in society, anywhere but in Rome' (22–3). Wild and abundant hair (with wayward tendrils) is commonly of note; there is always something a little 'off' or 'too much' about them. They are often typified by a plant or flower: Hester, by the wild rose that grows outside the Puritans' prison wall; Zenobia, first by the exotic, colourful hothouse flower she wears in her hair and then by the wild weeds that spring from her corpse; Beatrice, by the vivid purple bloom of her poisonous sister-plant, which she places on her bosom. They also, by their actions and in their backgrounds, fail to match Hollingsworth's typically nineteenth-century version of 'pure' and 'natural' womanhood:

> All the separate action of woman is, and ever has been and always shall be, false, foolish, vain, destructive of her own best and holiest qualities ... Man is a wretch without woman, but woman is a monster ... without man, as her acknowledged principal. ... were there any possible prospect of woman's taking the social stand which some of them – poor, miserable abortive creatures, who only dream of such things because they have missed woman's peculiar happiness, or because Nature made them really neither man nor woman! – if there were a chance of their attaining the end which these petticoated monstrosities have in view, I would call upon my own sex to use its physical force, that unmistakable evidence of sovereignty, to scourge them back within their proper bounds! (BR: 128)

This is a theme that Hawthorne takes up time and again. Not only are these women reminiscent of Freud's 'hysterics', defiant and then self-doubtingly compliant in turn, they are clearly placed as the kind of women, mythic or mundane, who have been represented as 'hybrid', unnatural, horrific and 'monstrous' – just like 'snaky Medusa', for example. 'Because the deities of the Olympiad identified her as a particularly dangerous enemy to the sky gods' succession and authority, mortal Medusa is especially interesting', writes Donna Haraway; 'the Gorgons turned men who looked into their living, venomous, snake-encrusted faces into stone. I wonder what might have happened if those men had known how to politely greet the dreadful chthonic ones' (2016a: 54).

It is a fable fit for the Chthulucene: the encounters that have involved the discrimination against those deemed to be Other, or 'earthly' and thus repellent in the view of sky god-dominated cultures, will (and have) become the instruments of far-reaching destruction, repressions that will erupt and return to haunt. What might the story have otherwise been, conjectures Haraway, and how might we now aim to redress the balance by honouring multiplicity and difference?

The myth of Medusa has informed many feminist analyses and projects, typifying as she does, the vengeful rage against misogyny. However, Medusa's multispeciesism or hybridity also offers new meanings. Donatello, the ambiguous character of *The Marble Faun*, is apparently reminiscent, even to conjectures about 'furry ears', of the mythical Faun of Praxiteles (c. 130 CE). The Faun, explains Hawthorne, was a creature who embodied 'all the pleasantness of sylvan life', of 'trees, grass, flowers' and who was 'neither man nor animal, and yet no monster, but a being in whom both meet on friendly ground', 'a poet's reminiscence of a period when man's ... fellowship with every living thing was more intimate and dear' (MF: 17). The narrative voice continues: 'In some long time past he must really have existed. Nature needed, and still needs, this beautiful creature; standing between man and animal, sympathizing with each, comprehending the speech of either race, and interpreting the whole existence of one to the other' (18). That the multispecies faun was not forced into a category – man or beast – and yet was not denigrated as a transgressive monster, as Hawthorne explains, is what renders him so relevant to the discussion here. Myth now abstracts such a creature as fanciful chimera, but Hawthorne thinks of this 'beautiful creature' of the past as a bridge, a mutual interpreter and model of species reciprocity. Haraway, on the other hand, is asking us to think the same way about the 'multispecies muddles' of the present and future rather than merely the mythic past. Medusa can be instructive by another route. The faun or satyr gets away with what Medusa cannot; Medusa represents horror and rupture while, for a time, the faun was interpreted as a rich combination. Medusa's snaky locks, her dragon-like body and her 'inhuman' face, the gaze from which turns *men* to stone, have been variously interpreted, often with psychoanalytic connotations: 'The terror of Medusa is ... a terror of castration' claimed Freud famously in 'The Medusa's Head' (1940). Medusa is many things; she is reptile and human and she is 'ugly' (where she once was beautiful, according to versions of the myth, until she was raped and punished for *her* crime). Rather than considering such a creature as utterly unnatural and repulsive, she should perhaps be seen as instructively plural. The garden in Eden's singular reptile, the snake, signifies unproblematised binaries (male/female; good/evil; natural/unnatural) and heralds the monotheism which in turn has fostered 'the sky gods' of the Capitalocene and Anthropocene.

CHERISHING THE DARK (COMPOST), THE WAYWARD (WEED), THE ENTANGLED (HYBRID) ...

One of the lessons that 'Rappaccini's Daughter' should help us learn in relation to gardens is that plants are never 'pure' and that commingling and admixture is inevitable and, indeed, essential for sustainable vigour. Plants have always been hybridising, with or without human control or ingenuity, and despite the come-lately but now long-standing anthropocentric views to the contrary. However, at the time of the story's setting it was seen to be intellectually unfounded and/or sacrilegious to think that plants were sexual beings (philosophers such as Aristotle and Theophrastus proclaimed that only species capable of movement could reproduce sexually), and this was overlaid with theological accounts of a Creation that 'furnished the world with an immutable set of plant and animal species (RD: 48). As Giovanni assesses the plants in Dr Rappaccini's garden, he finds them all shocking:

> their gorgeousness seemed fierce, passionate, and even unnatural ... Several, also, would have shocked a delicate instinct by an appearance of artificialness, indicating that there had been such commixture, and, as it were, adultery of various vegetable species, that the production was no longer of God's making, but the monstrous offspring of man's depraved fancy, glowing with only an evil mockery of beauty. (RD: 403–4)

This makes 'Rappaccini's Daughter', set in the late sixteenth or early seventeenth century, a tale of exceptional and, for the time, unlikely scientific modernity. Despite the establishment of botanical gardens at this time, Rappaccini's achievement of an entirely new plant species of his own invention would have been especially heretical, particularly after the Inquisition conducted by the Catholic Church, 'epitomized by the trial and humiliating condemnation of Galileo in 1633' (Thompson 2010: 54–5). As Peter Thompson points out, almost all academics at this time would be, if not actually ordained, compelled to abide by the Church's doctrines:

> That was a stumbling block highly likely to trip up anyone attempting to hybridize plants ... in order to 'create' new and improved varieties – the orthodox presumption being that if they were not present at the beginning, they could not be summoned into existence hereafter. (Thompson 2010: 55)

Thus it was, notes Thompson, that so 'many men of learning and academics' were able 'to disregard errant ideas that the very organs that make up a flower are blatantly sexual in purpose' (34). Carolus Linnaeus (1707–78), for example, famously developed a universal method for the scientific classification of plants which depended upon counting the number and type of sexual organs, but the approach was anything but objective. Rather, prim societal conventions and coy allegories of nuptials were projected anthropomorphically onto plants, where the evidence was entirely to the contrary. 'Rappaccini's Daughter' was written in the mid-nineteenth century, before the publication of Charles Darwin's ground-breaking *On the Origin of Species* in 1859, and is now being read in the twenty-first. Throughout the nineteenth century scientists before and including Darwin were cautiously conducting experiments to understand better plant reproduction and sexual selection, not least to further the cross-pollination and controlled hybridisation of plants. However, plants revealed some inconvenient models for human relations: 'polygamous', 'hermaphroditic', 'promiscuous'; 'bisexual', 'transsexual', 'parthenogenetic'. Not from plants could an endorsement or analogy be found for the strict binaries of cultural enactments.

It is not just women, of course, who fall prey to the arbitrarily controlling but, over time, normatised conventions of patriarchal capitalism. Miles Coverdale, the poet in *The Blithedale Romance*, is not simply a hapless bachelor who (lamely) professes his compulsorily heterosexual desire for Priscilla at the end of the novel; he is, rather, I maintain (Saguaro 2000: 197), a homosexual or bisexual man at a time and in a culture when this was illegal. Hollingsworth perhaps protests too much when he rails against just such an 'Unpardonable Sin', which is among the 'vile, petty, sordid, filthy, bestial and abominable corruptions ... cankered into our nature' and 'the portion of ourselves we shudder at' (BR: 76). It is Coverdale who, despite also having once been devoted to Hollingsworth, vociferously condemns the effects of his 'intensity of masculine egotism' on behalf of women (128): 'it is nonsense – and a miserable wrong – the result, like so many others, of masculine egotism – that the success or failure of women's existence should be made to depend wholly on the affections, and on *one species* of affection' (214, emphasis added). In opposition to Hollingsworth's obsessive utopian philanthropy and 'spick and span novelty' is Coverdale's preference for: 'creeping plants', 'moss to gather', trees', 'breadth of shadow' (133), darkness, decay and death – all as an integral part of life. This aligns the homoerotic, voyeuristic and melancholic poet, Coverdale, not just with the Gothic understanding that death is to be embraced as an inevitable part of living things, but with Hawthorne himself. Hollingsworth's refusal to have a graveyard as part of his new 'System', installed on an 'open hill side' is certainly reminiscent of Haraway's Capitalocenic 'Singletons' and 'sky god' astralisers (2016a: 31). Coverdale favours, tellingly, 'the backside of the universe' (BR: 147), the haphazard but luxuriant plots, full of runaway plants and wildlife feeding plentifully on the 'wormy earth' (147). Here too, we find Hawthorne challenging binaries, in this case of rural and urban. Rather, Coverdale finds these rich gardens in the urban wild, 'those nooks and crannies, where Nature, like a stray partridge, hides her head among the long established haunts of men!' (147). Hawthorne is clearly, as a fellow author, on the poet Coverdale's side. 'Romance and poetry, ivy, lichens and wallflowers need "ruin" to make them grow' (MF: 3). Imagining the opinions of his controlling, systematic and ruthless Puritan forefathers, Hawthorne conjectures that they would view him, a fanciful writer of storybooks, a 'degenerate fellow' (Hawthorne 1986: 42).

HUMUSISM: THE ABCANNY GOTHIC

These days, of course, a reading of 'Rappaccini's Daughter' brings to mind less the religious or cultural debates of the eighteenth and nineteenth centuries and more the contemporary debates about genetic modification (genetically modified crops), biotechnology and industrial-scale agribusiness. We now contend with the Olympian 'doctrines' of giant corporations such as Monsanto, 'the chemical giant ... turned "life sciences" giant' (Pollan 1998). In a well-known article, 'Playing God in the Garden', published in the *New York Times* in 1998 and later developed into a chapter in *The Botany of Desire: A Plant's Eye View of the World* (2001), Michael Pollan discusses Monsanto's 'New Leaf Superior' potatoes, which came genetically replete with their own insecticide. Although discontinued in 2001, these transgenic potatoes heralded a new era of botany and agriculture:

> For the first time, breeders can bring qualities from anywhere in nature into the genome of the plant – from fireflies (the quality of luminescence), from flounders (frost tolerance), from viruses (disease resistance) and, in the case of my potatoes, from the soil bacterium known as *Bacillus thuringiensis*. Never in a million years of natural or artificial selection would these species have produced these qualities. 'Modification by descent' has been replaced by ... something else. (Pollan 2001: 211)

Given all the compelling concerns about huge corporations such as Monsanto and their trademarked creations, there is no question that they are certainly an outcrop of the Capitalocene, and thoroughly implicated in the Anthropocene. Naomi Klein outlines the manner in which 'the six agribusiness giants including Monsanto and Syngenta' have responded to climate change, not just with some environmental Green Speak, but by seeing 'all kinds of business opportunities' (2014: 9): 'Between 2008 and 2010, at least 261 patents were filed', primarily by major agribusinesses, 'related to growing "climate-ready" crops – seeds supposedly able to withstand extreme weather conditions' (9) but which continue to reduce biodiversity in plants and flexibility for growers and consumers alike. Dr Rappaccini, it is easy to decide, is an early villain in the same vein, although today's power-plays and ensuing extinctions are more ubiquitous. However, Donna Haraway asks us to reflect on our continuing too-ready judgements of 'good' and 'bad', seeing them as falling into the very binary paradigms that have caused 'the trouble' and which she – and Hawthorne – are resisting: 'I cannot help but hear in the biotechnology debates the unintended tones of fear of the alien and suspicion of the mixed' (Haraway in Myerson 2000: 36). As George Myerson explains, even when it can seem most counter-intuitive, such as in the debates about genetically modified foods, 'you cannot exploit the logic of natural "kind and purity" at the end of the second millennium without setting foot on haunted ground' (36).

In a vein similar to Beatrice Rappaccini's kinship with her manufactured, poisonous, sister-plant, and Haraway's exhortation to establish and cherish 'oddkinships', Pollan also acknowledges a familial connection:

> What is perhaps most striking about the New Leafs coming up in my garden is the added human intelligence that the inclusion of the *Bacillus thuringiensis* gene represents. In the past, that intelligence resided outside the plant … One way to look at genetic engineering is that it allows a larger portion of human culture and intelligence to be imported … while my genetically engineered plants might at first seem like alien beings, that's not quite right; they're more like us than other plants because there's more of us in them. (Pollan 2001: 213)

In a posthuman world where humans live side by side with, say, Alexa or rely on Siri or another app or bot, the strict demarcations, especially in relation to 'intelligence' which hitherto was such an exclusively human attribute, are eroded. And whereas Pollan confidently claims that there is 'more of us in them', the measures of 'them in us' have not yet thoroughly been brought to bear. One of the most controversial aspects, perhaps, of the New Leafs is their provenance, developed by huge corporations who patent and delimit everything from off-the-shelf herbicides to soil-ready but trademarked seeds, tubers and plants. Clearly, Hawthorne, critical of the utopianism of Puritanism or the obsessive singular visions of nineteenth-century communitarianism in systems such as Brook Farm or its fictionalised version at Blithedale is, like Haraway, not a fan of monotheism or monoculturalism and is particularly against the obsessions (often construed as intense masculine egotism) which safeguard their interests. Both can be seen to favour an 'ethic of ambiguity' (de Beauvoir in Myerson 2000: 70) rather than the regulatory functions of vested interests and powerful institutions, as embodied in the Chthulucene, which Haraway articulates and which Hawthorne would, I speculate, endorse, even if it also shocks. As Myerson, again, explains:

> Capitalism manufactured objects, and in doing so it also manufactured a world, and the lives within it. Now something different is happening to the objects, and so, it follows, capitalism has taken a new turning. New objects are cascading among us … These things are neither natural nor unnatural in the old senses; they are beyond natural and unnatural. (Myerson 2000: 26)

Mary Shelley demonstrated as early as 1818, with Frankenstein's monster, that the offspring of new technologies are not inherently or incontrovertibly bad. The continuing lesson of feminism, and indeed, horticulture, is to challenge the very terms 'natural' and 'unnatural'. 'Staying with the trouble', says Haraway, 'requires learning to be truly present' and utterly entangled, rather than caught uselessly between debates about 'awful or edenic pasts and apocalyptic or salvific futures' (2016a: 1).

I suggest that the figures of hysteria and repression that so readily haunted a Gothic-garden sensibility need now to be replaced by something hitherto unimagined. Miéville muses on his own coinage, the 'abcanny', which, unlike the uncanny, is not 'reliant on the past' or on repression and repetition (Stachniak 2014). The distinctiveness and relevance of the abcanny is that it 'is without mythic resonance', unimpeded by the burden of meaning and thus, 'any future is implicitly possible' (Stachniak 2014). Haraway herself notes, 'the chthonic ones are not confined to a vanished past' (2016a: 56). Who can yet say to what figures the abject, tentacular, multifarious, contemporary 'chthonic ones', who have no mythological resonance, will give rise? Haraway is fond of her analogies of 'compost' and her multispecies 'critters'. But what of the massive landfills that never become humus? What about objects that are not even remotely 'critters'? And what speculative fabulations will be most fitting in the Chthulucene? One thing is certain; we must avoid Utopias. As China Miéville points out in an essay, 'The Limits of Utopia', and Hawthorne with his Puritan heritage knew well, Utopia 'has never been the preserve of those who cleave to liberation': 'There is a vision of the world as a garden, under threat. Choked with toxic growth. Gardening as war. And the task being one of ruthlessly eliminating the weeds that would deprive the better plants of nutrition, the air, light, sun' (Miéville n.d.)

Extending these metaphors, Haraway's remedy, albeit rhetorically, for a world garden in trouble is, instead, to rot down all the toxic rot of previous epochs to make a rich new humus of possibility: 'The unfinished Chthulucene must collect up the trash of the Anthropocene, the extremism of the Capitalocene, and chipping and shredding and layering like a mad gardener, make a much hotter compost pile for still possible pasts, presents and futures' (2016a: 57).

Even a twenty-first-century volume of academic essays such as this will share in that 'vision of the world as a garden under threat' and long for past idylls. As we have seen, gardens provide not just the allegories of ideology or the tropes of literature but, simultaneously, they are the venues in which we often unwittingly sow our prejudices and projections for survival. Pollan could not bring himself to eat the insecticide-laden, genetically modified, Monsanto-trademarked New Leaf Superior potatoes, understandably, no doubt; but here we are talking less about potatoes and more about paradigms. Beatrice Rappaccini might not have had to die, if a more tolerant view had been taken of her, by her father's competitor and by her terrified lover. Haraway – and Hawthorne long before her – asks us to interrogate much more thoroughly the paradigms by which we judge 'the natural world'. Nothing in the garden was ever 'pure' or designed to serve the hubristic purposes of the human species alone. Now

13 'Rappaccini's Daughter'. Illustration in Algis Valiunas (2011). 'The Last Temptation of Science', *New Atlantis*, 30: 119–35

the thorny entanglements of garden spaces must give rise to new allegories and modified tropes. As Toni Morrison noted when interrogating 'the kind of violent conflict that could happen ... to establish a Paradise ... it's really defined by who is *not* there as well as who is' (Morrison in Saguaro 2006: 156). Instead of Paradise, or Eden, or some new exclusive garden that is simply a version (however beguiling) of the old exclusive Garden, the time has come for a 'tentacular novum' fit for the 'terrapolis' of the Chthulucene. We must not expect it to be 'tidy', 'natural' or 'nice', in the ways that have brought us to this troubled juncture. It can still be beautiful, albeit redefined, but in so-far-unimagined ways.

WORKS CITED

Arment, Chad (ed.). 2013. *Flora Curiosa: Cryptobotany, Mysterious Fungi, Sentient Trees and Deadly Plants in Classic Science Fiction and Fantasy* (Greenville: Coachwhip Publications)

Endersby, Jim. 2016. *Orchid: A Cultural History* (Chicago and London: University of Chicago Press)

Freud, Sigmund. 1997. 'The Medusa's Head' (1940), in *Writings on Art and Literature* (Stanford: Stanford University Press), pp. 264–8

Haraway, Donna J. 2016a. *Staying with the Trouble: Making Kin in the Chthulucene* (Durham, NC: Duke University Press)

Haraway, Donna J. 2016b. 'Tentacular Thinking: Anthropocene, Capitalocene, Chthulucene' *e-flux journal*, 75, September, http://e-flux/journal/75/67125/tentacular-thinking-anthropocene-capitalocene-chthulucene/ [accessed 1 June 2020]

Hawthorne, Nathaniel. 1961. *The Marble Faun* (1859) (New York: New American Library)

Hawthorne, Nathaniel. 1981. *The House of the Seven Gables* (1851) (New York: Bantam Books)

Hawthorne, Nathaniel. 1986. *The Scarlet Letter* (Harmondsworth, Middlesex: Penguin)

Hawthorne, Nathaniel. 1987. 'Rappaccini's Daughter' (1844), in *Selected Tales and Sketches* (Harmondsworth: Penguin), pp. 386–420

Hawthorne, Nathaniel. 1996. *The Blithedale Romance* (1854), ed. by William Cain (Boston, MA: Bedford Book of St Martin's Press)

Klein, Naomi. 2014. *This Changes Everything: Capitalism vs. the Climate* (London: Allen Lane)

Lawrence, D. H. 1981. *Studies in Classic American Literature.* (Harmondsworth: Penguin)

Miéville, China. 2011. 'M.R. James and the Quantum Vampire', *Weird Fiction Review*, 29 November, http://weirdfictionreview.com/2011/11/m-r-james-and-the-quantum-vampire-by-china-mieville [accessed 1 June 2020]

Miéville, China. n.d. 'The Limits of Utopia', http://salvage.zone/mieville_all.html [accessed 1 June 2020]

Myerson, George. 2000. *Donna Haraway and GM Foods* (Cambridge: Icon)

Pollan, Michael. 1998. 'Playing God in the Garden', *New York Times*, 25 October, http://michaelpollan.com/articles-archive/playing-god-in-the-garden [accessed 1 June 2020]

Pollan, Michael. 2001. *The Botany of Desire: A Plants' Eye View of the World* (New York: Bloomsbury)

Rutherford, Sarah. 2015. *Botanic Gardens* (Oxford and New York: Shire Publications)

Saguaro, Shelley. 2000. '"Bosom Secrets": Decrypting Hawthorne's *Blithedale Romance*', *European Journal of American Culture*, 19. 3: 184–97

Saguaro, Shelley. 2006. *Garden Plots: The Politics and Poetics of Gardens* (Aldershot: Ashgate)

Stachniak, Alexander. 2014. 'Progressing from Definition to Heuristic: The Uncanny and the Abcanny', *Berfrois*, 21 January, www.berfrois.com/2014/01/the-uncanny-and-the-abcanny-alexander-stachniak/ [accessed 1 June 2020]

Thompson, Peter. 2010. *Seeds, Sex and Civilization* (London: Thames and Hudson)

8

Green is the new black: Plant monsters as ecoGothic tropes; vampires and *femmes fatales*

Teresa Fitzpatrick

Recent ecoGothic critics have drawn on ecofeminism 'to reconsider the role that the environment, species, and nonhumans play in the construction of monstrosity and fear ... by exposing interlocking androcentric and anthropocentric hierarchies, misogyny and speciesism, [that] seeks to question the mutual oppression of women, animals, and nature' (Del Principe 2014: 1). While late Victorian and Edwardian writers may have questioned 'assumptions about human supremacy' through the female Other as a spiritual conduit of nonhuman nature (Punter 2013: 55), '[g]othic fiction at its core is about transgression of all sorts' of boundaries, including national, social, sexual, and 'the boundaries of one's own identity', challenging established constructs and foreshadowing societal anxieties of impending change (Heiland 2004: 3). An ecoGothic approach pertains to examine these deep-seated fears through 'the interconnectedness of gothic and nature (ecology)' (Keetley and Wynn Sivils 2018: 3). Moreover, although 'femininity itself has been demonised in Gothic literature by way of the *femme fatale*, man-made monster, vampire and Medusa' (Mulvey-Roberts 2016: 108), these established Gothic tropes, particularly vampire and *femme fatale* figures, have not been extensively reconsidered as gendered Other in plant monsters, nor considered through an ecofeminist perspective. In fact, plant monster fiction has previously received little attention outside post-colonial Gothic criticism. Even more recent explorations, such as *Plant Horror* (Keetley and Tenga 2016), predominantly focus on environmental concerns in twentieth-century eco-horror rather than on plant monsters as Gothic tropes. Drawing on gender associations of nature and femininity within a Victorian framework, female Gothic and material ecofeminist theories, I offer a reading of two late Victorian Gothic texts: H. G. Wells's 1894 tale, 'The Flowering of the Strange Orchid' (2013: 63–71) and Howard R. Garis's 1905 short story, 'Professor Jonkin's

Cannibal Plant' (2013: 113–22), that create a place for plant monsters to bloom as ecoGothic tropes. Wells's short story depicts the orchid as a vampiric *femme fatale*, gendering nature to blur the lines between human and nonhuman through bodily transgression, while Garis's tale features a monster pitcher plant as uncanny eco-*femme fatale*.

French for 'deadly woman', the *femme fatale* is a well-established figure in literature: wickedly and sexually irresistible, this enchantress narcissistically manipulates the men around her into compromising and deadly situations. These characteristics are shared with the vampire figure; female vampires are often portrayed as draining male protagonists of their life force – that is, blood, energy or even money. When these demonised feminine qualities are projected onto flowering plants traditionally associated with the passive, caring female identity, the plant becomes a gendered Gothic monster. The 'peculiar commingling of the familiar with the unfamiliar' (Royle 2003: 1) in gendering these plants adds to their rendering as uncanny eco-(logical) *femmes fatales*. Through these gendered plant monsters, both tales engage with the contemporary anxieties and political sensitivities surrounding scientific progress, material change and rising feminism.

GENDERING THE PLANT MONSTER

Victorians were fascinated with plant-collecting, and the aspiration for green-houses, gardens and public parks reflected a modern age of imperial and patriarchal desire to demonstrate power over nature. Hardly surprising then, that '[t]he monstrous plant ... has proven an enduring object of fascination in literature and film, appearing everywhere from traditional folklore ... to hard science fiction' (Miller 2014: 470) as an embodiment of concerns about rapid social change and major scientific progress. Yet, although plant monsters 'may point to a deep unease about the boundary between taxonomic kingdoms' within animal studies, they are often overlooked in literary criticism (Miller 2012: 461). This seems strange since ecofeminism has increasingly focused on the intersectionality of cultural identities, with plant monster fiction offering a vehicle for considering national, racial and gendered 'Other' through the Gothic tropes of monstrous, grotesque and *femme fatale* figures. The long nineteenth century was one of 'explosive changes' which 'transformed the texture of everyday life', meaning 'social identities were dissolved and remade', with evolutionary theory providing 'a particularly rich source for Gothic plotting' and strange identities (Hurley 2001: 131–3).

The struggle to cope with these social changes in relation 'to nation, to race, to gender, to sexuality' accompanied fears of degeneracy that were frequently projected onto the vampire (Smith 2001: 64). The female vampire, however, challenges the 'power of the Victorian patriarch' with the 'voluptuous, voracious, immoral seductress' undermining the notion that 'women must appear pure and virtuous angels in the home' (Wisker 2012: 225). Amid such discourse on degeneration, invasion anxieties and the classification of national, racial and gendered Other, the *femme fatale* trope emerges 'from a phallocentric point of view' as the dark, chaotic, irrational, wild side of femininity (Stott 1992: 38). In Wells's tale, this dichotomous view of women is highlighted through the gendering of both human and nonhuman characters when novice plant collector Winter-Wedderburn purchases an unusual orchid rhizome at auction. After careful nurturing, it flowers beautifully, enticing the hapless gardener closer with its perfume, only to attack Winter-Wedderburn with its tentacle-like roots, revealing itself as a vampiric *femme fatale* in contrast to the conservative human housekeeper.

ORCHID AS *FEMME FATALE*

In the years following the Great Exhibition (1851), at which the engineering skill present in the Crystal Palace proved how well exotic plants from foreign lands could be kept in healthy abundance, Victorians became fascinated by orchids. An unusual, care-intensive, expensive and varied species, orchids were highly sought after at the time and required heated environments (hothouses) that replicated original habitats, meaning the ownership of both hothouse and orchids indicated wealth and social status. Victorian sensibilities encouraged the use of flowers to convey messages, and orchids were popular symbols of love, admiration and fertility. Hence, projecting socio-political concerns onto the 'flowering' of the 'strange orchid' within a Victorian Gothic context may well have resonated clearly with a contemporary reader. Having aerial roots, epiphytic growth, fused sexual structures and a symbiotic fungal relationship for germination (Arditti and Wing 2004: 69–70), orchids already offer Gothic potential with such unusual growing and reproductive methods. Charles Darwin's investigations into orchids also helped blur the boundaries between plants and animals, providing inspiration for writers to reflect the shifting relationship between the sexes (Endersby 2016). Orchids appeared to provide the Victorians with ready analogies for female sexuality.

Using this heightened sexualised femininity, Wells creates an eco-*femme fatale* figure through the orchid's transgressive nature and attack on the male gardener, reflecting contemporary concerns about socio-political change. Extolling his orchid growing, Winter-Wedderburn declares that in practising the 'mysteries of the orchid cultivator', his expensive rhizome could 'turn out to be a very beautiful orchid indeed' (Wells 2013: 66–7). In a gendered reading, the protagonist suggests the male 'orchid cultivator' must appropriately guide the orchid as 'woman' into the patriarchally constructed role. However, his rhizome produces a monstrous orchid that blurs the boundaries between beautifully benign and

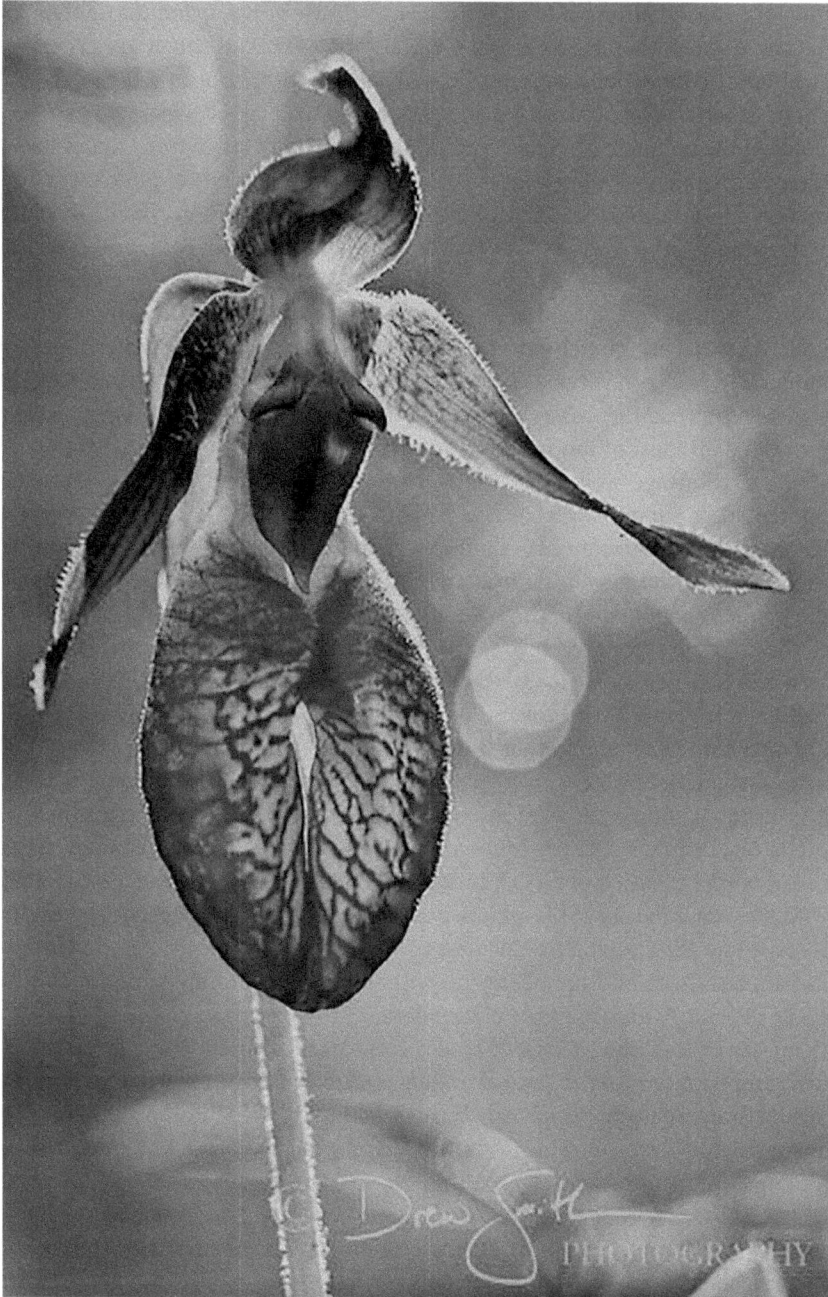

14 'Pink Lady's Slipper Orchid'

monstrously lethal, embodying the uncanny (Royle 2003: 2) and the dangerous nature of ecoGothic. Deleuze and Guattari argue that '[a] rhizome ceaselessly establishes connections between semiotic chains, organizations of power, and circumstances relative to the arts, sciences, and social struggles' (1987: 6–7), allowing the orchid to be considered as a gendered ecoGothic trope that reflects Victorian anxieties. They suggest modernity seen through a 'radicle-system' reflects a fragmented, chaotic world-view: '[t]he world has become chaos' while a 'rhizome as subterranean stem is absolutely different from roots and radicles' (5–6), providing a way of understanding the interconnectedness and increasing flux of cultural concepts. The aggressive nature of a generally benign flower underlines the multiplicity of anxieties stemming from the swift changes of modernity, such as evolving gender roles. On the one hand, the orchid reflects societies such as the Girls' Friendly Society and the Mothers' Union, which promoted an ideal of motherhood and femininity. Yet, the National Union of Women's Suffrage Societies and the women's movement were conversely influential in supporting social and political equalities, with members often lampooned publicly as monstrous despite many, in fact, being famously beautiful, such as British actress and suffragette, Cicely Hamilton. Hence, concerns about the increasing influence of these feminist and social movements on established gender roles are explored through Wells's orchid as a *femme fatale* figure.

While Rebecca Stott (1992), drawing on feminist theories of Hélène Cixous and Luce Irigaray, Toril Moi and Julia Kristeva, positions the *femme fatale* as Other within the dichotomous perspective of idealised/vilified woman in the male imagination, Mario Praz 'identifies the femme fatale as praying mantis, a vampire, a siren or a wanton courtesan' and sees 'sexual cannibalism and predatory instincts as a predominant characteristic of the fatal woman' (Praz in Luczynska-Holdys 2013: 4–5). In Wells's tale, Winter-Wedderburn is besotted with the exotic beauty of his orchid, described in suggestive overtones generally reserved for the sexual attractiveness of a human *femme fatale*. Andrew Smith has argued that Victorian obsession with 'normality' and the ostracisation of social deviants witnessed fears of degeneracy projected onto monstrous Others (2001: 164). Established gendered readings of nature alongside the characteristics of a vampire interpret the strange orchid as an alternative fatal woman. Winter-Wedderburn is always 'singularly busy in his steamy little hothouse … having a wonderfully eventful time', admiring 'his new darling', and when the orchid blooms, '[h]e stopped before them in an ecstasy of admiration' (Wells 2013: 66–8). The overt eroticism in his 'worshipping' the flowers, described as having a 'heavy labellum … coiled into an intricate projection' (69), portrays the orchid as a sexualised female protagonist in contrast to the conservative human (female) housekeeper, providing an uncanny rendering of females as symbols of either 'domestic happiness or unnatural monsters' (Hurley 1996: 121). Wells engages with contemporary anxieties about changing gender roles and early feminism, played out through the plotline of the power struggle between modern ideology (represented by the orchid) and conservative traditionalism (embodied in the housekeeper). After all, the *femme fatale* is a subversive figure that at any one time can be 'prostitute, suffragette, New Woman, virago, degenerate, Wild Woman, Free Woman' or witch, who threatens cultural, social, sexual, political and gender norms, representing unpalatable progressive changes of modernity (Stott 1992: 49).

When violence is exhibited by the fatal woman it is often 'displaced onto an inhuman and unfemale source' (Craciun 2009: 24–6), seen here as the plant monster. Also, in the late Victorian era, 'an independent woman was castigated as unfeminine or even openly presented as masculinised' (Luczynska-Holdys 2013: 11), and it is this change from feminine beauty to predatory violence nascent in the *femme fatale* that is portrayed through the plant monster discussed here. Investigating the 'predatory female as invading Other', Stott positions the *femme fatale* at the intersection of socio-cultural anxieties about invasion and the 'preoccupations with the all-powerful New Woman' (1992: 124–5). Using Joseph Conrad's *Heart of Darkness*, Stott aligns native females in colonial encounters with 'carnivorous jungle plants – *fleurs du mal* – alluring and deadly' (128). Drawing a direct and clear association between foliage, flower and female as a 'devouring femininity', Stott develops a compelling link between the *femme fatale* and exotic (carnivorous) plants as a means of addressing socio-political concerns through gender (137, 126–62).

Adriana Craciun, like Stott, argues that while women writers employed the *femme fatale* as a revolutionary figure in the 'liberation from the constraints of domesticity', the image of woman as bacchante was used by men during this period 'to justify restricting women's rights even further' (2009: 41). While Winter-Wedderburn is besotted with the orchid's unusual beauty, his housekeeper is not swayed. She describes the aerial rootlets as 'little white fingers poking out … trying to get at you', reminding her of 'tentacles reaching out after something' (Wells 2013: 67–8). Kelly Hurley (1996: 62) identifies tentacled beings or insects as the main nonhuman monsters in *fin-de-siècle* tales, building on the late Victorian obsession with the bizarre and fears of degeneration. Although Winter-Wedderburn's attitude towards the orchid reaffirms traditional associations of nature and femininity, the female housekeeper's reference to it as 'that horrid orchid' with 'tentacles' (Wells 2013: 67–9) highlights the transgressive nature of the plant. Through her attitude Wells characterises conservative fears of progress alongside anxieties of evolutionary regression.

THE BLURRED BOUNDARIES OF ECO-*FEMME FATALE*

Recent ecofeminist criticism calls for a reconsideration of anthropocentric views towards 'the movement across human corporeality and nonhuman nature'

(Alaimo 2008: 238). The orchid as an uncanny ecoGothic trope explores these blurred boundaries in the relationship between the plant (as female) and the (male) gardener. The female body has been 'so strongly associated with nature in Western thought that it is not surprising that feminism has been haunted' by, and largely responsible for reaffirming, gendered dualisms (240). Viewing Wells's blood-thirsty orchid as a *femme fatale* through an ecofeminist prism, however, materialises this gendered female body within nature, which 'fundamentally unsettles … the liberal humanist conception of the human subject as the only intelligent agent with the ability to control nonhuman others' (Oppermann 2015: 4).

Through the intersection of feminine nature, animalistic monstrosity and the grotesque, the orchid clearly claims its status as *femme fatale*. Winter-Wedderburn's obsession and the orchid's captivating perfume as his 'new darling' matures is the seduction tool of the fatal woman: '[T]here was a new odour in the air, a rich, intensely sweet scent, that overpowered every other', which at first beguiles him before the 'insufferable scent' causes him to swoon (Wells 2013: 68–9). The deliberate targeting of the plant monster's victim demonstrates the orchid's agency as *femme fatale*, reflecting socio-political fears of the emancipated woman. Shortly after succumbing to the orchid's scent, Winter-Wedderburn is duly rescued from the clutches of the seductive and beautiful vampiric orchid by his devoted housekeeper, who restores the natural order of things. Ergo, be wary of the consequences of modernity and the New Woman, referenced here as a sexually deviant, female vampiric orchid.

Cheryl Blake-Price (2013) has argued that the interactions of monstrous plants with their victims often depict a male domination over female victims. Gendering the plant as an aggressive female and the male gardener as the victim clearly disrupts phallocentric gender roles. The exotic orchid's femininity is undermined by its vampiric attack. Coupled with the atypical gender attributes of the human protagonists, established gender constructs are completely destabilised. This is a 'strange' orchid, and Winter-Wedderburn is keen to point out that fertilisation is not typically through the orchid flower, hence 'such queer things about orchids' are that 'some of them have never been found with seed' (Wells 2013: 67–8). The orchid flower's asexual identity and the grotesque descriptions of tentacled roots blurs the boundaries of plant, animal, human, nonhuman and gender associations.

Gendering the orchid within its Victorian context, Wells depicts its florid beauty and exoticism as a *femme fatale* of nature. In doing so, the 'strange' orchid's monstrous attack on Winter-Wedderburn reflects contemporary anxieties about rising feminism and expanding female roles through the key qualities of the fatal woman. Upon finding the prostrate Wedderburn 'lying, face upward, at the foot of the strange orchid' and within the clutches of its 'exultant tentacles' that were 'crowded together, … grey ropes, … stretched tight with their ends closely applied to his chin and neck and hands', the housekeeper struggles to 'pull him away from the leech-like suckers' (69). When snapped, 'their sap dripped red' and the orchid is completely revealed as a vampire plant (69). For Andrew Smith, 'images of vampirism' represent concerns about masculinity posed by modernist aesthetics as the 'power struggle between the sexes' in a way that 'suggests that masculinity loses control both over itself and over a feminine Other' (2001: 150–1). Using Victorian associations of flowers and femininity, Wells displaces concerns about embracing modern ideas of social equality onto the expensive orchid bulb, suggesting that supporting, nurturing and encouraging modern ideology could lead to gender anarchy. The struggle between conservative and progressive views are portrayed through gender and body at the end of the tale where the conservative housekeeper battles to free the gardener from the clutches of the modernist orchid: '[s]he tugged now with renewed strength at Wedderburn's motionless body', yet the orchid 'still clung with the grimmest tenacity to its victim' (Wells 2013: 70). The gender role reversal of hero-villain-victim (usually male-male-female) within the Gothic context and the reconfiguring of the flower as a sexualised body renders the situation and the orchid truly uncanny in that the familiar positions of both flowers and women are rendered alarming and strange.

MATERIAL ECOFEMINISM: HUMAN AS FOOD

Stacy Alaimo's concept of trans-corporeality explores the 'movement [of material substance] across human and more-than-human flesh' through 'food, since eating transforms plants and animals into human flesh' (Alaimo 2010: 12). Using this theory to examine the vampiric tendencies of the orchid as eco-*femme fatale* helps dispel any clear-cut boundaries between nature and culture through consideration of the material flesh of the gendered body. Within the Gothic context of 'other', the predatory orchid becomes a gendered eco-monster that engages with contemporary ideologies of femininity and resulting socio-political anxieties. As the gardener becomes plant 'food', the intra-actions of matter, discourses and cognitions (Barad 2007) reflect contemporary concerns about the disintegration of edified gender roles through a coemerging body. Plant, human and gender boundaries become temporarily blurred during the vampiric (sexual?) act in a momentary reflection of modern anxieties. The vivid imagery of a rotting corpse as the *femme fatale* orchid 'lay there, black now and putrescent', provides stark contrast to the rescued gardener as 'Wedderburn himself was bright and garrulous' (Wells 2013: 71); dichotomous gender ideology is restored through the separation of man and nature.

  ˎ Although the creepy personification of nature as *femme fatale* vampire in a quasi-domestic setting 'would separate human from nature' and may seem anthropocentric, 'trans-corporeality denies the human subject the sovereign, central position' (Alaimo 2010: 14–16). The orchid feeding on the human gardener exemplifies, albeit in reverse, trans-corporeality as 'the material interchanges between bodies (both human and non-human)' helping to 'cultivate a tangible sense of [human] connection to the material world' (16), highlighting the (hu)man's relationship with nature and his desire for control over it in the form of gardening. The orchid as vampire and physical consumption of the (human) gardener reflect Nancy Tuana's notions of porosity, which 'discloses ... the flow of information and discursive practices through bodies. Phenomena such as gender, sexuality, class, social practices, *and their narratives* are filtered through ... coemerging bodies' (Iovino 2014: 103, emphasis in original). The gender complexity and rhizomorphic quality of the orchid as an ecological *femme fatale* along with its vampirism provide an uncanny body that encapsulates these intersecting cultural concerns. Similarly, the anthropomorphic gendering of this predatory orchid seeks not only to question modernity's socio-political and cultural progressiveness but also to puncture the pervasive assumptions that (hu)man is superior and separate from nature and the environment.

A GENDERED SPACE: THE HOTHOUSE

The blurred boundaries of gender are typified by the description of the gardener, who from the outset is 'a shy, lonely, rather ineffectual man' whose only preoccupation is his 'ambitious little hothouse' (Wells 2013: 63). According to Marianna Torgovnick (quoted in Hurley 2001: 140), 'degeneration was associated with femininity (effeteness)', and ideas of masculinity are ambiguous in both gardener and hothouse.

The greenhouse follows social progress so closely that its development can be plotted from the orangery of the Restoration nobles to the 'highly decorative, social status' conservatory of the Victorians (Lemmon 1962: 121). Predominantly domains of scientific inquiry and the conserve of plant explorers, Victorian glasshouses have an ambiguous identification with the garden. Associated in Victorian literature with the construction of female identity as a nurturing gender role, the garden is considered a domestic space (Grasser 2005). Within Gothic texts, the garden is considered an extension of the house/home, a safe domestic space, with transgressive acts occurring in the garden rendered uncanny. Although greenhouse work was considered recreationally 'suitable for the women of the household', it took place in conservatories attached to the main house for the cultivation of out-of-season fruit and flowers as indicators of one's financial means and social standing (Lemmon 1962: 133). Botany, too, had previous been considered a feminine science (Endersby 2016), but during the late nineteenth century it became a manly pursuit of scientific inquiry and the detached glasshouse construction (hothouses) became more botanical laboratory than garden that 'called for a monklike [sic] devotion' and included only 'one

15 'In a conservatory lined with potted plants, a lady poses inside a doorway holding a plant in her right hand' (c. 1900). Photograph, collection no: 2006.012

or two curious or ugly objects … to show that there are such things' (Lemmon 1962: 157, 177). In Wells's tale, while Winter-Wedderburn invites his housekeeper to admire his orchid in the hothouse, it is not a space that she enters frequently nor feels comfortable in; this is a steamy, exotic, male space that implies sexual indiscretion. Situating feminised exotic plants grown by the male protagonist in a scientific (male) space underlines phallocentric dichotomies. The gendering becomes uncanny when it is disrupted through the *femme fatale* orchid's vampiric attack; when the domestic benign becomes aggressive.

In the end, the progressive New Woman (the orchid) is defeated in order to restore a traditional gender power balance. Although the tale appears to 'conclude with the triumphant transcendence of "man"' (Alaimo 2010: 16), it is the orchid's exposure to the elements that kills it. The female orchid was reliant on artificial conditions provided by the male gardener in his hothouse laboratory, in a reflection of traditional gender roles. The agency of the natural world intervenes to destroy the 'strange' as if issuing a warning against (hu)man's scientific interference with nature. Wells's uncanny orchid motif represents fears of how progressive modernity challenges normative constructions encompassed in both the rhizomorphic and vampiric nature of the flower. Yet despite being a human hors d'oeuvre, Winter-Wedderburn's lack of antagonism towards the man-eating plant monster suggests an acceptance of modernity's materialistic and progressive changes.

MAN-EATING PLANT MONSTERS AS ECO-*FEMMES FATALES*

Vampiric orchids are not the only eco-*femme fatale* figures. Victorians were 'avid botanists' of the unusual and carnivorous, being 'keen to obtain samples of sundews, pitcher plants, and venus flytraps for their collections' (Blake-Price 2013: 312). In 'Professor Jonkin's Cannibal Plant' (1905) by Howard R. Garis, the eponymous botanist also focuses his attention on his newly acquired pitcher plant; another rhizomatic growth where plant gendering is used to engage with contemporary concerns. With feminism as a term signifying the 'struggle for women's rights' in both European and American literature (Donawerth 2009: 213), Garis's *femme fatale* plant monster parodies unease with the changing gender roles resulting from the expanding women's movement in an American context.

Turn-of-the-century Americans were so concerned about the effects of women's education on the established gendered professions and politics that 'supporters of women's education ... separated themselves and their cause from women's rights, insisting that the well-educated woman longed only to enhance her sphere, not abandon it' (Gordon 2002: 227). Despite women having access to higher education, many colleges continued to limit opportunities for women to nurturing or teaching professions, with others such as clerks and librarians becoming 'feminized' and subsequently low-paid, dead-end careers (236). The language of flowers was popular in Victorian America as well as in Britain, with floral symbolism displayed by American writers within their own literature (Ingram 1869: 7). The use of eco-*femme fatale* imagery in the context of the assumed fragility of flowers to voice concerns about modernity and expanding female roles through education is compelling.

The narrator introduces Professor Jonkin as an experimental botanist who 'had, by skillful grafting and care, succeeded in raising a single tree that produced, at different seasons, apples, oranges, pineapples, figs, coconuts, and peaches' and as someone who 'was continually striving to grow something new in the

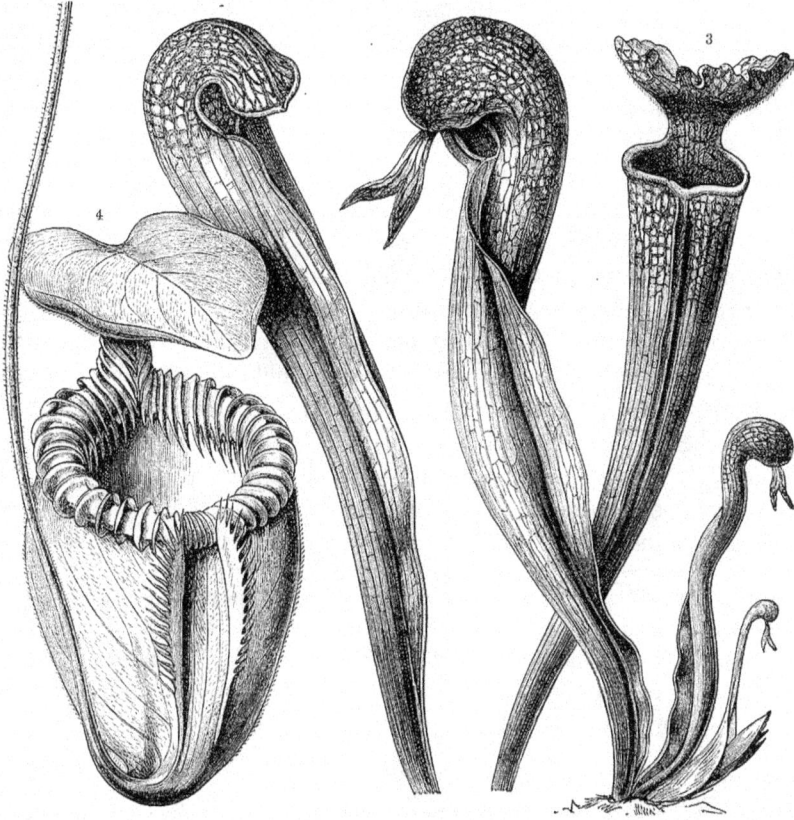

Schlauch= und Kannenpflanzen: 1 Sarracenia variolaris; 2 Darlingtonia Californica; 3 Sarracenia laciniata; 4 N
penthes villosa, um die Hälfte verkleinert. (Zu S. 311—314 und 318.)

16 *Nepenthes villosa, Sarracenia variolaris* (*S. minor*), *Darlingtonia californica* and
Sarracenia laciniata (*S. leucophylla*), from *Pflanzenleben: Erster Band: Der Bau und
die Eigenschaften der Pflanzen* (Leipzig and Vienna: Bibliographic Institute, 1900),
p. 309, fig. 4. Drawing, A. J. K. Marilaun (1831–98) and Adolf Hansen (1851–1920)

plant world' (Garis 2013: 113). Jonkin is the Dr Moreau of plants, meddling with
nature and scientifically creating vegetable hybrids. The professor's new acquisition is a South American pitcher plant from 'what Darwin calls the carnivorous
family of flowers' (114). Darwin's theories and botanical writings were well
publicised and his personification in *Insectivorous Plants* held implications for
human sexuality and not simply horticultural interest (Smith 2003). Indeed,
Darwin's evolutionary theory and botanical works inspired ideas of prehistoric
monsters that became frequently employed by contemporary sensation fiction,

linked to real-life events of sexual scandal and criminal behaviour that underlined late nineteenth-century anxieties (Hurley 1996: 60). Yet such monstrousness is not limited to nonhuman animal species. Insectivorous plants were likened to *femmes fatales* in both scientific writing and literature, described as 'lur[ing] their victims with enticing looks and tempting fragrances and empty promises of nectar, only to drown, dissolve, and dismember them' (Smith 2003: 144). The carnivorous nature of both Wells's orchid and Garis's pitcher plant not only destabilises gender perspectives, but their taste for humans as food upsets the balance of power in a way that reflects concerns about the gender power-shift of nineteenth-century female activism.

Jonkin's exotic plant is described in a similarly sensuous way to the orchid: 'a small plant with bright, glossy green leaves', with flowers described as female anatomy, '[h]e saw within a small tube, lined with fine, hairlike filaments' (Garis 2013: 114). Even when its carnivorous nature is demonstrated, the insects are 'attracted by some subtle perfume, as well as by a sweet syrup that was on the edge of the petals' (114). As in Darwin's scientific writings, Jonkin's pitcher plant is seen as *femme fatale* through the seduction and entrapment, when

> [t]he little hairlike filaments ... suddenly reached out and wound themselves about the insects feeding on the sweet stuff, which seemed to intoxicate them. In an instant the flies were pulled to the top of the flower shaft by a contraction of the hairs, and then they went tumbling down the tube into the miniature pond below, where they were drowned after a brief struggle. (Garis 2013: 115)

Jokingly suggesting the professor might 'train it to come to the table and eat like a human being' (115), the professor's friend aligns the plant in patriarchal tradition with children, savages and women as Other. Reading the tale through a post-colonial lens, the pitcher plant could represent a young, female, indigene from South America sent to the professor, possibly as a bride, who needs to be acclimatised for civil society. As Stott (1992) has argued, indigenous women and jungle plants have been closely associated in portrayals of colonial *femmes fatales* within racial discourse and concerns of degeneration. Notwithstanding such interpretations, the association of plant and female is particularly relevant to a gendered reading of the small pitcher plant as a young female. In the months that follow, the professor spends 'much time in that part of the glass house where the pitcher plant was growing' (Garis 2013: 115). Once more, the gardener appears to be enamoured with his 'mysterious pitcher plant' (116), portrayed as exotic female within a male scientific space subjected to the attentions of the male gardener. The small plant, 'about as big as an Easter lily', increases exponentially to its augmented carnivorous diet 'until the top was near the roof of the greenhouse, twenty-five feet above' (118). As a grotesque carnivorous monster, the beautiful flower becomes inherently Gothic.

YOU ARE WHAT YOU EAT: BLURRING BOUNDARIES
THROUGH CANNIBALISM

Garis engages with anxieties surrounding gender role reversal at the turn of
the century by exaggerating the plant's carnivorous tendencies in opposition
to Jonkin's 'healthy' diet as a vegetarian (117). 'Influenced by Darwin's theory
of evolution' and amid fears of degeneracy, Carole J. Adams argues, '[m]en who
decide to eschew meat-eating [in the nineteenth century] are deemed effeminate'
(1990: 34), querying the gender assignation of Jonkin as well. Feeding the giant
pitcher plant one of its three-a-day porterhouse beef steaks, the professor falls
victim to the plant himself. It is in attempting to eat the vegetarian professor
that the plant now becomes 'cannibal'. Humanising the plant and suggesting it
be named 'the cannibal plant instead' after it tries to eat Jonkin (Garis 2013:
122) implies a sense of equality between plant monster and human gardener.
The term 'cannibal' refers to humans eating the flesh of other human beings
or, more broadly, consumption of the same species as food, acknowledging the
Professor's vegetal subjectivity (Marder 2014).

   This blurring of the boundaries is a distinctly Gothic reflection of material
feminist theory that focuses on 'the interchanges between human corporeality
and the more-than-human world' (Alaimo 2008: 244). Jonkin's surrogate progeny's
meaty diet is increased steadily from 'chopped beef' to 'three big beefsteaks
every day' (Garis 2013: 118). George Beard claims (in Adams 1990: 30) that
'"Brain-workers" required lean meat as their main meal', suggesting a carnivorous
diet was important for male academia. Within the American author's contemporary context, a gendered reading of the plant's carnivorous diet symbolises
the educational opportunities for women that led to self-sufficiency and small
roles within predominantly male professions. The plant is anthropomorphised
as female throughout the tale, from training it to 'eat like a human being' to
deciding 'not to give it any supper or breakfast' as punishment 'for being naughty
... as if the plant were a child' (Garis 2013: 115, 122). Nick Fiddes argues that
foods 'are used to symbolise' cultural associations within society, although
these often signify 'our relationship with nature' (1991: 41–5).

   From an ecofeminist perspective, as a 'cannibal' this plant monster not only
underlines the interconnectivity of established dualisms, it also exemplifies
Alaimo's concept of trans-corporeality. For Alaimo, 'food, whereby plants or
animals become the substance of the human', demonstrates the interconnected
entanglements of 'human corporeality to the flesh of other-than-human' (2008:
253). In Garis's tale, the gendered semiotics of cannibal plant monster and
vegetarian human as food embeds this concept in reverse, destabilising patriarchal
constructs and questioning (hu)man's hubris in attempting to control the natural
world. Furthermore, the horror fiction degenerate is often depicted as eating
raw flesh (for example in the films *The Hills have Eyes* (1977); *Wrong Turn 1–7*

(2003–17)), and this 'transgression of the cannibalism taboo' is heightened when the consumer is female (Fiddes 1991: 89–90). Garis's plant monster is clearly portrayed as a female cannibal figure – a transgression that further adds to its status as a *femme fatale*.

When the professor begins feeding the plant larger meaty meals, the plant grows to nearly twenty-five feet tall and requires a scaffold to support the 'great flower, about eight feet long and three feet across the bell-shaped mouth' (Garis 2013: 119). The pitcher's exponential and rapid growth seems to mirror the socio-political achievements and continued influence of the women's movement on access to higher education for women in America and the resulting 'feminisation' of certain originally male professions (Gordon 2002). Andrew Tudor argues that the 'abstract threat to stability and order finds immediate and concrete expression in the monster' (1989: 19), evidenced here in the gigantism of the pitcher plant and its increasingly uncanny taste for more substantial flesh.

However, it is the intermingling of nature (the plant as consumer and human as food) and culture (the gendering of plant, gardener and space) that truly establishes the plant monster as an ecological *femme fatale*. It is the material ecofeminist reading of these plant monster stories that allows gendered nature to be reconsidered, not as a dualistic other, but as a complex interconnection that engages with multiple concerns of modernity. Sensitive gender and social issues were often displaced in Gothic texts onto a menacing otherness that allowed such debates to be removed from direct discourse. Like Wells, Garis projects contemporary fears about active feminism and similar socio-political changes onto the pitcher plant as monstrous female Other – as vegetable *femme fatale*. Ambiguous gendering of plant and gardener here engages with contemporary debates about expanding socio-political roles for both men and particularly, women.

CONCLUSION

A projection of these anxieties onto the plant monster through an ecofeminist perspective provides Stacy Alaimo's (2008) trans-corporeality and Karen Barad's (2007) intra-action with a concrete embodiment of human and nonhuman interconnection. Human gardener and plant monster become each other in an uncanny reflection of a narrative agency of matter as female nature gains the upper hand over male scientific endeavour. While the protagonists and the spaces in these stories appear to reflect dichotomous gendering, the uncanny mirroring and bodily transgression of human and plant interaction blurs the boundaries of nature and culture. Feminising exotic flowers and carnivorous plants draws on the *femme fatale* figure to highlight contemporary concerns about progressive modernity. Their interaction and subsequent overpowering of the male gardeners not only reflect anxieties about emerging gender power-shifts but underline how patriarchally constructed identities are no longer stable. Portrayed as female Other through the Gothic tropes of vampire and cannibal *femme fatale*, the authors project contemporary anxieties towards feminist movements onto nature as monstrous, but also open a wider debate about gender identity construction as well as androcentric attitudes towards nature and (hu)man's need to control it. Situating the exotic plant *femmes fatales* within a male-assigned space of the scientific hothouse further underlines contemporary concerns surrounding progressive modernity's obsession with controlling the environment and landscape alongside anxieties about expanding female roles within male-dominated professions. The transgression of gender-assigned roles onto both human and plant protagonists is distinctly Gothic, creating monstrous others within a gendered yet liminal space of the greenhouse, using established cultural constructs to underline the inextricable entanglement of human and nonhuman actors. Even when considering these transgressive Gothic monsters through a material-ecocritical lens, gender remains an important component used to collapse established concepts of Other, particularly when the human 'gardener' loses control and becomes plant food. After all, despite delusions of control, all humans become food for plants in the end.

WORKS CITED

Adams, Carol J. 1990. *The Sexual Politics of Meat: A Feminist-Vegetarian Critical Theory* (Cambridge: Polity Press)

Alaimo, Stacy. 2008. 'Trans-Corporeal Feminisms and the Ethical Space of Nature', in *Material Feminisms*, ed. by Stacy Alaimo and Susan Hekman (Bloomington: Indiana University Press), pp. 237–64

Alaimo, Stacy. 2010. *Bodily Natures: Science, Environment, and the Material Self* (Bloomington: Indiana University Press)

Arditti, Joseph and Yam Tim Wing. 2004. 'Raising Orchids from Seed', in *The Gardener's Guide to Growing Orchids*, ed. by Charles Marden Fitch (Brooklyn: Brooklyn Botanic Garden), pp. 69–81

Barad, Karen M. 2007. *Meeting the Universe Halfway: Quantum Physics and the Entanglement of Matter and Meaning* (Durham, NC: Duke University Press)

Blake-Price, Cheryl. 2013. 'Vegetable Monsters: Man-Eating Trees in Fin de Siècle Fiction', *Victorian Literature and Culture*, 41: 311–27

Craciun, Adriana. 2009. *Fatal Women of Romanticism* (Cambridge: Cambridge University Press)

Del Principe, David. 2014. 'Introduction: The EcoGothic in the Long Nineteenth Century', *Gothic Studies*, 16. 1: 1–8

Deleuze, Gilles and Felix Guattari. 2003. *A Thousand Plateaus: Capitalism and Schizophrenia* (1987) trans. by Brian Massumi (Paris: Editions de Minuit; London: Continuum)

Donawerth, Jane. 2009. 'Feminisms', in *Routledge Companion to Science Fiction*, ed. by Mark Bould, Andrew M. Butler, Adam Roberts and Sherryl Vint (Abingdon: Routledge), pp. 214–24

Endersby, Jim. 2016. 'Deceived by Orchids: Sex, Science, Fiction and Darwin', *British Journal for the History of Science*, 49. 2: 205–29

Fiddes, Nick. 1991. *Meat: A Natural Symbol* (London: Routledge)

Garis, Howard R. 2013. 'Professor Jonkin's Cannibal Plant' (1905), in *Flora Curiosa*, ed. by Chad Arment (Ohio: Coachwhip Publications), pp. 113–22

Gordon, Lynn D. 2002. 'Education and the Professions', in *A Companion to American Women's History*, ed. by Nancy A. Hewitt (Oxford: Blackwell), pp. 227–49

Grasser, Céline. 2005. 'Good Girls versus Blooming Maidens: The Building of Female Middle- and Upper-Class Identities in the Garden, England and France, 1820–1870', in *Secret Gardens, Satanic Mills: Placing Girls in European History, 1750–1960*, ed. by Mary Jo Maynes, Birgitte Søland and Christina Benninghaus (Bloomington: Indiana University Press), pp. 131–46

Heiland, Donna. 2004. *Gothic and Gender: An Introduction* (Oxford: Blackwell)

Hurley, Kelly. 1996. *The Gothic Body* (Cambridge: Cambridge University Press)

Hurley, Kelly. 2001. 'The Modernist Abominations of William Hope Hodgson', in *Gothic Modernisms*, ed. by Andrew Smith and Jeff Wallace (Basingstoke: Palgrave), pp. 129–49

Ingram, John H. 1869. *Flora Symbolica; or, The Language and Sentiment of Flowers. Including Floral Poetry, Original and Selected* (London: F. W. Warne and Co.)

Iovino, Serenella. 2014. 'Bodies of Naples: Stories, Matter, and the Landscape of Porosity', in *Material Ecocriticism*, ed. by Serenella Iovino and Serpil Oppermann (Bloomington: Indiana University Press), pp. 97–113

Keetley, Dawn and Angela Tenga (eds). 2016. *Plant Horror* (London: Palgrave Macmillan)

Keetley, Dawn and Matthew Wynn Sivils (eds). 2018. *Ecogothic in Nineteenth-Century American Literature* (New York and London: Routledge)

Kristeva, Julia. 1982. *Powers of Horror: An Essay on Abjection* (New York: Columbia University Press)

Lemmon, Kenneth. 1962. *The Covered Garden* (London: Museum Press)

Luczynska-Holdys, Malgorzata. 2013. *Soft-Shed Kisses: Re-visioning the Femme Fatale in English Poetry of the 19th Century* (Newcastle upon Tyne: Cambridge Scholars Publishing)

Marder, Michael. 2014. *The Philosopher's Plant: An Intellectual Herbarium* (New York: Columbia University Press)

Miller, T. S. 2012. 'Lives of the Monster Plants: The Revenge of the Vegetable in the Age of Animal Studies', *Journal of the Fantastic in the Arts*, 23. 3 (86): 460–79

Miller, T. S. 2014. 'Monstrous Plants', in *The Ashgate Encyclopedia of Literary and Cinematic Monsters*, ed. by Jeffrey Andrew Weinstock (Farnham: Ashgate), pp. 470–5

Mulvey-Roberts, Marie. 2016. 'The Female Gothic Body', in *Women and the Gothic, an Edinburgh Companion*, ed. by Avril Horner and Sue Zlosnik (Edinburgh: Edinburgh University Press), pp. 106–19

Oppermann, Serpil (ed.). 2015. *New International Voices in Ecocriticism* (Lanham: Lexington Books)

Punter, David. 2013. 'Algernon Blackwood: Nature and Spirit', in *Ecogothic*, ed. by Andrew Smith and William Hughes (Manchester: Manchester University Press), pp. 44–57

Royle, Nicholas. 2003. *The Uncanny* (Manchester: Manchester University Press)

Smith, Andrew. 2001. 'Vampirism, Masculinity and Degeneracy: D. H. Lawrence's Modernist Gothic', in *Gothic Modernisms*, ed. by Andrew Smith and Jeff Wallace (Basingstoke: Palgrave), pp. 150–66

Smith, Jonathan. 2003. 'Une Fleur du Mal? Swinburne's "The Sundew" and Darwin's "Insectivorous Plants"', *Victorian Poetry*, 41. 1: 131–50

Stott, Rebecca. 1992. *The Fabrication of the Late-Victorian Femme Fatale: The Kiss of Death* (Basingstoke: Macmillan)

Tudor, Andrew. 1989. *Monsters and Mad Scientists* (Oxford: Blackwell)

Wells, H. G. 2013. 'The Flowering of the Strange Orchid' (1894), in *Flora Curiosa*, ed. by Chad Arment (Ohio: Coachwhip Publications), pp. 63–71

Wisker, Gina. 2012. 'Love Bites: Contemporary Women's Vampire Fictions', in *A New Companion to the Gothic*, ed. by David Punter (Oxford: Wiley-Blackwell), pp. 224–38

9

Death and the fairy: Hidden gardens and the haunting of childhood

Francesca Bihet

There are fairies at the bottom of our garden!
It's not so very, very far away;
You pass the gardener's shed and you just keep straight ahead –
I do so hope they've really come to stay.
There's a little wood, with moss in it and beetles,
And a little stream that quietly runs through;
You wouldn't think they'd dare to come merrymaking there –
Well, they do. (Fyleman 1917: 34)

Fairies were a great Victorian and Edwardian obsession; they dominated children's picture books but were also 'strange and secret peoples' (Silver 1999: title). This chapter discusses how fairies haunted gardens during this period and in particular the liminal space at the bottom of the garden, a complex cultural habitat, and a space dominated by children's imaginations, in a distorted reflection of the adult world. David Punter highlights how the uncanny can be defined in terms of 'mischievous', 'malicious', 'supernatural', the 'mysterious' and uncomfortably strange (2007: 129). All these terms can also be applied to the darker folkloric fairies that haunt the British landscape. Other features of the uncanny such as repetition, animism, anthropomorphism and death are also relevant to Victorian fairies (131) as represented in art and print. They provide an uncanny experience, as Punter describes, familiar yet threatening, which 'continually overflows the bounds of reason', suggesting 'realms which hover just beyond the reach of our conventions and assumptions' (131). Tiny flower fairies, the most beneficent of the fairy species according to theosophist Edward Gardner (Silver 1999: 54–5), also point to darker animistic folkloric beliefs, worlds beyond the material realm and human problems far outside the garden.

The garden is a liminal space between the wild landscape and the domestic; it can be expressive of both nature and civilisation. Michael Waters highlights that in Victorian literature a garden's position should be understood 'in terms of its relations of equivalence' (1988: 149). For instance, in some texts gardens are 'virtually identical' to untamed nature and in others the garden is nestled 'among words denoting the world of social construction' (149). Harriet Ritvo points out that increasingly under British industrialisation 'wilderness' was 'no longer much of a threat but it might seem to be threatened' (1992: 375). She notes the term 'wild garden' no longer seemed an oxymoron as the categorical opposition at the end of the century was no longer between 'wild/tame' but 'living/dead' (Ritvo 1992: 375). William Robinson in *The Wild Garden* advocated 'naturalizing or making wild innumerable beautiful natives of many regions of the earth in our wood, wild and semi-wild places' in 'unoccupied places' around gardens and pleasure grounds of any kind (1870: 7). Similarly, Dion Calthrop in *The Charm of Gardens* highlights the desire for wildness in a garden, noting how the 'well-ordered garden with its high walls' is but a 'prison house' for plants, nothing like the roadside flowers of the 'Garden of England' (1910: 8). Little wild spaces within the garden walls reflected a hedgerow wilderness, the beauty of the outside within.

The concept of the bottom of the garden heightens the ambivalent nature of a domestic, yet wild place. As middle-class Victorian town houses proliferated, so their gardens became spaces with defined borders surrounded by the urban landscape. In country villages or grand estates the bottom of the garden might still lead to wild nature itself. Catherine Alexander explores the 'intimate relationship between the English small, back garden and the house' (2002: 858). For her the garden is metaphor of a domestic space, she considers the 'third area', 'beyond the lawn' for 'baser functions', such as 'vegetables (if grown), sheds, and compost heaps' for 'regeneration and transformation' (864). But traditionally beyond the back of the garden is wildness, an area in which children adventure out to play. The bottom of the garden with its fairies can also be viewed as a *heterotopia*. These are 'places outside of all places, even though it may be possible to indicate their location in reality' (Foucault and Miskowiec 1986: 24). In gardens there is 'excess, inversion, a festive exuberance. Action here is unrestrained' (Alexander 2002: 867). The bottom of the garden, and just beyond, becomes an important physical and metaphoric space for the fairies. It can be seen as a supernatural landscape where imaginations run wild; through play, children explore and negotiate the complex relationship between wild and civilised 'natureculture' (Haraway 2003: 15). Both fairies and gardens straddle the human and the more-than-human world.

BEING FAIRY

The most common contemporary depiction of the fairy is of a small, benign, gauzy-winged flower fairy wearing clothes made from petals. Folklorists generally employ the term 'loosely to cover a range of non-human yet material beings with magical powers' (Simpson and Roud 2000: 115). Jenni Bergman considers elves as 'Others, not humans, not the same' (2011: 4). Fairies can be broadly expressed as nonhuman others, they are defined by humans and in relation to humans, but are not *quite* human. They can voice a multitude of human fantasies, social difficulties, uncomfortable issues and fears. Fairies provide a key which can unlock awareness of human culture because they sit on its margins, timeless, in liminality, in fantasy. They come in all shapes, sizes, social classes and temperaments. Fairies can be good, evil, mischievous or just amoral.

The Victorian and Edwardian miniature flower fairy retains some of the ambivalence and liminality of her wilder folkloric cousins. Julian Wolfreys argues that 'spectrality appears in a gap between the limits of two ontological categories', which can be 'between life and death, though neither alive nor dead' (2002: x). Fairies, of any kind, stand in this role. Yuki Yoshino points out that 'fairies do not exist, but they haunt', 'they are projections of self, rather than the other', blurring borders between 'reality and fantasy', 'authenticity and forgery' and 'presence and absence' (2011: 4). Nicola Bown argues that the Victorians, confronted by the 'power of modernity' that was 'overwhelming', used fairies as a 'smaller, more fragile, more magical version of themselves' to express their hopes and fears (2001: 11). In Walter Crane's illustrations for *A Floral Fantasy in an Old English Garden* (1899), a butterfly-winged fairy guides the reader around the anthropomorphised flower friends, who are almost flower fairies. Fairies haunting the bottom of the garden prove a persuasive combination for the manifestation of spectrality. The tiny flower fairy is thus an uncanny animism, a spectre of imagination projected upon the apparent safety of the garden.

Freya Mathews suggests engaging with the environment through panpsychism, noting that to 'enter the terrain of faerie is to step through the veil of everyday appearances into a realm in which everything holds the possibility of transformation and transfiguration' (2003: 17). She describes how walking through a fairy tale is like a 'landscape filled with cryptic presences'; upon entering such a landscape you pass through 'a field of subjectivity, in which everything is already alive with a life of its own or charged with the psychic life of the world at large' (18). In such a way, Mathews suggests, the fairy tale metaphor of 'falling in love' can help awaken us to realise the permeability between us and nature, eventually forming a 'permanent way of being' (21). Fairies help engage communication between human and nature and can, therefore, help us understand the Victorians' fear of and connection to uncontrolled nature and our own.

THE SECRET GARDEN AND THE MANIFESTATION OF MAGIC

Frances Hodgson Burnett's *The Secret Garden* provides an excellent example of the garden as a *heterotopia* (Foucault and Miskowiec 1986: 25–6). Orphan

17 'The Fairy Queen Takes an Airy Drive in a Light Carriage, a Twelve-in-hand, Drawn by Thoroughbred Butterflies', from Richard Doyle and William Allingham. 1870. *In Fairyland: A Series of Pictures from the Elf-World* (London: Longmans). Engraving, Richard Doyle (1824–83)

Mary Lennox goes to live with her uncle in an eerie, Gothic country house bordering the Yorkshire moors. She discovers an abandoned, locked garden which she nurses back to life, and she teaches her sickly cousin to walk within it. Upon first opening the garden door Mary proceeds as if 'she were afraid of awakening someone' (Burnett 1911: 98). Being in this garden 'seemed almost like being shut out of the world in some fairy place' (111); even its grey arches are 'fairy-like' (98). The garden is overgrown, forgotten and wild, representing a space where normal order has broken down. Mary encounters ideas of fairies and magic while she plays; her friend Dickon has panpsychic encounters with the material garden (Mathews 2003: 79). He 'can charm foxes and squirrels and birds', he even feels 'as if he was a bird or rabbit himself' (Burnett 1911: 181). As a rural working-class child, living on the peripheral moor, Dickon is representative of the folk, the kind of people who believe in fairies; indeed, he is virtually a 'sort of wood fairy' (139). Waters (1988: 163) highlights the 'fundamental topographical dichotomy of exposed wildscape and enclosed park' as exhibited in classically Gothic-influenced literature such as *Wuthering Heights*. In *The Secret Garden* this is explored in the difference between the bleak moor and the cultivated gardens surrounding Misselthwaite Manor.

18 Illustration from Frances Hodgson Burnett. 1912. *The Secret Garden* (London: William Heinemann). Illustration by Charles Robinson (1870–1937)

The locked garden sits as a liminal and mediating space between the two landscape types.

Through their engagement with the wildscape, it is paradoxically the children who support the process of 'degothicization' (Chang 2019: 112): restoring cultivation, civilisation and order to the house. By teaching her cousin Colin to walk in the garden, Mary defies the rules of both doctor and housekeeper who aim to keep the sickly boy secure from perceived external danger. His restoration to health is brought about by a process of 'Mystery and Magic and wild creatures' and the 'odd companionship' of playing with other children in the garden (Burnett 1911: 373). Furthermore, Mary plants seeds in defiance of her uncle's order to lock up and abandon the garden. Her seeds 'grew as if fairies had tended them' (296); the child harnesses fairy power to cultivate the garden. Unexpectedly the 're-vivifying qualities of the natural world' are found in 'highly cultivated' or perhaps re-cultivated locations, rather than the moorland (Chang 2019: 108). The power of nature, like the wild fairies, comes into the garden. Adult disharmony is removed through the occult harmonies played out by the children and their encounters. The garden is tended again; her grieving uncle returns home from his restless travels and her sickly cousin plays as any ordinary child.

Burnett capitalises the word 'Magic' throughout the book, denoting it as the title of a force running through the story like an animistic presence making the characters and plants blossom. Colin describes nature as driven by Magic, 'always pushing and drawing and making things out of nothing' (Burnett 1911: 300). Dickon describes this 'Magic' as the 'same Magic' that made the crocuses in the earth grow (284). As the children grow flowers in the garden, 'it seemed as if Magicians were passing through it drawing loveliness out of the earth and the boughs with wands' (233). The garden becomes a supernaturalised microcosm hinting at forces far beyond its walls. Elizabeth Chang highlights that *The Secret Garden* absorbed 'constant and repetitive narrative energy' reimagining envisioned layers of past, present and future, both material and immaterial (2019: 108). Similarly, Calthrop describes how in a cottage garden 'with children playing eternal games with dolls', we see the 'whole world, cares, joys, birth, death and marriage' (1910: 59). The garden provides a spirit realm in which the forces of nature might convene with human hopes and dreams. In *The Secret Garden* fairies and magic act as leitmotifs to describe anything natural or close to nature, a force closely tied to the act of gardening. Through engagement with this theme the children overturn a distorted patriarchal family which ultimately regains equilibrium, allowing the children to play and grow normally in the garden.

THE COTTINGLEY FAIRY PHOTOGRAPHS AND ARTHUR CONAN DOYLE'S SPIRITUALIST SPRITES

On a summer's afternoon in 1917, armed with a Midg camera, some hat pins and delicate tracings of fairy pictures from *The Princess Mary Gift Book*, two young girls, Elsie Wright and Frances Griffith, captured some fairy images (Cooper 1990: 21–4). These are the Cottingley photographs, described by Richard Sugg as a 'British National Treasure' in which 'the once ubiquitous pagan elves of Britain' become 'trapped' in 'flat picture frames' (2018: 64). Rose Fyleman's poem 'There Are Fairies at the Bottom of our Garden' was published in *Punch* in May 1917, and Joe Cooper argues it inspired the Cottingley girls to produce their famous photographs (1990: 131). The girls lived in a row of cottages with a small linear back garden, as seen in many Victorian terraces (Doyle 1997: 34). Cottingley Beck ran through a wood at the bottom of their garden. It was here where they set up the camera shots, which Sir Arthur Conan Doyle would spread around the world as proof that fairies really existed (1920: 463–8). Doyle discovered the photographs through theosophist Edward Gardner: 'Fairies Photographed: An Epoch Making Event' headlined the Christmas 1920 *Strand Magazine*. After the Cottingley photographs became internationally famous they were intensely scrutinised and often ridiculed. The garden fairy became a figure of mockery.

Within the Cottingley photographs the bottom of the garden becomes a landscape whose narrative we can read. Anne Spirn notes, '[l]andscape is loud with dialogues, with story lines that connect a place and its dwellers' (1998: 17). Stories of sad loss, deep mourning, vanished childhood play and the futility of war are all elements which become connected at the bottom of this Cottingley garden. Juliette Wood notes the Cottingley case is 'a richly textured event that polarises belief and scepticism, and involves an intuitive understanding of legend formation and the social nuances of early twentieth-century English Society' (2006: 288). After the losses of World War I, Doyle hoped to employ the Cottingley photographs to promote an acceptance of the metaphysical realm (1997: 32). He hoped recognition that fairies existed would 'jolt the material twentieth-century mind out of its heavy ruts in the mud' and 'make it admit that there is a glamour and mystery to life' (Sugg 2018: 59). The phrase 'ruts in the mud' conjures up images of trench warfare, where no life flourished, here juxtaposed by the fairies 'glamour'. In this phrase, Sugg argues, 'feminine grace, gentleness and nurture', even childhood innocence is opposing masculine 'violence and cruelty' (59–60). For Doyle, they represented a landscape of small yet tangible hopes, an attempt to reconcile himself with terrifying mortality. Wolfreys argues that 'to be haunted is the on-going process of coming to terms with one's being' (2002: 18), and fairies as the nonhuman other did this spectacularly well in the Cottingley case. Doyle tries to generate hope for the whole of human afterlife from the tiny flower fairies and in doing so the bottom of the garden becomes, for him, a site of resurrection for the lost children of World War I.

Prior to the Great War, the Victorian fairy intersected with the era's crisis of faith through spiritualist beliefs and attempts to find tangible proof of another realm. After the publication of Charles Darwin's *On the Origin of Species* (1859), the religious and secular landscapes told different stories. The displacements and anxieties of the era caused 'widespread religious doubt' and it is unsurprising that some people turned to spiritualism to re-enchant the scientific Victorian world (Bown 2001: 2). Furthermore, after the 'devastating losses' of the war, spiritualism 'flourished anew' (Owen 1994: 66). Joseph McCabe, making a reference to Robert Browning's poem 'Mr Sludge: "The Medium"' (1864: 171–238) while criticising Doyle's spiritualism, noted, a 'war which removed 5 million men in adolescence or early manhood inevitably gave the opportunities and the Sludges of the world came out of their dark corners' (McCabe 1920: 439). Through spiritualism people sought tangible proof for the afterlife, to validate the lives of their lost loved ones and soften their grief. The Cottingley flower fairies were placed among the 'occult beings' of seances such as spirits and poltergeists (Silver 1999: 4). Taken from the world of childhood play and adapted, the photographs were interpreted and presented through the lens of adult spiritualism.

The Coming of the Fairies (1922), Doyle's investigation of the Cottingley photographs, ends with a chapter on 'The Theosophic View of Fairies' by Doyle's 'co-worker', aptly named Edward Gardner. By framing this as Gardner's opinion, Doyle aims to retain his investigative Sherlock Holmes-styled narrator's voice. Gardner's fairies form a key component in the growth of flowers; their role furnishes 'the vital connecting link between the stimulating energy, of the sun and the raw material of the form' (1997: 101). He depicts fairies as naturalised in a garden, like any blackbird. Despite sun, seed and soil, plant growth 'would never take place if the fairy builders were absent' (101), a belief that the children in *The Secret Garden* might endorse. Like children, fairies skip, dance and exhibit 'a gay abandon suggestive of the keenest delight in the experience. It is evidently "time off" for the fairy when it is not tending to the plants' (102). Spirn notes that gardening represents 'a life-embracing act, an act of faith and hope, an expression of commitment to the future' (1998: 70), and for theosophists the garden fairies become, like children, a symbol of growth and new hope for the future.

The Cottingley images became inextricably linked to spiritualist photography. Supernatural photography was often taken at face value, appearing to be the 'end result of a scientific process and therefore acceptable as proof', standing as seemingly 'straightforward visual representations of reality' (Van Bronswijk 2001: 107). Indeed, the medium of photography heightened the images' sense of haunting. The very modern medium of photography also allowed 'spectres' to become representable within it (Wolfreys 2002: 2–3). This made fairies 'as vulnerable to the paparazzi, as any other superstar' (Purkiss 2000: 284). Furthermore, the fairy figure haunts the photographs, '[n]either material nor non-material', traversing between 'matter and the abstract, between the corporeal and the incorporeal, incorporating itself within both, while never being available corporeally' (Wolfreys 2002: 24). The photographs claim to represent materially something intangible. Wolfreys argues that 'the promise of the gothic was – and still is – a promise of a certain return, a cyclical revenance' (10). Fairies, familiar as fictional figures from children's books, become the doubly haunting spectres of Doyle's alternative reality. The Cottingley figures echo old picture books, like Crane's *A Floral Fantasy* (1899) where flowers become anthropomorphised. By this the Cottingley photographs, claiming to be real fairies, created 'a disruption that is other to the familiarity of particular structures' (Wolfreys 2002: 6). Like a haunting, the photographs also keep returning: the photographs capture a moment in the past and repeat it as a 'haunted trace' through reprints in magazines, books and now on the internet (119). Through their constant replication the Cottingley images literally haunt British popular culture.

The aesthetics of the Cottingley photographs provide a fascinating insight into the world of childhood play and the garden as a scene of the uncanny imagination. Alexander notes the 'garden is a place of dreams and fantasy' which 'encourage people to create different worlds' (2002: 868); the Cottingley girls were re-enacting their own games with the photographs. Their first image, 'Frances and the Fairies', shows a little girl wearing a garland of flowers in her hair with a waterfall in the backdrop and a troop of fairies dancing around her as she looks into the camera. It looks like a stage set, except for the stream in the background, which is blurred with movement. Like the stream, real fairies, as these claimed to be, should have suggested movement as they flew and danced around; however, in the photograph they stand unusually static and frozen in the frame. Despite being cut-outs of flower fairies, they tap into deep cultural substrates and sit as mnemic symbols of more fearsome fairies. Such fairies live in streams where children also play: fearsome sprites such as Peg Powler, Jenny Greenteeth and Nelly Long-Arms were said to drag children into the water as they played on riverbanks (Simpson and Roud 2000: 275, 381). The photographs point to and obscure the dangers lurking at the bottom of the garden with semi-anthropomorphised beings used to express the power of water. Another image captures Elsie sitting on grass coaxing a gnome against a backdrop surrounded by trees, highlighting the natural habitat of the fairies. This gnome with his cap, feather and jacket is a sinister little figure, hinting at folkish menacing goblin creatures. The iconography resembles William Allingham's frightening 'wee folk', with '[g]reen jacket, red cap, [a]nd white owl's feather' (1883: 2), who steal children and put sharp thorns in people's beds as acts of revenge. While their iconography speaks of childhood play and innocence, Cottingley fairies symbolically reference the darker folk fairies.

Another two images are taken among the foliage with the fairy cut-outs carefully suspended from the leaves and branches. A final image, the fairy sunbath, is a smudgy double exposure, showing some fairies standing in the grass. All the images apart from the last show the girls posing with the fairies. The girls are the protagonists as the fairies appear to play them music, or offer them posies, fairies reduced to props in a human world of play. The Cottingley images undermine the popular photographic motif of little girls being posed with 'fairies' in gardens. *Finding a Fairy* (1917) by Carine Cadby is a children's story book liberally illustrated with photographs of a little girl posing with an ornately dressed doll acting as the fairy (Bown 1996: 75–7). The *Sphere* magazine (Anon. 1918: 146) also published 'A Fantastic Invasion of a Modern Garden', showing a scene similar to the Cottingley images, just before they had become public. The title suggests that fairies sit awkwardly in the 'modern garden', they are outside invaders, belonging to the wild and their presence is out of place. Yet children invite them, and in this sense they are uncanny spectres haunting the garden.

Alex Owen argues the Cottingley images represent a 'fragment of 1917 childhood which Conan Doyle appropriated and invested with new meaning, and the intentions and dreams of the girls were subsumed in the process' (1994: 79). Conan Doyle's uncle was the eminent Victorian painter Richard Doyle (50), whose illustrations to *In Fairyland* (1870) show fairies flying in butterfly-drawn carriages, riding snails, playing around mushrooms and with birds, all comparable to the Cottingley fairies. Similarly, Conan Doyle's father, Charles Doyle, as a patient of Montrose Royal Lunatic Asylum in 1889, kept an illustrated diary full of watercolour fairy pictures (Crawley 1983: 118). For Conan Doyle, if the Cottingley fairies existed, it would redeem Charles, showing that he had the 'evolved sensibilities' of a clairvoyant, rather than being 'mad' (Lycett 2007: 409). The Cottingley images spoke to Doyle in a deep and personal way. Michel Foucault and Jay Miskowiec note that a *heterotopia* 'is capable of juxtaposing in a single real place several spaces, several sites that are in themselves incompatible', citing traditional Persian gardens as bringing together four parts of the world in a sacred space, a 'sort of microcosm' (1986: 25–6). The Cottingley case develops this type of *heterotopic* space for Doyle. The garden forms a supernatural, miniaturised landscape upon which images from his past could grow small hopes for his future.

The Cottingley girls used illustrations from Alfred Noyes's poem 'A Spell for a Fairy' from *The Princess Mary Gift Book* (1914: 101–4) to trace their fairy figures (Gettings 1978: 71), a poem of contrasts between urban and rural.

> Bring an old and wizened child
> Ah, tread softly and speak low
> Tattered, tearless, wonder-wild,
> From that under-world below;
> Bring a withered child of seven
> Reeking from the City slime,
> Out of hell into your heaven.
> Set her knee-deep in the thyme. (Noyes 1914: 103)

The image of a wizened city slum child seems like a deformed changeling, robbed of the joy of nature, contrasted with the redemptive image of magic performed in the wild natural setting of a 'hill top in dawn'. The spell requires 'buds of the hazel-copse', 'crushed red wild thyme tops' and 'the four-leaved clover' (102–3).

It implies that a city child is more truly at home, *Heimlich*, on the hilltop rather than in the actual home of 'city slime'. Elizabeth Tucker highlights a distinction that '[w]ildness is the opposite of civilization' in children; as opposed to their apparently well-ordered caregivers, children are considered 'wild by nature' (2012: 395). Karin Lesnik-Oberstein explores the connection between children's literature and nature, which goes back to the 'origins and developments' of children's books (1998: 209) She argues it is 'taken for granted almost as a truism' that a child is 'natural' (Lesnik-Oberstein 1998: 210). Both the 'child' and 'nature' were considered 'essential', 'unconstructed' and 'uncontaminated' and were 'assigned the status of being prior to, above and beyond man' [human], 'and therefore man's language, history and culture' (210). The poem and the Cottingley photographs play into this polarisation. Children do not belong in the spoiled factory landscape but with nature among the fairies. Indeed, this plays into the common folkloric motif of fairies who steal human infants and replace them with their withered fairy changelings (Simpson and Roud 2000: 53).

KIPLING AND THE WILD CHILDREN

Rudyard Kipling's books *Puck of Pook's Hill* (1906) and its sequel *Rewards and Fairies* (1910) incorporate a motif anticipating some Cottingley themes: two children playing in a space just beyond the realms of their garden where they encounter fairies. Puck lives in an ancient hill at the bottom of Dan and Una's garden, he is the last fairy in England and through him they meet a whole cast of historical characters. Dan and Una act *A Midsummer Night's Dream* three times on Midsummer's Eve just under Pook's Hill, thus conjuring up the mischievous elf. There is also a brook at the bottom of their garden, with their little rowing boat the *Golden Hind* (Kipling 1906: 61). Along the 'overgrown banks just beyond their garden' they pull their boat upstream using low branches (61). It is a space where they experiment with danger and role play at being adult explorers. Like the Cottingley children, this bottom-of-the-garden wilderness allows them the freedom to explore nonhuman nature; to understand the dangers of this landscape but also to explore supernatural elements away from the manicured flowerbeds.

Dan and Una also have their 'very own kingdom' in the garden, a 'little fenced wood' where even the gardener could not go (Kipling 1916: 33). The gardener controls nature, he manicures their parents' garden; their 'kingdom' is a wilderness space, away from adult order. It is reflective of Robinson's descriptions of the *Wild Garden*, a spare unused space, given over to the children and hedgerow flowers. However, Puck may enter their kingdom without permission; his status as a fairy, playmate and nonhuman exempts him from the ban. The bottom of the garden and the liminal area beyond is a space for children and fairies to play. It is a place where the adult world is not (quite) allowed. While playing, the children encounter villagers such as 'their particular friend old Hobden, the hedger' (Kipling 1906: 12). His toil involves the world of wild flowers, hedgerows and trees, representative of nature, not the authoritarian rules of the nursery or their parents' world. Even Hobden's name conjures up the 'hob' household brownie type of fairy (Simpson and Roud 2000: 178). The hedger is a figure who in Victorian England was expected to believe in fairies. He was working class and therefore paralleled with the children as opposed to their educated middle-class parents, under whose paternal control the countryside and nation, like the garden, were kept in logical order. The garden is a site where wildness and fairies meet civilisation. Waters argues that while gardens in Victorian literature are associated with 'civility and refinement', 'wildscapes' are associated with 'brutality'; gardening thus becomes a 'cultivating' act in more than one way (1988: 161). While gardens cultivated nature, they also tamed fairies, who still stand as miniaturised wild elements in the garden.

However, Cottingley exposes the absent presences in gardens, as explored by Robert Louis Stevenson in his anthology *A Child's Garden of Verses*. The title, as Anne Colley highlights, draws strongly on Stevenson's nostalgia for the 'landscape of his childhood' (1997: 304). The garden for him represents the 'topography' of a child's world, their own play kingdom in which adults are 'outsiders' (307). 'To Any Reader', explores the theme of growing up:

> As from the house your mother sees
> You playing round the garden trees,
> So you may see, if you will look
> Through the windows of this book,
> Another child, far, far away,
> And in another garden, play.
> But do not think you can at all,
> By knocking on the window, call
> That child to hear you. He intent
> Is all on his play-business bent.
> He does not hear; he will not look,
> Nor yet be lured out of this book.
> For, long ago, the truth to say,
> He has grown up and gone away,
> And it is but a child of air
> That lingers in the garden there. (Stevenson 1901: 76)

Speaking in grief, the poem expresses the death of childhood into adulthood. The child is a spectre haunting the garden. 'Such hauntings can also cause us to feel unsafe, uneasy, in places where we had always felt at home' (Wolfreys 2002: 111). For Stevenson, like Conan Doyle's presentation of Cottingley, the garden, the place of childhood play and safety, becomes a scene in which the fears of growing up and what lies ahead are projected. Likewise, Stevenson's nostalgia 'barely touches what it desires; it can never fully revitalize what it hopes to recover' (Colley 1997: 315). Both men's scenes of nostalgic childhood solace are perpetually haunted by their adult fears.

Nostalgia for childhood, especially imagined play violence, makes the garden with its fairies a heterotopic space in which adults' fears are manifested. In Stevenson's 'The Dumb Soldier', a toy soldier is buried in the ground (1901: 61).

> He has seen the starry hours,
> And the springing of the flowers;
> And the fairy things that pass,
> In the forests of the grass. (Stevenson 1901: 62)

While the little boy in this poem is darkly re-enacting his potential fate, the soldier, the adult, is watching his childish fairy-imaginings pass him by. Robert Graves's poems from *Fairies and Fusiliers* also reflect these themes. The poem 'I'd Love to Be a Fairy's Child' is followed by 'The Next War':

> You young friskies who to-day,
> Jump and fight in Father's hay,
> With bows and arrows and wooden spears. (Graves 1919: 51)

Young friskies, a word-play on the Cornish piskie, links the images of fairies back to the previous poem. These children make 'long-bows from the garden ash' (51). Fairyland is a space where children imagine what it is like to be adult and adults nostalgically locate their own lost childhoods. For Stevenson and Graves this is an emotional garden which provides an imaginary space to enact fairyland and project make-believe, of children looking to the outside world and adults looking wistfully in. But their nostalgia is coloured by adult knowledge. The bottom of the Cottingley garden represents this same emotional garden for Conan Doyle, haunted by nostalgic fairies, like his uncle's illustrations, which become tainted with adult worries about war and afterlife.

Seen through adult eyes, the garden of childhood play can become an unsettling world of terror and fear. John Hall-Edwards, 'the famous authority upon radium' (Doyle 1997: 44), wrote to the *Birmingham Weekly Post* criticising Cottingley, suggesting that encouraging wild childhood imagination could create dark disorder:

> I believe that the inculcation of such absurd ideas into the minds of children will result in late life in manifestations of nervous disorder and mental disturbances. Surely young children can be brought up to appreciate the beauties of Nature without their imagination being filled with exaggerated, if picturesque, nonsense and misplaced sentiment. (Hall-Edwards 1997: 45)

Cooper states Hall-Edwards vocalised fears that any 'excursions into the realms of fairies, witches and spirits have links with black magic and all the gory

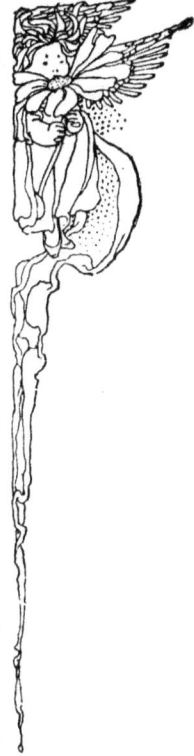

19 Frontispiece to Robert Louis Stevenson. 1909. *A Child's Garden of Verses*
(London: John Lane). Illustration by Charles Robinson (1870–1937)

trappings of horror films' (1990: 58). Hall-Edwards's criticisms draw upon wide-ranging fears of the occult and supernatural world and the possible effect this might have on children. While the concept of Magic haunting *The Secret Garden* was mysterious, yet ultimately nurturing and beneficial, its inversion could also be viewed as deeply threatening. The Cottingley girls, with their flower fairies, unwittingly tapped into a rich cultural vein of terror and fear surrounding fairies and the occult. Margaret Murray's infamous history *The Witch-Cult in Western Europe* (1921) similarly portrayed fairies as ancient savages worshipping a pagan horned-god cult, which later evolved into satanic witchcraft practices. The seemingly innocent flower fairy held the cache of a much darker past.

THE FAIRIES TAKE THEIR LEAVE?

Diane Purkiss notes that '[b]efore the war, fairies were what one wrote about if one was going to be a writer' (2000: 278); after World War I this changed. After the Cottingley controversy, fairies were no longer considered a serious adult topic and a silence fell upon them. Silver highlights that 'ostensible proof of the actual existence of the fairies, deprived the elfin peoples of their grandeur and status' (1999: 190). They had become predominant in children's literature and were 'virtually dislodged' from adult culture (185). Yet fairies have always represented a distorted reflection of humanity, including their fears and desires. During the nineteenth century, with vast industrialisation, wildscapes might be seen as something to 'cherish and protect against the encroachments of city and cultivated landscapes alike', the garden could 'accommodate within an unmistakably humanized framework, vestigial elements of nature's wilder forms and processes' (Waters 1988: 170). Likewise, the wilder folkloric fairies had become tamed in the gardens of children's literature. These blossom beings later became epitomised by Cicely Mary Barker's *Flower Fairies of the Spring* (1923). They were a quaint simulacrum of what fairies had once been. Since then fairies have sat at the bottom of the garden as concrete statuettes presiding over tiny ornamental fountains, sad mossy monuments to the creatures they once were.

However, there is a folkloric theme that fairies are always leaving but never quite leave. In *Puck of Pook's Hill* Puck may have been the last of his kind, but he still sat waiting for the children to conjure him up and guided them with his wise knowledge. Fairies have never truly vanished and are resurfacing as mediators in early twenty-first-century environmental crises, again reflecting human fears. Andy Letcher examines how eco-protest culture harnesses fairy imagery. He describes how 'Eco-paganism, as it is called, combines ideas from Wicca and Druidry, the New Age, Buddhism and theosophy, with anarchist politics, feminism, and 1960s psychedelia, all with an itinerant lifestyle incorporating green radicalism and direct action' (Letcher 2001: 148). Sabina Magliocco points to neo-pagan belief in fairies that uses 'kataphatic practices' – for example, guided meditations – which 'move narrative into experience' (2017: 329). She notes that fairy narratives can 'reenchant the natural world at a time of unprecedented ecological crisis' (329), but also that pagans can 'work with fairy energies because the fairies have been stripped of most of their negative powers' (330). Similarly, in *The Secret Garden* Burnett's concept of Magic, as a natural agent of healing and growth, shows how through gardening and play children can develop a close, enchanted and material relationship with nature. The Cottingley fairies' images still resonate today as so much is represented in their iconography. Some simple photographs at the bottom of a garden capture a moment that speaks down the decades in the nation's collective memory. Perhaps we need to understand that the fay folk are within us all and are part of nature and therefore not something separate. We walk with them; hear the call of the wild wood beyond the safety of the garden wall.

WORKS CITED

Alexander, Catherine. 2002. 'The Garden as Occasional Domestic Space', *Signs*, 27: 857–71

Allingham, William. 1883. *The Fairies: A Child's Song* (London: Thos. De La Rue and Co.)

Anon. 1918. 'A Fantastic Invasion of a Modern Garden', *Sphere*, 9 February: 146

Barker, Cicely Mary. 1923. *Flower Fairies of the Spring* (London: Blackie)

Bergman, Jenni. 2011. 'The Significant Other: A Literary History of Elves' (unpublished doctoral thesis, Cardiff University)

Bown, Nicola. 1996. 'There Are Fairies at the Bottom of our Garden', *Textual Practice*, 10: 57–82

Bown, Nicola. 2001. *Fairies in Nineteenth-Century Art and Literature* (Cambridge: Cambridge University Press)

Browning, Robert. 1864. *Dramatis Personae* (London: Chapman and Hall)

Burnett, Frances Hodgson. 1911. *The Secret Garden* (New York: Frederick A. Stokes)

Cadby, Carine. 1917. *Finding a Fairy* (London: Mills & Boon)

Calthrop, Dion. 1910. *The Charm of Gardens* (London: A. & C. Black)

Chang, Elizabeth Hope. 2019. *Novel Cultivations: Plants in British Literature of the Global Nineteenth Century* (Charlottesville and London: University of Virginia Press)

Colley, Ann. 1997. '"Writing Towards Home": The Landscape of "A Child's Garden of Verses"', *Victorian Poetry*, 35: 303–18

Cooper, Joe. 1990. *The Case of the Cottingley Fairies* (London: Robert Hale)

Crane, Walter. 1899. *A Floral Fantasy in an Old English Garden* (London: Harper)

Crawley, Geoffrey. 1983. 'That Astonishing Affair of the Cottingley Fairies Part 6', *British Journal of Photography*, 4 February: 117–21

Doyle, Arthur Conan. 1920. 'Fairies Photographed: An Epoch Making Event', *Strand Magazine*, December, pp. 463–8

Doyle, Arthur Conan. 1997. *The Coming of the Fairies* (1922) (London: Pavilion Books)

Foucault, Michel and Jay Miskowiec. 1986. 'Of Other Spaces', *Diacritics*, 16: 22–7

Fyleman, Rose. 1917. 'There Are Fairies at the Bottom of Our Garden', *Punch*, 23 May: 34

Gardner, Edward. 1997. 'Notes', in *The Coming of the Fairies*, ed. by Arthur Conan Doyle (London: Pavilion Books), pp. 99–106

Gettings, Fred. 1978. *Ghosts in Photographs* (Montreal: Optimum Publishing)

Graves, Robert. 1919. *Fairies and Fusiliers* (London: Heinemann)

Hall-Edwards, John. 1997. 'Article from *Birmingham Weekly Post*', in *The Coming of the Fairies*, ed. by Arthur Conan Doyle (London: Pavilion Books), pp. 44–5

Haraway, Donna J. 2003. *The Companion Species Manifesto: Dogs, People, and Significant Otherness, Vol. 1* (Chicago: Prickly Paradigm Press)

Kipling, Rudyard. 1906. *Puck of Pook's Hill* (New York: Doubleday, Page and Co.)

Kipling, Rudyard. 1916. *Rewards and Fairies* (New York: Doubleday, Page and Co.)

Lesnik-Oberstein, Karin. 1998. 'Children's Literature and the Environment', in *Writing the Environment: Ecocriticism and Literature*, ed. by Richard Kerridge and Meil Sammells (London: Zed Books), pp. 208–17

Letcher, Andy. 2001. 'The Scouring of the Shire: Fairies, Trolls and Pixies in Eco-Protest Culture', *Folklore*, 112: 147–61

Lycett, Andrew. 2007. *The Man who Created Sherlock Holmes: The Life and Times of Arthur Conan Doyle* (London: Weidenfeld and Nicolson)

McCabe, Joseph. 1920. 'Scientific, Men and Spiritualism', *English Review*, 30: 439–48

Magliocco, Sabina. 2017. '"Reconnecting to Everything": Fairies and Contemporary Paganism', in *Fairies, Demons, and Nature Spirits: 'Small Gods' at the Margins of Christendom*, ed. by Michael Ostling (London: Palgrave Macmillan), pp. 325–48

Mathews, Freya. 2003. *For Love of Matter: A Contemporary Panpsychism* (Albany: SUNY Press)

Murray, Margaret. 1921. *Witch-Cult in Western Europe* (Oxford: Clarendon Press)

Noyes, Alfred. 1914. 'A Spell for a Fairy', in *Princess Mary Gift Book* (London: Hodder and Stoughton), pp. 101–4

Owen, Alex. 1994. 'Borderland Forms: Arthur Conan Doyle Albion's Daughters and the Politics of the Cottingley Fairies', *History Workshop*, 38: 45–85

Punter, David. 2007. 'The Uncanny', in *Routledge Companion to Gothic*, ed. by Catherine Spooner and Emma McEvoy (London: Routledge), pp. 129–36

Purkiss, Diane. 2000. *Troublesome Things: A History of Fairies and Fairy Stories* (London: Penguin)

Ritvo, Harriet. 1992. 'At the Edge of the Garden: Nature and Domestication in Eighteenth- and Nineteenth-Century Britain', *Huntington Library Quarterly*, 55: 363–78

Robinson, William. 1870. *The Wild Garden* (London: John Murray)

Silver, Carol. 1999. *Strange and Secret Peoples: Fairies and Victorian Consciousness* (Oxford: Oxford University Press)

Simpson. J. and S. Roud. 2000. *Oxford Dictionary of English Folklore* (Oxford: Oxford University Press)

Spirn, Anne Whiston. 1998. *The Language of Landscape* (London: Yale University Press)

Stevenson, Robert Louis. 1901. *A Child's Garden of Verses* (New York: Charles Scribner's Sons)

Sugg, Richard. 2018. 'Fairy Magic and the Cottingley Photographs', in *Magical Folk*, ed. by Simon Young and Ceri Houlbrook (London: Gibson Square), pp. 54–64

Tucker, Elizabeth. 2012. 'Changing Concepts of Childhood: Children's Folklore Scholarship Since the Late Nineteenth Century', *Journal of American Folklore*, 125: 389–410.

Van Bronswijk, Renske. 2001. 'Enchanted: The Fairy Tale as Meeting Place in the Late-Victorian Period' (unpublished doctoral thesis, University of Birmingham)

Waters, Michael. 1988. *The Garden in Victorian Literature* (Aldershot: Scolar Press)

Wolfreys, Julian. 2002. *Victorian Hauntings: Spectrality, Gothic, the Uncanny and Literature* (Basingstoke: Palgrave)

Wood, Juliette. 2006. 'Filming Fairies: Popular Film, Audience Response and Meaning in Contemporary Fairy Lore', *Folklore*, 117: 279–96

Yoshino, Yuki. 2011. 'Desire for Perpetuation: Fairies Writing and Re-Creation of National Identity in the Narratives of Walter Scott, John Black, James Hogg and Andrew Lang' (unpublished doctoral thesis, University of Edinburgh)

10

Presence and absence in Tennyson's gardens of grief: 'Mariana', *Maud* and Somersby

Sue Edney

Not wholly in the busy world, nor quite
Beyond it, blooms the garden that I love. (['The Gardener's Daughter': 33–4] in
   Tennyson 1991)

Tennyson was a poet of gardens, who 'affected garden-consciousness' throughout the Victorian period, influencing cultural outputs in such a way that other writers and artists were often unaware 'ever of having consumed' the impressions (Waters 1988: 99). 'The Gardener's Daughter', for example, is better remembered as a poem about a garden than it is about the daughter; the garden 'fires the poem', comments Christopher Ricks (1989: 94). Alfred Austin, a notably mediocre poet and sorry representative of laureateship after Tennyson's death, attacked Tennyson's position as the Victorians' 'great' poet in garden terms: 'His flowers of poesy are flowers of the garden – a beautiful, exquisite, tasteful, sweet-smelling, brightly-glittering garden, but – a garden' (1870: 15). Not for Tennyson the 'mountains, the far-stretching landscape ... the planets, the intolerable thunder, grim murder, vaulting ambition, mad revenge' (17). Not for most people, in fact; Byron would not do for the railway age, but grim murder, vaulting ambition and mad revenge were as prevalent in Victorian Britain as they were in Romantic Italy and Germany. And their actions were often played out in gardens; in *Maud*, mad revenge and grim murder are alive and well and living in a Victorian country house, complete with rose garden and wooded landscape walks.

Austin comments on the lines above from 'The Gardener's Daughter', noting the 'mine of confession and suggestiveness' in them; Tennyson's 'heart is partly in the city and partly in the fields' (22). In other words, Tennyson was a poet who wrote about what he knew, like many another writer considered to be 'great'. Yet, Austin has picked out two terms that apply to much of Tennyson's best writing – it is both confessional and suggestive, half revealing and half concealing, not in the 'busy world, nor quite / Beyond it'. In this it demonstrates the way uncanniness can suffuse poetic expression without the writer's will or even knowledge, and much more so in the imagined garden, the space between the world and the field, porous, adaptable and wholly, deliberately affective.

In Victorian culture the association between poets and nature had changed, even by 1830 when Tennyson's early poems were published; the nonhuman could no longer be commandeered in support of personal fulfilment. It had become the 'age of the public scientific lecture, the laboratory demonstration and the introductory textbook', writes Richard Holmes, adding that science, in all its forms of experiential knowledge formed 'the basis of a new, *secular* philosophy of life' (2009: xix, emphasis added), with the potential for adjusting human/nonhuman reciprocal relations which made the 'wild' Romantic project look increasingly solipsistic and antithetical to the public good. Human emotional status can be affected by gardens surreptitiously, without the astonishment and awe promoted by sublime landscapes or Romantically inspired immersion in wilderness: in general, gardens are assumed to work with their guardians. However, the quiet infiltration of garden into human consciousness permits deeper, closer naturalcultural connections (Haraway 2003); nondualistic relationships socially and materially formed.

Freya Mathews considers the position of nonhuman 'matter' as envisaged by 'disinterested' science (Holmes 2008: xviii) and sees it as risking becoming 'unendowed with meaning, purpose, or agency, either in its own right or as a result of "occult" interventions' (Mathews 2005: 9). Mathews is discussing a 'strict materialism' (9) in which matter is reduced in its ability to be 'encountered' (2003: 10) – is, in fact, impossible to relate to in anything other than objectifying terms – arguing that the potential for reductionism in science ultimately results from that same 'thoroughly secular view of empirical reality' (2005: 8). By secular, she implies the rejection of a wealth of 'occult' interventions, which may be theistic, animistic or related to ancestral modes of living and being-in-the-world. Whatever they are, their insistence on 'being' is more apparent as they are pushed aside, not less. Mathews uses 'panpsychism' as a term to 'ascribe ... a mentalistic dimension to all of matter' (14), which is not, in her opinion, the same as ascribing agency to material objects, rather that the physical world is in communion with itself, including human subjects. The nonhuman acts in relation to the human in whatever way is possible; many of these acts result in uncanny situations to be dealt with by humans who are attempting to create familiar normalities out of some exceedingly disruptive behaviours – disruptive for a human sense of order, that is.

It is this type of materialism – seeking and being open to encounter with matter – that ecocritical materialism wishes to address. How far an 'occult' interpretation of nonhuman 'agency' can be applied is open to scrutiny; however, for my purposes, 'occult' is exactly the right name for those encounters beyond human that Tennyson tries to grapple with in his personal life and his poetic experiences of Otherness. In this chapter, I will consider the notions both of agency in matter and of encounter with matter as a means of 'occult' knowing in the garden. Vegetal co-workers' engagement with human experience and action can go astray, and neither human nor vegetal agent has full control of the outcomes, particularly for Mariana in her gloomy garden-that-was and for the hero of *Maud* whose only friends seem to be Others, but also for Tennyson himself, in the Somersby rectory garden filled with absent presence, especially that of Arthur Hallam. In gardens, nature and culture are conspirators as well as co-workers. Entangled cooperation is more subtly represented in 'Mariana' and *In Memoriam* than in *Maud*, so I will leave talking flowers and their plots to the chapter's end.

MATERIAL SENSATIONS

In 1831, in support of Tennyson's first poetry collection *Poems, Chiefly Lyrical* (1830), Arthur Hallam published what might be called a mission statement for the type of poetry he thought his friend represented; Tennyson was a poet of 'sensation', like Keats, in Hallam's opinion, with a 'tendency of imagination to a life of immediate sympathy with the external universe' (Hallam 1831: 617). Poets of sensation 'are not descriptive; they are picturesque' (617). Picturesque was not loaded with the same freight in 1831 as it had been in 1768 when William Gilpin coined the term as 'that peculiar kind of beauty which is agreeable in a picture' (1768: 2), partly because the picture had changed. Human dwellers in the Gothic landscapes of Horace Walpole and Ann Radcliffe were placed in sites which invoked a delicious terror in the minds of Romantic readers, as in the craggy artwork of Salvator Rosa, or sites of idyllic contrast to the characters' emotional distress and isolation (Kröger 2013: 18–20). Both kinds of landscape are disruptive for different reasons and reflect more than fictive spectres. Disruption is an important constituent of remaking whereby the '"ghosts" of former times in landscapes ... or just the sudden sensory perception of a smell or a sound' can trigger deep responses and create encounters (Berberich et al 2015: 14). These experiences are 'embedded with affective memories ... bringing us up to a halt' in our everyday processes (14).

Ruins reminded most readers of the pragmatic inevitability of loss and decay, but Gothicised ruins were supplemented by the once-human or never-human Other that leaked out of the crumbling mortar and peered from beneath the ivy. Ruined landscapes might cause materiality to be reduced to an 'emphasis on aesthetic effects' (Hunt 1992: 186); in the right hands, however, that

sensation resonates through other cultural outputs to support much wider
varieties of naturalcultural encounter. By 1830, the picture of picturesque had
been domesticated into 'the sketchable country scene and the modest cottage
garden' (Waters 1988: 79). Turn-of-the-century garden designer Humphry Repton
was concerned to keep the focus on what gardens were for, not just what their
aesthetic principle might be. Repton is quick to point out that 'the *antiquated
cot*, whose chimney is choked up with ivy, may perhaps yield a residence for
squalid misery and want' (1795; Loudon 1840: 100, emphasis in original), and
not a pretty picture. In 1830, 'Mariana' encapsulates not only Tennyson's but
also the 'sensation' artist's aesthetic and personal difficulties – how to write
material nature; how to picture loss in words; how to image absence, and how
to give poetry a modern voice. 'His attention to the experience of nature', as
Donald Hair points out in *Tennyson's Language*, is embedded in his 'element
of word-painting' (1991: 42) – it is indeed his element, as water is to fish. Hair
notes that both Hallam and Tennyson were particularly influenced at Cambridge
by Bishop George Berkeley's use of sensation, association or 'suggestion' in
the perception and realisation of material objects, specifically in his *Theory of
Vision, Vindicated and Explained* (1709). Berkeley's theories of 'immaterialism'
or 'idealism' (Downing 2013) – part of which imply that things as matter exist
only when experienced – were useful to painters and poets alike, because of
the reliance on the immediacy of senses in order to create experience, whether
the theories were accepted or not.

Far from creating immateriality, sensation poetics enables Tennyson to attach
materiality to images that, while they are *symbols* of distress, the reader is
drawn immediately into the physical as well as the emotional location of disturbance by association. 'The effectiveness of the language of "Mariana" thus
depends upon two assumptions the reader must share with the poet: first, that
our sensations ... are real and true', whether of internal emotion or external
material; 'secondly, that these sensations are ... a language established by
association, which makes sensations signs of other sensations' (Hair 1991: 55–6).

> With blackest moss the flower-plots
>   Were thickly crusted, one and all:
> The rusted nails fell from the knots
>   That held the pear to the gable-wall.
> The broken sheds looked sad and strange:
>   Unlifted was the clinking latch;
>   Weeded and worn the ancient thatch
> Upon the lonely moated grange. (['Mariana': 1–12] in Tennyson 2007)

From the opening 'with', the reader is pulled into a garden that is unable to
flourish, suffocated by moss, pear trees unsupported, thatch full of weeds,

sheds unused. Characteristically, Tennyson uses a negative that implies a positive, or has at least positive potential – it is by association that he creates the illogical but emotionally authentic connection between a 'latch' that is 'unlifted' yet continues to clink. Juxtaposition of the familiar with the unexpected creates uncanny discomfort for readers; we agree with Christopher Ricks when he comments on how we 'strain our ears ... for "uplifted"' (1989: 45). In our minds, we hear the sound of absence; 'He cometh not', says Mariana, and he continues not to come for the length of the poem. 'Mariana' is a poem of stifling claustrophobia, filled with nonhuman Others attempting to expand the enclosing space while Mariana herself blocks every overture, whether innocent or sinister, refusing access and resisting an encounter with any material reality other than her own self. The uncanny appropriation of selfhood by more-than-human nature returns to haunt sections of *In Memoriam*, in the very material garden of the Somersby rectory, a place of happy memory for Tennyson – as long as it was Hallam he was remembering.

UNHOMELY HOMES

Tennyson's difficult relationship with home caused him to resist localising his poems, yet Lincolnshire is present in his entire life, and in 'Mariana' and *In Memoriam*. There is a fear of presence in home, however, characterised by his persistent physical restlessness, even when apparently settled with his wife and sons. For this anxious discomfort we can thank Dr George Clayton Tennyson, the poet's father, a simmering pot of familial resentment, coupled to violent alcoholism (2). 'After the family left Somersby in 1837', comments Patrick Scott, Tennyson 'never went back for any extended period'; he looked for a home 'almost anywhere except Lincolnshire' (1996: 41). In the Somersby garden of memory, Tennyson attempts to re-create the idyll, while trying to extricate himself from the actuality of distress.

> Unwatched, the garden bough shall sway,
>> The tender blossom flutter down,
>> Unloved, that beech will gather brown,
> This maple burn itself away;
> Unloved, the sun-flower, shining fair,
>> Ray round with flames her disk of seed,
>> And many a rose-carnation feed
> With summer spice the humming air. ([*In Memoriam*: CI. 1–8] in Tennyson 2007)

An 'unwatched', 'unloved' garden is flourishing still, in transitory and sensually expressive abundance; swaying, fluttering, burning, shining, feeding and humming. Take away the negatives, and this is a typically Tennysonian English garden. Even in his regret, Tennyson is pragmatically aware of the cycles of regeneration. The unity of human and nonhuman in 'association' moves dispassionately round the years, until other families dwell in the landscape.

> Till from the garden and the wild
> A fresh association blow,
> And year by year the landscape grow
> Familiar to the stranger's child. ([*In Memoriam*: CI. 17–20])

There is an undercurrent of deliberate absenting here; what is familiar to a 'stranger's child' is unfamiliar to the current adult who is no longer 'at home'. By the time *In Memoriam* was published, Tennyson had moved away from the poetics of 'sensation' that he and Hallam had explored in their Cambridge days, yet the use of juxtaposition in order to disrupt assumption and expectation remained a feature of his writing. In this case, 'un' jars with 'loved' to create a garden that yearns for sensory involvement, to be touched, heard, smelled, while Tennyson leaves it behind, never to return. A thing familiar to strangers carries an uncanny doubleness in its construction, yet there is also a sense of relief in this line, that Tennyson can relinquish what is unhappily familiar to what is happily unfamiliar, the classic paradox of *heimlich/unheimlich*.

Mariana is eager to displace herself from her situation, without being able to untie the emotional knot that binds her to her environment. This appears to be a dismal home for any being, and yet many beings make it their dwelling. How they dwell in the 'moated grange' is precarious, contingent, uncanny – and picturesque. The 'weeded' thatch was a staple of late eighteenth- and early nineteenth-century 'cottage door' painting (Barrell 1983: 70), in which domesticity is celebrated as a national public good in miniature, the small garden offering glimpses of an intimate interior, complete with 'surprisingly well turned-out' women and children (70). Tennyson has no such thoughts; discomfort and alienation reign supreme in the moated grange. Gerhard Joseph comments on Tennyson's affinity for 'remote and abandoned places that reflected the psychic strangeness of their inhabitants' (1973: 421). Tennyson's picturesque is complicated by 'a terror at the ease with which vegetative and inorganic life – weeds, insects, and houses – take on a morally ambiguous animation and a menacing sentience' (421). John Dixon Hunt makes the point that there were moral considerations in picturesque aesthetics: a garden landscape should 'satisfy the mind's understanding of its schemes as well as the eyes' pleasure ... fine aesthetic taste denotes excellence of moral character' (1992: 166).

The morality of picturesqueness as a concept had been supplanted during the early nineteenth century in favour of what pleased the eye alone, something Repton resisted and for that reason brought back into direct view useful garden elements: walled kitchen gardens, flower borders, fish ponds, as might be found in a medieval English Gothic 'grange', traditionally the centre of a productive, often monastic, hub. That the grange is 'moated' implies an ancient site where the moat would be used in part for defence but also to keep fish (McLean 1981: 56–7). The gardens would have been arranged as several enclosures and packed with flowers, vegetables and herbs grown for the benefit of various communities. Thus, the nominal setting of the poem, although never really alluded to outside the epigraph from *Measure for Measure*, is the antithesis of what Mariana experiences and makes the frantic activity of nonhuman life around her immobility even more poignant.

The 'ancient' thatch is only one element in 'Mariana' of classic Gothic decay; the grange is fast falling into ruin: outhouses 'broken', life-giving channels filled with 'blackened water' [38], internal panelling now 'mouldering' away [64]. Waters notes that the communitarian values of rural estates as ordered unities is 'subverted' here: 'all distinctions between past and present are grotesquely collapsed' (1988: 103). In fact, they are deliberately decomposed by organic nonhuman material acting on the assumptions and expectations of teleologically minded humans; time is meaningless, as constantly expressed by Mariana and practised in the repetitive, cyclical behaviours of life around her. At Somersby, Tennyson employs repetition, in text and in his journey through grief, as part of a cooperative work with nature; Mariana is so placed that she ignores cycles of decay and renewal until, ultimately, they confront her with potentially disastrous outcomes.

SIGNS OF ABSENCE

In *In Memoriam*, while Tennyson is quite prepared to meet his friend's ghost in their old haunts, the rectory garden, the fields, woods and streams around Somersby, he deliberately eschews imagined phantoms. Longing for his friend, but understanding that longing creates 'spiritual presentiments' [XCII. 14] rather than presences, Tennyson knows: 'I shall not see thee' [XCIII. 1]. And yet he remains prepared to hope at least, but not in gloomy ruins.

> When summer's hourly-mellowing change
>> May breathe, with many roses sweet,
>> Upon the thousand waves of wheat,
> That ripple round the lonely grange;
> Come: not in watches of the night,
>> But where the sunbeam broodeth warm,
>> Come, beauteous in thine after form,
> And like a finer light in light. [*In Memoriam*: XCI. 9–16]

This section of *In Memoriam* is part of a canto sequence in which Tennyson comes closest to a spiritual connection with Hallam, among the rectory garden leaves and 'the noble letters of the dead', both 'fallen leaves which kept their green': 'The living soul was flashed on mine' [XCV. 23, 36]. It must be a soul-to-soul connection, not some phantom, a 'canker of the brain' [XCII. 3], in Tennyson's terms, but a true 'encounter'. Moreover, although the domestic landscape around the rectory is far removed from Mariana's, *In Memoriam* contains allusions to 'Mariana' that create an uncanny association between the two (Ricks in Tennyson 2007: 435): in this section, the 'lonely grange', for example, and the 'thick-moted sunbeam' ['Mariana': 78] that almost certainly 'broodeth warm' across the empty rooms. If readers are willing to support A. H. Hallam's proposal that late Romantic poetry was moved by 'sensation' suggestive of continuing engagement with imaginative growth, then Mariana's neglected, distorted garden haunts Tennyson's later grief. For so many months, Tennyson lingered in a grange of absences, filled with unwanted presences, much like his earlier victim of loss – '"He will not come," she said' ['Mariana': 82].

There are several absences here, including the lover, Mariana's lost hope and the garden that was, or might be again. The blurring of material boundaries in dynamic flow, which is itself a presence in the domestic landscape, has implications for the ecoGothic uncanny, in that what was familiar becomes Other; what is Other is no longer recognised as dreadful or dangerous but can be assimilated into the material world, for good or ill. 'Occult' carries within it the suggestion of secrecy; like 'uncanny', occult implies knowledge that is hidden for good reason, as well as the potential for deeper spiritual communication. For many Victorians, occult and spiritualist practices were part of everyday life; they enhanced quotidian reality by extending the boundaries between worlds. In *In Memoriam*, Tennyson asks, 'What hope of answer, or redress? / Behind the veil, behind the veil' [LVI. 27–8]; the 'veil' alluded to was 'a conductor, its porosity encouraging transactions and transmissions across time and space' (Kontou and Willburn 2012: 8). These transmissions are not (and, perhaps, should not be) universal but 'particularistic' (Mathews 2005: 111). The 'poetic language of particulars', writes Mathews, 'speaks through *this* landscape, through *these* individual women and men, through the tangled psychic terrain of *this* gathering' (111, emphasis in original). In these Tennyson poems, the tangled gathering is that of vegetal, animal and more-than-human others pressing their conversation upon the human ear.

SOUNDS OF PRESENCE

> About a stone-cast from the wall
>   A sluice with blackened waters slept,
> And o'er it many, round and small,
>   The clustered marish-mosses crept.
> Hard by a poplar shook alway,
>   All silver-green with gnarléd bark:
>   For leagues no other tree did mark
> The level waste, the rounding gray. ['Mariana': 37–48]

20 Tennyson's rhododendrons at Farringford, Isle of Wight. Photograph,
Sue Edney (2010)

A stone thrown from a wall of stone signifies the futility of action in this place, where even the water-channels sleep, but still other beings attempt a different kind of vitality. Tennyson knew the 'little marsh-moss lumps that float on the surface of water' (Ricks in Tennyson 2007: 5); he would have seen them in the Fens, they creep over the dormant surface and match the mossed flowerbeds. One tree, a poplar, which might be an aspen as it 'shook alway', marks the flat land and dominates her night. Its shadow sways in the wind 'when the moon was low' and looms 'upon her bed, across her brow', watching her sleep [53–6]. Sleep, though, is probably a relative state here, with little to distinguish it from wakefulness; Mariana is awake to hear the 'night-fowl crow' and the 'oxen's low' [26, 28]; small wonder she is 'aweary, aweary' [35]. The apparent lack of change in the human is contrasted with the organic cycles of vegetal, animal and more-than-human others. Morning and evening bring the dews and dry them, bats flit and sparrows 'chirrup' [73], it is all one to Mariana. Christopher Ricks comments fittingly on the 'stagnancy' of her environment, which remakes 'the vegetable kingdom as a soft-footed reclaiming, a sinister stealth … where only unseen movements are permitted' (1989: 44). Joseph notes the 'deliquescent mood' of the theme 'emerges obliquely through the details of a dimly ominous landscape' (1973: 421). Not everything is smothered by soundless vegetal creeping:

at the other extreme, 'cold winds woke the gray-eyed morn' and 'shrill winds were up and away' in the low moonlight [31, 50]. But as the night draws into day, these 'wild' tearaways are 'bound within their cell' [54], made ecoGothic prisoners as the voiceless poplar shadow takes over.

The implication of an ecoGothic takeover is increased by growing nonhuman clamour; although the house may be 'dreamy', 'All day … The doors upon their hinges creaked':

> The blue fly sung in the pane; the mouse
>   Behind the mouldering wainscot shrieked,
> Or from the crevice peered about.
>   Old faces glimmered through the doors
>   Old footsteps trod the upper floors,
> Old voices called her from without. ['Mariana': 61–8]

The phantasmal more-than-human echoes the nonhuman Otherness of an uncanny environment – these were presences familiar to the house, now absences familiar to Mariana's desolation, yet she is unable (or unwilling) to respond. By the final stanza, the clock ticks a slow counterpoint to the sparrow's chirrup, and the wind conspires in sound with the poplar to confirm Mariana's lonely status.

>   … the sound
> Which to the wooing wind aloof
>   The poplar made, did all confound
> Her sense; but most she loathed the hour
>   When the thick-moted sunbeam lay
>   Athwart the chambers, and the day
> Was sloping toward his western bower. ['Mariana': 74–80]

What was quiet has become loud, and culminates, to her distress, in the illuminating sun leaning into Mariana's dusty life and persuading her to an ending. The poem's structure juxtaposes the possibility of progression with the inevitability of defeat in a cycle of repetition, the essence of haunting – this poem is also haunted by itself. 'Mariana' keeps to a strict stanza form, even though the subjects of the stanzas are erratic, wayward and unstable. The boundedness of Tennyson's poetic form, his invention (Ricks in Tennyson 2007: 3), acts like a garden border in which the occupants have free rein, the constraints enabling a more pronounced uncanniness of disturbance. We expect order; we get disorder in the border; yet the structure allows for orbital movement, never ending a *verse* cycle in the same place. By this means, the monotonous *refrain* acts as an unconscious invocation to the garden world and the internal house-dwellers: the more she offers up her weary, dreary self, the more they respond either in stagnant sympathy or in determined activity.

From the beginning, the human was going to be overtaken by Others, noticeable from the outset in an ordered garden dissolved into moss and rust, a 'model for rotting garden poems', as Waters remarks (1988: 102). 'Blackest' moss is slinking over the flowerbeds, not merely 'black', and certainly not a healthy green like most garden-related mosses even when displaying their seasonal pink-brown sporophytes. But this moss has become a plot of its own, linked to the 'marish-mosses' in their 'blackened' waters, creeping over any sign of cultivation.

Whether the pear tree has become a vagrant in this derelict garden we are not told – only that it was secured to the house for human use; now it may please itself, no longer 'held to the gable-wall' [4]. Tennyson had originally chosen the 'peach' for this fruit tree, however, Ricks notes that Tennyson thought '"peach" spoils the desolation of the picture' (in Tennyson 2007: 4). 'Pear' has that downward movement consistent with nails, tears and shadows falling throughout the poem. In the next stanza, dusk brings 'the flitting of the bats' followed by night falling, 'When thickest dark did trance the sky' [17–18]. It appears that Gothic sensation has the upper hand, by association alone. 'We are not aware', comments Hair, 'that we are judging our visual experience' in our response to 'nouns like "moss" and "nails"; we think only that, through long use and custom, those words are linked with those objects' (1991: 54). Dark night, trances, bats and black moss connect the reader to images of ruin, horror, phantoms and incarceration – none of which is actually present in the story. The words 'fall into a configuration' (55) with Mariana's largely self-imposed state of physical and emotional immobility, and also with the picturesque Gothic aesthetic that allows for fantastic conjurations. *Measure for Measure* creates more problems here than it solves: Mariana does, eventually, marry Angelo who had rejected her for so many years, but under such strange circumstances that one might expect her to refuse. However, John Stuart Mill considers the Shakespearean relevance to be nominal; we should only 'retain' the moated grange 'and a solitary dweller within it' (1835; 2002: 87). Her 'dreariness ... speaks not merely of being far from human converse and sympathy, but of being *deserted* by it' (87, emphasis in original). Yet if this were viewed from the position of nonhuman Others, Mariana is far from solitary and deserted. Indeed, the vegetal, animal and even mineral elements of the moated grange could be striving to rescue her from herself, to get up, to engage with nonhuman nature burgeoning around her visionless self-absorption. Jane Bennett speaks of material life – that is the 'life' of any matter, including human or nonhuman animal – as a 'positive, active virtuality, a quivering protoblob of creative élan' (2010: 61). Life 'draws attention ... to an interstitial field of nonpersonal, ahuman forces, flows, tendencies, and trajectories' (61). Finally, the refrain resolves into Mariana's definitive acceptance of her own condition – for better or worse, we can only conjecture: "'He will not come ... Oh God, that I were dead!'" [82, 84].

CONVERSATIONAL FLOWERS

The encounters between human and vegetal in Maud's garden are even more disorienting, although in many ways less affective or haunting than those of Mariana's disintegration. As a study in solipsistic derangement, familial desperation and violence, *Maud* shares many features with its Gothic and mid-century sensation fiction cousins, yet it may be because it has more affinity with them and less with Tennyson's personal environmental preoccupations that the relationships between human and nonhuman are not only strained in the tale but also in its telling, and its subsequent reception. We lose sympathy with the hero and with his nonhuman collaborators; the human presences – Maud, her brother and her arranged suitor – are shadows compared with the glittering depictions of sky and sea, heath and woodland, bird and flower, yet these seem dangerously over-wrought and untrustworthy. It is too obviously 'Gothic' without the subtlety of 'uncanny'. There are, though, connective moments which can be associated with Mariana's ecoGothic and Tennyson's own panpsychic encounters in the Somersby garden of *In Memoriam*. Mariana's shrieking mouse returns ([*Maud*: I. VI. 260] in Tennyson 2007), and Maud's phantom is dismissed as a 'blot upon the brain' [IV. VIII. 200], similar to Tennyson's fear that Hallam's spirit would prove a 'canker'. This ghost appears in the inserted lyric, 'O that 'twere possible' [IV. I. 141], originally written in 1833–34 and deeply expressive of Tennyson's anguish 'After long grief and pain' [IV. I. 142], representing a textual haunting and the persistence of loss 'that *will* show itself without' [IV. VIII. 201].

> Come into the garden, Maud,
>   For the black bat, night, has flown,
> Come into the garden, Maud,
>   I am here at the gate alone;
> And the woodbine spices are wafted abroad,
>   And the musk of the rose is blown. [*Maud*: XXII. I. 850–5]

Publisher John Boosey extracted this famous section and sent it to Victorian opera composer and singer Michael Balfe (1808–70), who translated a poem of obsession and death-wish into a popular parlour song (1857), possibly the most uncanny event of all in this story. The Gothic 'black bat' settles over the entire tale after this climactic invitation to a potentially blissful union between human and more-than-human. Here, the lover has said goodbye to his beloved; she returns to the Hall to attend a dance in her honour; he follows and lingers by her garden gate, willing her to come out, which she does, but is fatally intercepted by her brother.

The narrator, our unlikely hero, seems unable to 'make reliable contact with an external world' (Peltason 2009: 201); at the beginning, he broods on his father's death 'all by myself in my own dark garden ground':

> Listening now to the tide in its broad-flung shipwrecking roar,
> Now to the scream of a maddened beach dragged down by the wave,
> Walked in a wintry wind by a ghastly glimmer … [*Maud*: I. III. 97–9]

Throughout the poem, the speaker has a heightened sense of Other presences and their entanglement with human sensation. Shunning human company, he has either become unhinged through family and personal dysfunction, or he just might be better attuned to the more-than-human Otherness of his environment. There is a necessity, to some extent, for characters in Gothic-inflected stories to be emotionally hyperactive; this tale has influences from Walter Scott's novel *The Bride of Lammermoor* (1819): a lost ancestral home, thwarted love, murder, madness, duelling and deaths. There are also ghosts, either living versions, as at the start of the poem when pale Maud haunts the speaker's dreams, or at the end, when dead Maud appears 'In a cold white robe before me' [IV. IV. 159]. In fact, Francis O'Gorman points out a 'persistent oddity', a doubt as to 'whether she is alive' at all: being 'lain in the lilies of life' [I. IV. 61], for example, 'sounds uncomfortably close to a corpse in a funeral parlour' (2010: 304). The lilies and roses play active parts in this drama.

> Maud has a garden of roses
> And lilies fair on a lawn;
> There she walks in her state
> And tends upon bed and bower. [*Maud*: XIV. I. 489–92]

Lilies and roses had religious and hierarchical status as well as being emblems of love (Seaton 1995: 43), yet they were often simultaneously rejected by churches as symbolic of luxury and frivolity (Goody 1993: 89). Stately Maud attends her garden as queen and virgin, 'bed and bower' become privileged subjects, certainly much more governed than Mariana's overgrown plot. Although the garden contains many of the elements of a *hortus conclusus* with Maud as the 'Madonna-in-a-garden' (116), the bed and bower imply a more erotic seclusion, made obvious in her suitor's frantic attempts to reach her:

> And thither I climbed at dawn
> And stood by her garden-gate;
> A lion ramps at the top,
> He is clasped by a passion-flower. [*Maud*: XIV. I. 493–6]

In the Victorian sentimental language of flowers, the passion flower signified faith, with the flower's interior 'symbolizing the crucifixion' (Seaton 1995: 48), but that might have been lost on *Maud*'s audience given the showy appearance of the flower, which in this case is ominously wrapped around a lion.

Faith, though, is probably a more helpful quality than passion in this story. While the hero walks to the rose garden, a 'rivulet' joining the Hall to his dark wood brings down a 'garden-rose'. The rose, however, is 'lost in trouble and moving around' trying to 'pass to the sea', and is 'forgetful of Maud and me' [XXI. 837–43]. Maud has already been figured as a rose: 'Rosy are her cheeks, / And a rose her mouth' [XVII. 577–8]; this rose demonstrates an anxious independence. Yet, perhaps Maud has sent it, 'saying in odour and colour, "Ah, be / Among the roses tonight"' [XXI. 848–9]. This is how one might expect a flower to communicate, with the 'woodbine spices' and the 'musk of the roses' fading with the dawn. 'Through their crafty use of chemical language', writes Monica Gagliano, 'plants are able to breathe out their message by encoding it with a single scented word that nonetheless conveys multiple meanings depending on the intended recipients' (2017: 90). Gagliano is referring to other plants and potential pollinators, not (necessarily) human recipients, yet Luce Irigaray reminds us that we used to inhabit a 'vegetal world' (2017: 126) that is no longer available to us, reduced as it is in terms of both pollen-bearers and pollinators, with which we could not avoid communicating in former times.

However, the flowers in *Maud* talk in human language, to each other and the hero, and in a passionate and yearning unity that both supports and undermines human endeavours to reach a happy ending. As he stands by the gate, he strikes up a conversation with lily and rose, expatiating on Maud, her intended 'lord-lover', and how she 'is weary of dance and play' [XXII. 871, 878], so the hero believes. And, as he waits, and the flowers listen to the dance and to his distressed impatience, so 'the soul of the rose went into my blood, / As the music clashed in the hall' [XXII. VI. 882–3], an encounter remarkably similar to Tennyson's description of Hallam's 'living soul' which was 'flashed on mine' in *In Memoriam*. Maud has been rose-like from the early moment of the hero's involvement; now the hero has assumed single-minded rose-nature. Rose has entered him in an erotic and a spiritual climax with the plant; by this means, he appears able to command emotional support and encouragement from other vegetal beings. Most of them sleep their own sleep, 'But the rose was awake all night for your sake' [XXII. VIII. 898]. Rose seems to have a pact with the hero to bring Maud into the garden. After this apparent vegetal/human transcendence, the flowers do all the talking:

> The red rose cries, 'She is near, she is near;'
>   And the white rose weeps, 'She is late;'
> The larkspur listens, 'I hear, I hear;'
>   And the lily whispers, 'I wait'. [*Maud*: XXII. X. 912–15]

Lily, the emblem of purity, sounds a note of caution in the roses' triumph; she only whispers, 'I wait', because our hero notes that in his heightened rose state, even his dead dust would hear Maud and 'tremble under her feet, / And blossom in purple and red' [XXII. XI. 922–3].

In his later madness, after he has killed Maud's brother, fled the scene, and Maud herself has died, this intense sensation comes to him again: that lily and rose were over-encouraged by the music, and the garden only produced flowers,

21 'There has fallen a splendid tear / From the passion flower at the gate.' Albumen print. Sitter is Mary Ann Hillier. Alfred, Lord Tennyson. 1875. *Idylls of the King and Other Poems* (London: Henry S. King). Illustrated with photographs by Julia Margaret Cameron (1815–79)

'no fruits'; it was sterile. And, anyway, 'I almost fear they are not roses, but blood' [Part II. V. VIII. 315–16]. Is the man blaming the flowers for his violence? Matthew Hall discusses plant behaviour in the context of other beings, which can depend on how a plant interacts with those in its path; increased well-being is its ultimate goal, and a plant will 'learn' through 'continual assessment and the ability to make behavioural corrections' (2011: 145). Hall adds, 'there is some direct experimental evidence for the existence of intention and choice in plants' (146). Their complex intercommunication systems, within themselves and in combination with their kin and other species indicates a recognition of 'self' and 'not self' (150); this is especially noticeable in their root systems, in connection with fungi, microbes and other plants and creatures. However, Hall asks that plants be included within human-based 'moral consideration ... as it both recognizes and reveals plant sentience' (156). But one problem with any aspect of attaching human moral value to nonhuman others is that we might demand behaviour inappropriate for nonhuman lifeforms. Plants behave like plants; our present misfortune is that we are unclear about what this might signify for human and other beings, or how we can interpret vegetal threads in animal lives. As Michael Marder points out, 'the literal plant, the plant itself, remains untranslatable' (2017: 109). 'For scientists, "language" means "communication"', writes Marder, plants as 'emitters and receivers of information' (117) without their story. The vegetal beings in these poems are 'untranslatable' in literal terms, but can be encountered in uncanny relationships, not in analysing their behaviours.

Maud's talking flowers are the least affective among these plant/human interactions *because* they are talking flowers. They have been made to fit a human-framed story – the only speaker, in fact, is human. If 'it is through encountering the world ... that we shall actually acquire [a] sense of spiritual kinship' (Mathews 2003: 79), then we need to hear nonhuman Others differently, with what George Steiner calls 'vital comprehension' (1998: 25); 'familiarity ... will facilitate understanding' through 'the transforming energies of feeling' (25). The occult creates a multidimensional environment whereby human and nonhuman across time and space can tell the story of naturalcultural phenomena, which will inevitably prove uncomfortable. The nonhuman in 'Mariana' and *In Memoriam* is entangled in human contact, is encountered on its own strange terms, disconcerting for human others, but ultimately unifying even in ecoGothic turmoil. In between-worlds of encounter, the liminality of gardens, growth and renewal become possible for Mariana and for Tennyson in Somersby, where only death is the final encounter in Maud's garden of roses.

WORKS CITED

Austin, Alfred. 1870. *The Poetry of the Period* (London: Richard Bentley)
Barrell, John. 1983. *The Dark Side of the Landscape* (Cambridge: Cambridge University Press)

Bennett, Jane. 2010. *Vibrant Matter: A Political Ecology of Things* (Durham, NC: Duke University Press)

Berberich, Christine, Neil Campbell and Robert Hudson. 2015. 'Introduction', in *Affective Landscapes in Literature, Art and Everyday Life: Memory, Place and the Senses*, ed. by Christine Berberich, Neil Campbell and Robert Hudson (Farnham: Ashgate), pp. 3–17

Downing, Lisa. 2013. 'George Berkeley', in *The Stanford Encyclopedia of Philosophy*, ed. by Edward N. Zalta, https://plato.stanford.edu/archives/spr2013/entries/berkeley/ [accessed 1 June 2020].

Gagliano, Monica. 2017. 'Breaking the Silence: Green Mudras and the Faculty of Language in Plants', in *The Language of Plants*, ed. by Monica Gagliano, John C. Ryan and Patricia Vieira (Minneapolis: University of Minnesota Press), pp. 84–100

Gilpin, William. 1768. *An Essay upon Prints* (London: Robson)

Goody, Jack. 1993. *The Culture of Flowers* (Cambridge: Cambridge University Press)

Hair, Donald S. 1991. *Tennyson's Language* (Toronto: University of Toronto Press)

Hall, Matthew. 2011. *Plants as Persons: A Philosophical Botany* (Albany: SUNY Press)

Hallam, Arthur Henry. 1831. 'On Some of the Characteristics of Modern Poetry, and on the *Lyrical Poems* of Alfred Tennyson', *Englishman's Magazine*, 616–28

Haraway, Donna J. 2003. *The Companion Species Manifesto: Dogs, People and Significant Otherness, Volume 1* (Chicago: Prickly Paradigm Press)

Holmes, Richard. 2008. *The Age of Wonder* (London: Harper Press)

Hunt, John Dixon. 1992. *Gardens and the Picturesque: Studies in the History of Landscape Architecture* (Cambridge, MA: MIT Press)

Irigaray, Luce. 2017. 'What the Vegetal World Says to Us', in *The Language of Plants*, ed. by Monica Gagliano, John C. Ryan and Patricia Vieira (Minneapolis: University of Minnesota Press), pp. 126–35

Joseph, Gerhard J. 1973. 'Poe and Tennyson', *PMLA*, 88. 3: 418–28

Kontou, Tatiana and Sarah Willburn. 2012. 'Introduction', in *The Ashgate Research Companion to Nineteenth-Century Spiritualism and the Occult*, ed. by Tatiana Kontou and Sarah Willburn (Abingdon: Routledge), pp. 1–18

Kröger, Lisa. 2013. 'Panic, Paranoia and Pathos: Ecocriticism in the Eighteenth-Century Gothic Novel', in *Ecogothic*, ed. by Andrew Smith and William Hughes (Manchester: Manchester University Press), pp. 15–27

McLean, Teresa. 1981. *Medieval English Gardens* (New York: Viking)

Marder, Michael. 2017. 'To Hear Plants Speak', in *The Language of Plants*, ed. by Monica Gagliano, John C. Ryan and Patricia Vieira (Minneapolis: University of Minnesota Press), pp. 103–25

Mathews, Freya. 2003. *For Love of Matter: A Contemporary Panpsychism* (Albany, NY: SUNY Press)

Mathews, Freya. 2005. *Reinhabiting Reality: Towards a Recovery of Culture* (Albany, NY: SUNY Press)

Mill, J. S. 2002. '*Poems, Chiefly Lyrical* (1830) and *Poems* (1833)' (1835), in *Lord Alfred Tennyson: The Critical Heritage* ed. by John D. Jump (London and New York: Routledge), pp. 84–97

O'Gorman, Francis. 2010. 'What is Haunting Tennyson's *Maud* (1855)?' *Victorian Poetry*, 48. 3: 293–312

Peltason, Timothy. 2009. 'What the Laureate Did Next: *Maud*', *Victorian Poetry*, 47. 1: 197–219

Repton, Humphry. 1840. *Landscape Gardening and Landscape Architecture of the Late Humphry Repton, Esq*, ed. by J. C. Loudon (London: Longman)

Ricks, Christopher. 1989. *Tennyson*, 2nd edn (Basingstoke: Palgrave Macmillan)

Scott, Patrick. 1996. 'Tennyson, Lincolnshire, and Provinciality: The Topographical Narrative of *In Memoriam*', *Victorian Poetry*, 34. 1: 39–51

Seaton, Beverly. 1995. *The Language of Flowers: A History* (Charlottesville and London: University Press of Virginia)

Steiner, George. 1998. *After Babel: Aspects of Language and Translation*, 3rd edn (Oxford: Oxford University Press)

Tennyson, Alfred. 1991. *Alfred, Lord Tennyson: Selected Poems*, ed. by Aidan Day (London: Penguin)

Tennyson, Alfred. 2007. *Tennyson: A Selected Edition*, ed. by Christopher Ricks (Harlow: Longman)

Waters, Michael. 1988. *The Garden in Victorian Literature* (Aldershot: Scolar Press)

11

Blackwater Park and the haunting of Wilkie Collins's *The Woman in White*

Adrian Tait

First published in 1859–60, Wilkie Collins's *The Woman in White* quickly establishes its hold over the reader. A young drawing-master named Hartright is walking home late one night when, out of nowhere, he is 'brought to a stop by the touch of a hand laid lightly and suddenly on [his] shoulder' (Collins 2003: 23): 'There, in the middle of the broad, bright high-road – there, as if it had that moment sprung out of the earth or dropped from the heavens – stood the figure of a solitary Woman, dressed from head to foot in white garments' (23–4). 'Few readers will be able to resist the mysterious thrill of this sudden touch', said *Blackwood's Magazine*; '[t]he sensation is distinct and indisputable' (quoted in Page 1974: 118). *Blackwood's* was correct. Overnight, it seemed that Collins had succeeded in creating what contemporaries regarded as an entirely new sub-genre: the sensation novel (Mangham 2013: 1). As an outstanding instance of what Timothy Morton has called 'environmental creepiness' (2010: 54), Collins's novel is equally compelling. Place is often evoked in disturbing ways; gardens and garden-like spaces play an important role in shaping the narrative. Of these spaces, the most notable is a landed estate called Blackwater Park, a landscape garden that is at once thoroughly ordinary yet profoundly strange. As the novel unfolds, it becomes clear that Collins's apparently realistic tale of marital deceit and madness is inseparable from his haunting depiction of this latter-day instance of the Gothic (Botting 1998: 131).

For the ecocritic, the relevance is that the Gothic might itself represent a latent form of ecological awareness. As Andrew Smith and William Hughes have argued, the Gothic originates in the same critique of modernity that gave rise to Romanticism: 'shared critical languages exist between the two' (2013: 1). Unlike their Romantic counterparts, however, Gothic writers did not feel bound to present 'Nature' as benign or, for that matter, passive. To the contrary, they often presented Nature not only as morally ambivalent, but active, even agential (Botting 1998: 2–3). This is the basis of what Smith and Hughes have called an 'ecoGothic', which 'variously questions, compromises and challenges the way in which the world has been understood' (2013: 1, 4). In particular, it challenges modernity's emphasis on reductionist, rationalistic and atomistic epistemologies, while opposing a Romanticised construction of Nature, which ecocritics have come to regard as in itself problematic (Morton 2007: 1–2; 2010: 7). But ecoGothic also suggests that the nonhuman and more-than-human worlds are themselves active parts of the world they co-constitute, creating an uncanny and often unsettling sense of their proximity to the human. This is a strangeness with which we are intimately entangled, but also strangely familiar: it is, as Sigmund Freud suggested in his discussion of the uncanny experience, that which 'has been repressed and now returns' (Freud 2003: 147).

In light of the material turn in the humanities – a turn associated with the work of, among others, Karen Barad, Jane Bennett and Stacy Alaimo – it is this last point that may be the most intriguing. As Barad has argued, what we call 'reality' is in fact a complex dynamic constituted through the intra-action of material and discursive phenomena (2007: 32–5). This processual understanding of the relationship between the two domains suggests new ways in which to re-evaluate matter as agential, while nevertheless acknowledging the importance of discourse as itself constitutive of reality. Barad's theory of agential realism also suggests a way of rereading the Gothicised landscapes in Collins's fiction and exploring their importance as instances of an ecoGothic. From his depictions of the Shivering Sands to the Paris Morgue, Collins is famous for the way in which he 'creates a "sensational" atmosphere through the use of location' (Wheeler 1994: 104). Furthermore, Collins's responsiveness to place – his sense of its transgressive, agential materiality – reflects his enduring fascination with the Gothic (Pykett 2005: 4, 7). As Collins's narratives also suggest, the agentiality of the material world is above all disturbing because, as Freud observed, 'this uncanny element is actually nothing new or strange, but something that was long familiar to the psyche and was estranged from it only through being repressed' (Freud 2003: 148).

In this chapter, my aim is, therefore, to reread Collins's depiction of Blackwater Park as a latter-day example of an ecoGothic garden. Neglected by its current owner, Sir Percival Glyde, the Park is reconstituting itself, much to Glyde's consternation. But while the material turn underlines the importance of Blackwater's landscape garden as an instance of agential materiality, it also highlights the processual, performative dimension of intra-activity. All those who come into contact with Blackwater Park respond to it in different ways, as Marian Halcombe records in her own account of her experiences there. As I also argue, Marian's narrative plays a central role in determining (perhaps even over-determining) the reader's own response to Blackwater Park as itself

22 'At the Park Gate' (1878). Oil on canvas, John Atkinson Grimshaw (1836–93)

an agential, but also a haunting presence. This is Gothicised landscape as revenant: 'it *begins by coming back*', as Jacques Derrida suggested (1994: 11, emphasis in original). As I conclude, there is another dimension to what Derrida called 'the logic of haunting' (10): the withdrawal or erasure that Blackwater's return presupposes. Even as it enacts a Gothic-like resurgence of the more-than-human world, *The Woman in White* constitutes a 'work of mourning' (9).

The loss that such a work implies is already reflected in the novels of another, much earlier nineteenth-century writer: Jane Austen. As I explain in the first of the chapter's three sections, Austen's literary response to the changing nature of the landscape garden goes some way to explaining Blackwater's own troubled – and troubling – past, as grand estates and parks fell out of favour, and improvement gave way to neglect.

THE CHANGING NATURE OF BLACKWATER PARK

In *Mansfield Park*, first published in 1814, Jane Austen's heroine Fanny Price rues the loss of an avenue of trees that, for her, symbolise a symbiotic relationship between people and place (Austen 1996: 48). To Fanny, their removal signals the imposition of a new kind of landscape garden whose primary purpose is simply to please the eye. Quoting Cowper's *The Task* in their defence, Fanny makes it quite clear that this is a loss that matters, as it mattered to Austen herself. Everywhere, Whig 'improvements' were radically transforming country estates. Entire villages were sometimes displaced, customary rights over-ridden, and an 'austerely abstract … canvas of rolling green lawns [and] sinuous lakes' substituted for a working rural landscape (Gold and Revill 2004: 129). This was the 'bare "natural"' style of Lancelot 'Capability' Brown, a 'large-scale overhauling of nature' to which Cowper's *The Task* was itself a highly critical response (Uglow 2004: 172, 165).

In the eyes of those like Austen, what was lost was a lived and living landscape, and with it, an intimate relationship between people and place. In fact, these changes were not quite as radical as Austen's narratives imply. By definition, gardens have always combined different functions: as flower-gardens, they may please the eye, or as kitchen gardens, provide food for the table. Although bold, the Whig expansion of gardens and estates into the large-scale vistas of the country park simply reflected that duality. Moreover, and while these 'improved' and expansive landscapes often survived their historical moment, they quickly fell out of fashion. By the mid-Victorian period, a now industrialised and urbanised nation was turning its attention to *rus in urbe* and, in particular, to life in the suburbs, where the new middle classes created their own versions of the landed estate in the gardens of their villas. A rural bias persisted, but on the landed estates themselves, the great parks were in decline. As Jane Fearnley-Whittingstall points out, '[t]he new money, the money for making gardens, was no longer in the countryside – it was in suburbia' (2003: 185). In turn, it was to the middle classes that a fresh generation of landscape designers, like John Claudius Loudon, profitably directed their attention (183).

In *The Woman in White*, Collins picks up where Austen leaves off, with a country estate whose trees have already been cut down, perhaps by a Brown or Repton. As Marian Halcombe notes, taking in the prospect for the first time, 'I suspect there must have been a ruinous cutting down of timber, all over the estate, before Sir Percival's time' (Collins 2003: 204). At some stage, however, Glyde's predecessors have felt the need to replant the park's trees, 'an angry anxiety', as Marian puts it, 'to fill up all the gaps as thickly and rapidly as possible' (204). Consequently, firs have been planted. Fast-growing and straight, firs can be planted very close together, creating a dense, dark screen. The house is now 'stifled by them' (204). Whether the firs were planted to make hasty amends for the loss of the estate's trees, as the phrase 'angry anxiety' suggests, or were themselves intended as a cash-crop, the effect is one of enclosure, even entrapment.

In other ways, the Park's changing nature reflects human neglect rather than intervention. Left to its own devices, the more-than-human world is reasserting itself. Beyond the firs lies the lake that gives Blackwater Park its name, a dark and sullen body of water that is now more or less silted up, 'all puddles and pools' (230). As Glyde remarks, '[s]ome people call that picturesque' (230), perhaps because of its pleasingly ruinous appearance and abandoned air. Glyde himself resents the result, finding it somehow disquieting.

Like the owners of many other great estates at the time, however, Glyde lacks the resources to (re)impose himself upon the landscape. Resenting his powerlessness to affect it, Glyde calls the lake a 'blot on a gentleman's property' (230). 'I wish I could afford to drain it', he says of the lake, 'and plant it all over' (230). Perhaps he hopes to do so with neat rows of fir trees. As Marian later observes, Glyde has 'a mania for order and regularity' that prompts him to rage at the servants 'if there is a crease in the tablecloth, or a knife missing from its place at the dinner-table' (214). But perhaps there is more to Glyde's annoyance than the fact that he cannot bend the landscape to his will. At the time, it was assumed that stagnant bodies of water bred typhus; several London parks had recently had their lakes drained (Sutherland 1998: xix). Glyde may fear the lake's impact on his health, an anxiety heightened by his own guilty recognition that its moribund waters are the result of his own neglect; the lake is, after all, a 'naturalcultural' construct – or more exactly, 'practice' (Barad 2007: 32) – that requires his intervention if it is to keep its pleasing aspect, or be prevented from becoming a source of waterborne disease. Ironically, it is Marian, not Glyde, who later falls ill with typhus: readers may nonetheless have linked her illness to the lake, an association that would have reinforced their sense of it as an active and, because of its mistreatment, a malign, even vindictive presence.

In spite, therefore, of the ways in which Blackwater's identity is or might be constituted, it dominates the text as a transgressive, even vengeful entity, abnormal by virtue of the way in which it deviates from the domesticated norm of Nature. Rather than offer open vistas with views of the country beyond, or charming but secluded gardens, it is characterised primarily by its gloom, its strangeness, and by a suffocating sense of enclosure. As Chris Baldick has pointed out, the Gothic 'effect' often embodies some form of 'claustrophobic enclosure in space' (quoted in Luckhurst 2006: xv). In Tamar Heller's reading of Collins's novel, however, this sense of enclosure is the basis of a specifically 'female Gothic' that looks back to both Ann Radcliffe's Udolpho and Charlotte Brontë's Thornfield, where another 'madwoman' is imprisoned (Heller 1992: 113).

> 'Suffocated' by trees, the claustrophobic Blackwater represents women's experience in true Gothic style as a kind of stifling prison sentence; it is here that Marian Halcombe laments she is 'condemned to patience, propriety, and petticoats, for life'. Not surprisingly, Marian is imprisoned by Fosco in the most crumbling and Gothic section of the mansion. (Heller 1992: 113)

In Heller's view, Blackwater – house and grounds alike – represents a 'carceral [sic] world' (113). Yet Blackwater is also characterised by the resurgence or reactivation of the more-than-human world. This may be the most striking aspect of the novel. Collins's narrative gives the reader a glimpse of what has been suppressed, then forgotten and neglected, but is always present: 'matter-in-the-process-of-becoming' (Barad 2007: 179). Moreover, Collins's narrative constructs the reader's sense of that processual reality in a way that amplifies its uncanny dimension as a 'species of the frightening that goes back to what was once well known and had long been familiar' (Freud 2003: 124). Famously, Collins presented the novel as a series of first-person narratives, all written by those directly involved in the action, all caught up in the world – and entangled with the words – in which (to paraphrase Barad (2007: 133)) they have their being.

It is, however, Marian who introduces the reader to Blackwater Park, and her experience of it supplies the reader with a sense of its agency. It is also Marian who conveys a sense of Blackwater as a haunting, Gothic landscape, a reading that is all the more powerful because the sensible Marian is by nature sceptical. '[A] haunting needs an outside, interpretive presence', notes Ruth Heholt: 'a haunting is an intervention, an encounter' (2016: 5). In consequence, the next section of this chapter looks in more detail at the way in which Marian's own encounters – and the encounters that she records – together construct the reader's experience of Blackwater.

MATERIAL INTRA-ACTIONS: MARIAN HALCOMBE AND THE UNCANNY PRESENCE OF BLACKWATER PARK

With her sister married to Glyde, Marian takes up residence at Glyde's 'ancient and interesting seat' (Collins 2003: 196), there to wait the return of the married couple. It is through her eyes that we first see Glyde's home, itself partly ruined (202–3). Marian is, however, spirited, independent and active; she is not one to take fright at a place simply because it is 'five hundred years old' (197). She is rather more concerned that its 'regions of dust and dirt' may spoil her clothes (202). She is, therefore, happy to find that 'the habitable part of the house' has been 'repaired and redecorated' (203). 'It is', she tells her diary, 'an inexpressible relief to find that the nineteenth century has invaded this strange future home of mine, and has swept the dirty "good old times" out of the way of our daily life' (203). Yet even as she awaits her beloved Laura's return, Marian's narrative signals sometimes unwitting anxieties.

> Eleven o'clock has just struck, in a ghostly and solemn manner, from a turret over the centre of the house, which I saw when I came in. A large dog has been woke, apparently by the sound of a bell, and is howling and yawning drearily, somewhere round the corner. I hear echoing footsteps in the passage below, and the iron thumping of bolts and bars at the house door. The servants are evidently going to bed. Shall I follow their example? (Collins 2003: 197)

Bell, dog, footsteps, bolts and bars; Marian has a rational explanation for all these noises off, though any one of them is perfectly capable of freezing the marrow of a more susceptible (and conventional) heroine. Even as Marian explains them away, however, her narrative betrays both her irrational fears and her unavoidable indebtedness to the Gothic. Bells are not solemn, and a howl cannot be dreary, but Marian has no other language with which to communicate the way these noises reach out to her. Simply, they possess an 'effectivity' – but also an affectivity – that her coolly reasonable mind denies (Bennett 2010: ix).

Understandably, Marian cannot sleep; her excited state amplifies both the sheer strangeness of her new home, with its 'half-ruined wing' (Collins 2003: 203) and 'dark and dismal' galleries (202), and the influence of that new home over her. The power and agency of Blackwater is made all the more obvious when, at midnight, Marian glances out of her open window. Those suffocating trees, 'dimly black and solid in the distance, like a great wall of rock', have 'shut out the view on all sides', and in the 'airless calm' they create, 'the echoes of the great clock hum ... long after the strokes have ceased' (202). This world seems to work according to its own rules, rules over which its human inhabitants have less control than they might wish or expect. Even the stars 'are dull and few' (202). 'I wonder how Blackwater Park will look in the daytime?' Marian asks herself, in a tone that is suddenly no longer as brisk or jaunty; 'I don't altogether like it by night' (202).

Marian discovers the next day when she walks the grounds. There is a perfectly pleasant fish pond and circular belt of grass in the 'great square ... formed by the three sides of the house' (204), but beyond it, the more-than-human world is felt more actively, and intra-actively. There is a flower-garden, 'small and poor and ill-kept', but Marian is quickly swallowed up 'in a plantation of fir-trees' (204). 'Daylight confirmed the impression which I had felt the night before, of there being too many trees at Blackwater', notes Marian (204). By the time Marian finally reaches the lakeside itself, she is already predisposed to think it sinister, and to see its grass as 'rank', its willows as 'dismal', its waters as 'poisonous', and even a spot of sunlight as 'sickly' (205). 'Far and near, the view suggested the same dreary impressions of solitude and decay', she observes (205). Yet solitude is simply another word for a place that has been left to its own devices, and decay is simply what humans call the result of it; place has reasserted itself in the wake of humankind's impositions. Literally, it has come alive. 'The frogs were croaking, and the rats were slipping in and out of the shadowy water, like live shadows themselves'; a snake basks, 'fantastically coiled' (205). The world that Marian encounters is full of what Jane Bennett has called a vibrant, lively matter (2010: viii–ix), and Marian feels herself threatened by it. The plantation is not, after all, a tame construct, but a 'wilderness of trees' (Collins 2003: 209), and an entity in its own right; with its 'twining reeds and rushes' (204), the 'wide, wild prospect of the lake' (205) reveals a reality that has long since exceeded the artful arrangement of the original park.

Collins's largely middle-class readership would have shared Marian's dismay. They saw the garden as the corollary of the cult of the home, and their ideal, by the 1860s, was the country cottage-style garden (Brown 1999: 152). By contrast, Marian's narrative suggests an untamed wilderness, its many agentialities conspiring to wreck (rather than work with) the identity that is intended for them. As Marian's narrative also records, Blackwater has a disconcerting way of affecting all those who come into contact with it. A week or so later, Marian returns to the lakeside. This time, she is accompanied by Glyde and Laura, now returned from honeymoon, but also by the sinister Count Fosco. At once, Glyde seems to catch the 'dreary', 'lonely' mood of the lake (Collins 2003: 231). 'Look at it now!' he exclaims (230–1). 'My bailiff (a superstitious idiot) says he is quite sure the lake has a curse on it, like the Dead Sea. What do you think Fosco? It looks just the place for a murder, doesn't it?' (230–1). If this intra-action tells us something about Glyde's own lurking unease at the ambivalent agency of the lake, Fosco's reply is still more revealing. Count Fosco is, of course, one of Collins's greatest creations, an 'overweight comic grotesque' (Lycett 2013: 192) whose florid manners and extravagant politeness cannot quite conceal his villainous intentions.

> 'My good Percival!' remonstrated the Count. 'What is your solid English sense thinking of? The water is too shallow to hide the body; and there is sand everywhere to print off the murderer's footsteps. It is, upon the whole, the very worst place for a murder that I ever set my eyes on ... If a fool was going to commit a murder, your lake is the first place he would choose for it. If a wise man was going to commit a murder, your lake is the last place he would choose for it.' (Collins 2003: 231)

Like the Count's listeners, Laura and Marian, the reader is left to wonder at the kind of man who quite clearly keeps an inventory of the kind of places that *are* fit for a murder. Is it Fosco's intention to signal this to Laura and Marian, and encourage them to comply with his plans? Or has he too been affected, in spite of his professions to the contrary, by 'the waste of the lake', made 'doubly wild, weird, and gloomy' (230) on this windy, cloudy day, by the rapid play of light over it?

By now, it is perhaps apparent that the intra-actions between people and place have shaped in Marian's mind, as in the minds of others around her, an impression of Blackwater that is quite at odds with its apparently unremarkable identity as Glyde's ancestral seat. Blackwater has intruded itself upon the narrative in ways that anticipate the story's direction, or that shape it; it is the mist 'over the lake' (262) that enables the woman in white to draw near to Marian and Laura, and 'the black depths of the trees' that allow her to follow them so closely that, although she remains unobserved, they can hear her 'long, heavy sigh'

23 'Schoonoord Historical Garden', Rotterdam. Nineteenth-century 'English' garden created from eighteenth-century reclaimed water meadow

(263). It is also, as we have seen, Blackwater's brooding presence that prompts – or provokes – both Glyde and Fosco to reveal something of their own inner natures. Forewarned by revelations such as these, Laura and Marian try their best to elude the plot they feel is gathering against them.

Yet they are sabotaged by their own efforts. Determined to eavesdrop on the plotters, Marian climbs out of her window at night and listens to Fosco and Glyde as they talk below. The weather is not on her side. It rains, and she contracts a fever that reduces her to 'a useless, helpless, panic-stricken creature' (334), rendering her more or less insensible for weeks. It is the opportunity for which Fosco and Glyde have been waiting. The house is immured by the trees; now, Marian is immured in 'the most desolate part of that desolate house' (395). It as if house and ground together conspire to keep her trapped. With Marian subdued and in effect subjugated, Fosco and Glyde are able to advance their plot to strip Laura of her fortune.

There is a further, still more unsettling dimension to Marian's experience. As Barad has insisted, the corollary of her theory of agential realism is the fact that human lives are never independent of, because humans are themselves never isolatable from, the more-than-human world. This is not to make a case for determinism; it is to insist that 'intra-actions are constraining' (Barad 2007: 177). Bodies 'are not objects with inherent boundaries and properties; they are material-discursive phenomena' (153). Marian has already been troubled by prophetic dreams that signal her entanglement with the supra-human world, just as they also mark Collins's willingness to entertain the non-rational (Wheeler 1994: 104). Now, Marian's fevered state draws specific attention to the question of bodily boundaries (Barad 2007: 153), but also, as Alaimo has argued, to the vital effect of 'dematerializing networks' (2010: 2). As fever overtakes her, Marian ceases to be legible; literally, her words disappear from the page, leaving only 'blots and scratches of the pen' – until, that is, none other than Fosco himself takes up her story ('Admirable woman!') (Collins 2003: 336). Well-to-do Victorian women were always expected to absent themselves from their own bodies and transcend (but in effect erase) their own bodily identities. Here, Marian's illness acts as a locus for what Alaimo has called 'a trans-corporeal materiality' through which 'social power and material/geographic [and biological] agencies intra-act' (2010: 63). Chillingly, these agencies in effect complete society's erasure of an unconventional and independent woman, much as Blackwater's own agentiality was once suppressed through improvement; both Marian and Blackwater are allowed to be themselves only when forgotten, overlooked or, as in Blackwater's case, neglected.

As Marian's story underlines, she is variously caught up with other agencies. In particular, Marian's entanglement with her surroundings – an entanglement made all the more poignant by her own determination to regard Blackwater as a passive and submissive object to her active and independent subject – underlines the fact that Glyde's home cannot simply be read as 'a palimpsest on which are inscribed the traces of symbolic meanings that encompass not only gender but also class and history itself' (Heller 1992: 119). It is rather a co-contributor to the construction of its own meaning, which is also to say that its meaning does not exist independently of its intra-actions with Marian, Glyde, Fosco or the woman in white. Each intra-acts with and creates a further iteration of Blackwater's identity; in turn, each is inseparable from Blackwater, in a quintessential instance of Barad's performative reading of an agential reality (Barad 2007: 132–3).

For all those exposed to it, therefore, Blackwater is a felt presence: as Heholt notes in her own discussion of haunted landscapes, 'there is no haunting without a material bodily experience of it' (Heholt 2016: 5). Useful as the formulations of agential realism may be in understanding these intra-actions, however, there is a sense in which Blackwater remains indecipherable, elusive. In the next, concluding section, the chapter considers the way in which some part of Blackwater always remains out of reach, a haunting reminder not only of the limits or finitude of human understanding, but of the more-than-human world's own withdrawal and even erasure.

WITHDRAWAL AND ERASURE: A BLACKWATER BEYOND REACH

As critics have noted, Collins's novel reflects (and never entirely resolves) an inherent tension between the Gothic's resistance to logical explanation, and the realist novel's need for 'narrative disclosure' (Bernstein 1993: 293). In re-adapting the Gothic for a modern world, the sensation novel creates as many mysteries as it solves; this is, in part, why Collins's novel continues to be read and reread. But this air of uncertainty or indecipherability also hovers around Blackwater's own material-discursive formation. To reduce it to the sum of its intra-actions is to overlook the fact that 'the solemn mystery of its stillness' (Collins 2003: 262) is left unexplained. Somehow, Blackwater lingers in the memory as a place which is, yet is not the sum of its performative identities. Even as it touches the lives of Marian, Laura and Glyde, it withdraws from their understanding.

The impression given by Blackwater's strange landscape is, in part, a function of the way in which the sensation novel was constructed, and the way in which it focused on the reader's sensitivities or sensibilities. The sensation novel was, as Matthew Sweet has pointed out, a very careful attempt to collapse some if not all of the formalities that separate text from reader (2003: xvi–xvii). As we have seen, *The Woman in White* is notable in part because it has no (omniscient) narrator. Instead, it is composed of a succession of different voices, each more or less reliable, partial or privileged. These narratives offer 'the authority that comes from direct observation and experience', as Lyn Pykett has pointed out, and it is precisely this sense of intimate embodiment and entanglement that reveals the agential materiality of the more-than-human world (2011: 58). At the same time, however, and as Pykett has also noted, 'it is not the totalizing realism that we tend to associate with the mid-Victorian novel' (58). We are instead party to what Raymond Williams called the 'fragmentation of the narrative voice', and by extension, the disappearance of the kind of 'knowable community' that, for example, Jane Austen's fiction so confidently invoked (quoted in Pykett 2011: 58, 59). The reader is left in the paradoxical position of experiencing more, but knowing less; of being intimately involved in the narrative, but denied the opportunity to see it in its entirety.

At the same time, however, Collins succeeds in making strange what readers would otherwise have found familiar. As a nonplussed reviewer from the *Dublin University Magazine* remarked, '[y]ou are bidden to look at scenes of real modern life, described by the very persons who figured therein, and you find yourself, instead, wandering in a world as mythical as that portrayed on the boards of a penny theatre or in the pages of a nursery tale' (quoted in Page 1974: 107–8). In other words, and as Henry James would later write, Collins's work 'of science' had stumbled on the sheer strangeness of the everyday (quoted in Page 1974: 124). These are the grounds of 'the Gothic terrors of Blackwater Park' (Pykett 2011: 36). There was no need for a 'castle in the Apennines', James remarked: the 'stern reality' of a country house and its garden was 'infinitely the more terrible' (quoted in Page 1974: 123).

Amid everything that is so familiar, the reader is consequently left with a sense of the narrative's strangeness, and by extension, the strangeness of the world it describes. Confronted for the first time by the 'black shadows' of lake and plantation, it seems to Marian that 'the glorious brightness of the summer sky overhead, seemed only to deepen and harden the gloom and barrenness of the wilderness on which it shone' (Collins 2003: 205). With the view literally closed off (205), this is a garden in name only, a place of shadows not of light, and of desolation rather than consolation.

That sense of estrangement opens up another, productive way of rereading Collins's use of the Gothic. The idea of a once-familiar, even comforting, but now strange and withdrawn reality finds its correspondence in the concept of *hantologie*, a term coined by Jacques Derrida to describe an irreducible 'element' that belongs neither to life nor death (1994: 63). As Colin Davis has explained, hauntology 'supplants its near-homonym ontology, replacing the priority of being and presence with the figure of the ghost as that which is neither present nor absent, neither dead nor alive' (2005: 373). The ghost – or, in the Derridean reading, the spectre – is 'a wholly irrecuperable [sic] intrusion in our world, which is not comprehensible within our available intellectual frameworks, but whose otherness we are responsible for preserving' (373).

As Davis has pointed out, however, hauntology may also point to a different, historicised explanation of the role and status of the ghost: not that it is and always has been withdrawn, but that it has become withdrawn; that its withdrawal is, specifically, a function of and response to modernity (378–9). The loss of the knowable community, and the values it encoded, is itself an aspect of that process; it creates in its wake the Blackwater from which Marian recoils, recognising in its thickly planted, fast-growing firs an angry but also anxious and ultimately futile attempt to restore a once-valued wooded landscape and the network of relationships it embodied (Collins 2003: 204). It could even be argued that the agential materiality of the more-than-human world once formed an integral part of human doings, and that the relationship was knitted into an oral tradition whose loss was itself a function of modernity. Walter Benjamin called the traces of that agentiality 'an aura' (1999: 216–17); Freud saw it as uncanny, but also recognised in it the residue of an 'old *animistic* view of the universe' (Freud 2003: 147, emphasis in original). We might speak of a haunting; as Julian Wolfreys has observed, '[a] spectre haunts modernity, and the spectral is at the heart of any narrative of the modern' (2002: 2).

If, therefore, the Gothic may be seen as an attempt to reassert the agential materiality of the more-than-human, but also supra-rational, the disappearance of the Gothic genre – and its replacement by the realist novel – may itself be read as an aspect of that withdrawal. As Wolfreys has argued, there is 'a transition in the nature of the gothic from the end of the eighteenth century onwards, an irreversible movement from genre to trope, from structural identity to that which haunts the structures of narrative … marked by an inward turn perhaps, an incorporation which is also a spectralization' (25). What we encounter as a consequence in our reading of Blackwater are 'the fragments and manifestations of a haunting, and, equally, haunted, "gothicized" sensibility' (25).

Arguably, this is precisely what Collins exploited so deftly, but also shamelessly. He was widely criticised as a mere 'manufacturer of stories' (quoted in Page 1974: 104), and his plots were dismissed 'as a type of soulless modern machinery' (Heller 1992: 110), ingenious, but themselves exploitative. Collins, his critics contended, was simply playing with the reader's feelings to elicit his or her involvement, and Gothic devices were merely a way to achieve the effect. In gesturing towards the Gothic, Collins was not seeking to revive it as a form so much as cannibalise it to create his own. In effect, *The Woman in White* is itself a symptom of modernity; even as it allows Blackwater a partial place in its narrative, the novel is gesturing towards its erasure, just as it gives us the independent, spirited Marian, only to make her another victim. The spectral Blackwater has, in returning, already signalled its retreat (Wolfreys 2002: 2).

To readers, however, Blackwater seemed all too real, and its readers have always played a particularly, perhaps peculiarly, important role in constituting the novel's significance. *The Woman in White* was a sensation; readers spoke of its 'genuine enchantment' (quoted in Page 1974: 93). Their reaction is important because the sensation novel exploits but also makes explicit what other forms of fiction prefer to elide: that its meaning is co-constituted by text and reader, in a dialogue (which is itself a material-discursive intra-action) over which the novelist has no final control. Collins's novel possessed a life of its own, a point that can also be made about Blackwater and its lake, even as they fade 'in the gathering darkness, to the faint resemblance of a long wreath of smoke' (Collins 2003: 262).

At the level of both content and form, therefore, the novel reveals its troubling sense of being haunted, and haunted not least by the uncanny agency of the more-than-human world embodied in Blackwater. Whether its meaning is constituted, moment by moment, in the multiple intra-actions of characters and context, people and place, or in the reader's own response to Collins's textual construction of this haunted and haunting locale, or whether its meaning is, ultimately, withdrawn from human comprehension and hence intervention,

Blackwater remains a ghostly presence, beyond our reach – beyond, therefore, of our objectification. It is this last explanation that fits most closely most with the Derridean interpretation of hauntology (Davis 2005: 373). For Derrida, the spectre cannot and should not be put into words; it is not awaiting human intervention, since it exists independently of it; its 'ethical injunction consists on the contrary in not reducing it prematurely to an object of knowledge', therefore gesturing towards 'a still unformulated future' (379). Morton has spoken of an ecological awareness that is 'dark-depressing [but also] dark-uncanny … a dark pathway between causality and the aesthetic dimension, between doing and appearing, a pathway that dominant Western philosophy has blocked and supressed' (2016: 5). Derrida's own sense of the spectre offers a positive to this negative, by pointing to the possibility of respecting even that which cannot properly be understood.

And so Blackwater's Gothic landscape recedes, in its own way as inscrutable as the woman in white who haunts its fringes. Improbable as its isolation might seem, in England's populous south, its self-seclusion and indecipherability was and remains part of its appeal (Page 1974: 90). But if, as Wolfreys remarks, '[t]he gothic is always with us' (2002: 25), it is because that withdrawal is only ever temporary: behind the haunting power of the (eco)Gothic lies the recognition that a garden like Blackwater can never finally be repressed or suppressed. Like Marian, it recovers from any attempt to erase or expurgate it. Its return is a reminder of the limits of our own agentiality, frightening because, as Freud suggested, it insists on what we have always known but chosen to forget: that a supposedly passive and pliable world is itself radically alive.

WORKS CITED

Alaimo, Stacy. 2010. *Bodily Natures: Science, Environment and the Material Self* (Bloomington: Indiana University Press)

Austen, Jane. 1996. *Mansfield Park* (1814), ed. by Kathryn Sutherland (London: Penguin)

Barad, Karen. 2007. *Meeting the Universe Halfway: Quantum Physics and the Entanglement of Matter and Meaning* (London: Duke University Press)

Benjamin, Walter. 1999. 'The Work of Art in the Age of Mechanical Reproduction', in *Illuminations*, ed. by Hannah Arendt, trans. by Harry Zorn (London: Pimlico), pp. 211–44

Bennett, Jane. 2010. *Vibrant Matter: A Political Ecology of Things* (London: Duke University Press)

Bernstein, Stephen. 1993. 'Reading Blackwater Park: Gothicism, Narrative, and Ideology in *The Woman in White*', *Studies in the Novel*, 25. 3: 291–305

Botting, Fred. 1998. *Gothic* (London: Routledge)

Brown, Jane. 1999. *The Pursuit of Paradise: A Social History of Gardens and Gardening* (London: Harper Collins)

Collins, Wilkie. 2003. *The Woman in White* (1859–60), ed. by Matthew Sweet (London: Penguin)

Davis, Colin. 2005. 'Hauntology, Spectres and Phantoms', *French Studies*, 59: 373–9

Derrida, Jacques. 1994. *Specters of Marx*, trans. by Peggy Kamuf (London: Routledge)

Fearnley-Whittingstall, Jane. 2003. *The Garden: An English Love Affair* (London: Weidenfeld and Nicolson)

Freud, Sigmund. 2003. *The Uncanny*, trans. by David McLintock (London: Penguin)

Gold, John R. and George Revill. 2004. *Representing the Environment* (London: Routledge)

Heholt, Ruth. 2016. 'Introduction: Unstable Landscapes', in *Haunted Landscapes: Super-Nature and the Environment*, ed. by Ruth Heholt and Niamh Downing (London: Rowman & Littlefield), pp. 1–20.

Heller, Tamar. 1992. *Dead Secrets: Wilkie Collins and the Female Gothic* (London: Yale University Press)

Luckhurst, Roger. 2006. 'Introduction', in *Late Victorian Gothic Tales*, ed. by Roger Luckhurst (Oxford: Oxford University Press), pp. ix–xxxi

Lycett, Andrew. 2013. *Wilkie Collins: A Life of Sensation* (London: Hutchinson)

Mangham, Andrew. 2013. 'Introduction', in *The Cambridge Companion to Sensation Fiction*, ed. by Andrew Mangham (Cambridge: Cambridge University Press), pp. 1–6

Morton, Timothy. 2007. *Ecology Without Nature: Rethinking Environmental Aesthetics* (London: Harvard University Press)

Morton, Timothy. 2010. *The Ecological Thought* (London: Harvard University Press)

Morton, Timothy. 2016. *Dark Ecology: For a Logic of Future Coexistence* (Chichester: Columbia University Press)

Page, Norman (ed.). 1974. *Wilkie Collins: The Critical Heritage* (London: Routledge & Kegan Paul)

Pykett, Lyn. 2005. *Wilkie Collins* (Oxford: Oxford University Press)

Pykett, Lyn. 2011. *The Nineteenth-Century Sensation Novel*, 2nd edn (Tavistock: Northcote House)

Smith, Andrew and William Hughes. 2013. 'Introduction: Defining the EcoGothic', in *Ecogothic*, ed. by Andrew Smith and William Hughes (Manchester: Manchester University Press), pp. 1–14

Sutherland, John. 1998. 'Introduction', in Wilkie Collins, *The Woman in White* (Oxford: Oxford University Press), pp. vii–xxiv

Sweet, Matthew. 2003. 'Introduction', in Wilkie Collins, *The Woman in White*, ed. by Matthew Sweet (London: Penguin), pp. xiii–xxxiv

Uglow, Jenny. 2004. *A Little History of British Gardening* (London: Chatto and Windus)

Wheeler, Michael. 1994. *English Fiction in the Victorian Period, 1830–1890*, 2nd edn (London: Longman)

Wolfreys, Julian. 2002. *Victorian Hauntings: Spectrality, Gothic, the Uncanny and Literature* (Basingstoke, Palgrave)

Afterword: *Z Vesper*, the Wilderness Garden, Powis Castle

Paul Evans

Thoughts fly from the light of life like birds in a wild evening.
Piofu de Gou (2019)

As the crow flies, from a rough-hewn bench under oaks in Wales, the view sweeps over the river valley, crossing the shoulder of Long Mountain towards Corndon Hill and Caer Caradoc in England, to turn again on the border, at the standing stones on Stapeley Common, and gaze back to where I sit on a bench at the edge of the Wilderness Garden, the woodland garden of Powis Castle near Welshpool, Powys.

I have been sitting here, on and off, sometimes once or twice a year, sometimes visiting only by thought, much of my adult life, looking. Returning today, March light flashes a mile away on windscreens along the A458 between Welshpool and Newtown running parallel to the Heart of Wales railway line, parallel to the Shropshire Union Canal, parallel to the River Severn/Afon Hafren, parallel to Marcher ridges of Powys and Shropshire up where the border burrows between tree roots and stream banks and worms along Offa's Dyke. This is also the axis of the vernal equinox, poised on the balance; the weight of an extra hour when clocks go forward tips us into British Summer Time. The prospect twists like a Mobius strip and loops back to the refuge oaks (as if I were watching myself from the other side of a bridge) to the needs-oiling song of chiffchaff, the freshly laundered whites of wood anemone and fallen-cloud, as John Clare calls violets. The oaks are dark still but in vernation, cells in their leafbuds fan like hands of cards to bet again on three hundred springs.

Thinking about the view from these trees across fields and woods to those hills on the horizon, I turn to the geographer Jay Appleton's theory of prospect and refuge. Appleton says our aesthetic taste for landscape is an acquired preference for satisfying inborn desires – opportunity (prospect) and safety (refuge) (1975: 70–4). This comes from an evolutionary impulse: the predator scanning for potential prey or danger from a concealed vantage point. The aesthetic experience is enhanced by vistas over wide-open space, with mountains, lakes and an expanse of sky viewed from a cave, grotto, over a wall, behind a gate or within a grove of trees. Satisfying an innate and largely unconscious watchfulness from a safe place is used in the design of urban planning and landscape architecture; prospect and refuge are determining factors in landscape aesthetics. The Old English *landscipe* and the Dutch *landshap* – region, district – became 'landskip', the Georgian movement for the design of land based on the work of painters and poets, to 'landscape' as a description of a tract of land that can be seen (painted or photographed) from a single view. Such a prospect observed from safety shapes a human preference for savannah-like habitats, open forest, wood pasture and the parkland and landscaped gardens that replicate that preference, re-creating the aesthetic of landskip painting in rural and urban environments.

Desires for opportunity and safety may not be as passive as they at first appear; they become the way landscape is created, managed, inhabited and represented. Desires that find their expression in a deep bond with the land may also express feudalism, territorialism, nationalism, xenophobia and a proprietorial entitlement to exploit Nature as a resource – natural capital, ecosystem services – as long as the prospect's visual integrity and the refuge's security are preserved. The view of the countryside I see from here may look very similar to how I saw it forty years ago or someone else saw it 140 years ago, but it is not – its ecocultural field of nonhuman and human dwelling is invisibly coming undone. This passive aesthetic relationship with place, that the ethologist Konrad Lorenz calls 'to see without being seen' (1961: 181), is the desire transferred to film, cinema and television; the prospect can be ever more dangerous because the refuge is so much safer; in virtual reality, internet prospect and refuge are becoming ever more complex and problematic. Transferring the virtual back to the physical reality is place porn.

In this anthropocentric view, the capacity of what is being watched to return the predatory gaze and the capacity of the sanctuary to enclose and retain the darkest of desires, is not considered in the aesthetic. The landscape, and indeed the Nature it re-presents, is assumed to be neutral and indifferent. Nietzsche says, 'We love the open countryside so much because it has no opinion concerning us' (1995: 181). Is this true?

The bench I occupy is at the edge of the woodland garden, called (without a trace of irony) the Wilderness, part of the world-renowned gardens of Powis Castle near Welshpool, Powys. I lived and worked here from 1973 to 1980; seven years – as many years at it takes cells in the human body to change, and they have changed several times since. I may not be entirely the same person but I come back every now and then to reconnect with the magic of the gardens and inevitably end up here, looking out, as if coming up for air. My habit of sitting in this place for a moment begins many years ago without my knowing why. It may have begun before I came to live here: cycling home from work at the nursery in Shrewsbury I stop on a railway bridge to look out at the hills of Shropshire and Powys and wonder what it is like to live there. When I move here I'm looking back the other way. This dreamy experience, although hard to describe, seems to come from the place itself; it has become a kind of ritual observance, and I still don't know why. John Dewey, the American philosopher and educational reformer, says, 'Through habits formed in intercourse with the world, we also in-habit the world … How then can objects of experience avoid becoming expressive?' (quoted in Howarth 1995: 108). The feeling created by the prospect of this view of the Marches hill country from the refuge of this garden bench becomes an expressive object of experience. This is not a Cartesian meditation through which I become aware of my own existence in this landscape. This feels instead like receiving something from the nature of this place, something uncanny that takes me over like a mood.

'They descend upon us without reason, stay without permission and leave without cause', is how philosopher Jane Howarth describes moods (113). In discussing how emotion terms are ascribed to Nature – angry skies, melancholy seasons, joyful brooks – Howarth says it is Nature that is expressive of these emotions; it has no feelings or intentions but then, not all human behaviour that arises from emotion is intentional, some is expressive or irrational and may be an instinctual residue of evolution, as are the desires for prospect and refuge. Many emotional ascriptions we make to Nature are, says Howarth, easily thought of as mood ascriptions in that Nature can 'echo' our moods because it moves in similar, if mysterious, ways. Moods are sometimes described using emotion terms such as lively, edgy or gloomy, but many are much subtler than this and are not so easily differentiated. Often, in my experience, the uncanny – a being-watched, a mood that falls from the gaze of something unseen – cannot be communicated as a specific emotion and refuses to be fixed to something I can identify as anxiety, even though it may cause it. Howarth claims that it is the backdrop that specifies the mood; different environmental features – hills, woods, rivers, sky – although lacking in specific object, have an atmosphere that seems to spread out to impinge on consciousness. I see the uncanny as part of Nature that consciousness is conscious of, a mood I receive from a place and not something my consciousness projects onto the backdrop. It is my recognition of the backdrop's atmosphere that specifies the mood which in turn colours my surroundings and the way I feel.

When I think about the atmosphere in this garden observatory facing the backdrop of the Welsh Marches, it is not passive like a stage set; I sense a protagonist's spirit, a specific and metaphysical objectness of hills, trees, birdsong, stories, an ontology of objects Graham Harman (2018) regards as human, nonhuman, natural, cultural, real or fictional. The atmosphere from this bench at the edge of Powis Castle gardens is charged with a kind of radiation from the hill country itself. According to Helen Glenny (2019), geophysicists have discovered that humans have an ancient ability to sense magnetic fields; our magnetorecepetion, like that of many bacteria, and migrating birds, insects and fish, is a built-in compass based on magnetite, iron crystals aligning to the Earth's magnetic field somewhere in the cells of our nervous system sending signals to the brain. This 'sixth sense' does not appear to be one we are conscious of and it opens the possibility of other unconscious forms of perception.

This is contested borderland, fought over, killed for, medieval castles, Iron Age hillforts, Bronze Age stone circles, an archaeology stretching back to the Palaeolithic, wolves, aurochs, eagles, giants – wilderness. Seen by those looking out, the 'kings of the castle', built as the Welsh Castell Coch, the Red Castle – red for its bloody history as much as its stone – becomes English with the imperialist's I in the spelling of Powis in the Welsh kingdom of Powys, and a vault for Clive of India's looted treasure. For those looking in, we 'dirty rascals', this has been a land at various times under the castle's protection and a land laying siege to it – home ground and enemy territory. For wildlife, it is an arena for ritual or casual slaughter dressed as ethnic pageantry. This is the land A. E. Housman, with nostalgic amnesia, calls the 'blue remembered hills' (1896: XL. 3). For poet-novelist Mary Webb, who writes from inside the 'expressive object of experience', it is a place 'betwixt and between … a land half in, half out of faery', it is a borderland between different states of being (Cole 1978: 145). Absorbing this hazy atmosphere leads to a lapse into daydream: thoughts fly into shadows moving across the mountain, others return as bumblebees, traffic noise, a pheasant. 'The world is not the world manifest to humans', says Graham Harman, 'to think a reality beyond our thinking is not nonsense but obligatory' (2011: 26). So, I'm obliged but conscious of a sadness beyond my thinking. This could be how the Welsh word *hiraeth* feels – not unlike homesickness, not dissimilar to a melancholy of missing, an ache in the soul. There is no English word for looking back the other way. But although I may feel a nostalgia for the time I lived here, it does not account for having the same feeling all those years ago when I did. Even though I get angry and despondent about forces that continue to ignore the unfolding ecological catastrophe they cause sucking the marrow out of this landscape, those changes to the countryside are everywhere and they are less visually pronounced here. This feeling of missingness then, the *hiraeth*, is an aftertaste.

A pair of ravens call to each other, they toll a dark space through a clear sky; in the river valley, white dots of gulls rise and fall in flood meadows echoing wood anemones here under oaks. From the bench at the edge of the garden, I become aware that the uncanniness of the mood does not come solely from

24 The Lady's Bath, the Wilderness Garden, Powis Castle

the atmosphere of the prospect but resides in the refuge, the garden; it is enclosing, enveloping, an enchantment.

This week, out of the blue, someone who was a horticultural student at Powis sends me a photograph he took in 1978 of four of us gardeners standing outside the Orangery. We look funny, happy, mischievous, standing to attention – one with a spade, one with secateurs – we have planted little box plants grown from cuttings to make a new hedge backing a lawn to replace parterres. Today, the Orangery box hedge looks as if it's been there forever and I haven't seen the gardeners in over forty years and don't know if they're still alive. In the photograph, plants on the wall have changed, so has the light, the colours of the air, stone, leaves, clothes; although I've seen other snaps of the period I find it difficult to recognise myself; my comrades remain the same in my memory as the day I last saw them. It suddenly feels so long ago. The photograph is a shock.

Four years before this image is taken, Maria and I, with our babe-in-arms, walk around the garden talking to the extraordinary head gardener Jimmy Hancock during my interview for a craftsman gardener's job. As we walk along eighteenth-century terraces for which Powis is internationally famous, listening to Jimmy's plans to rejuvenate the moribund herbaceous borders and breathe

25 The Orangery Terrace, Powis Castle Gardens

new life into the way the garden is run, we hear voices from a wooded ridge across the Great Lawn which was once an Italianate water garden. The echoing voices sound like young women, laughing and calling excitedly. The garden is not open to the public today so I assume it's a private party and Jimmy doesn't seem to notice. When we reach the wooded ridge, Jimmy explains the history of the Wilderness Garden and the tradition of growing trees and shrubs collected from temperate parts of the world in native woodland as idealised versions of 'wilderness' found in North and South America, the Himalayas and China. At the point where we heard the women's voices is the Lady's Bath, a square sunken pool backed by a tufa rockery of ferns secluded in the trees. Today, the sign says it's a plunge pool built in the 1770s, 1.4m deep, for plunging into cold spring water to cure ailments and promote a healthy mind. This accounts for the wildly joyful, erotic laughter, but the women have disappeared; it is not possible for them to leave without being seen or heard.

Maria and I look at each other quizzically, Jimmy carries on talking without paying attention to it; I don't think he hears them. Perhaps the ladies of the Lady's Bath do not exist. For those of us who watch Nigel Keane's *The Stone Tape* (1972), a television drama about the ability of stones in old buildings to store, record and transmit sounds and images of haunting apparitions, paranormal experiences (if that's what they are) can be represented by fringe science, accessible through knobs and dials like radio. Perhaps the bathers we hear are what psychical researchers call a veridical hallucination – an experience that conveys the idea of truth and yet is something unknown. Rosalind Heywood claims such apparitions 'are genuine, though non-physical, phenomena, of which many people are aware by means of some form of ESP [Extra Sensory Perception]' (1975: 14). H. H. Price, who set up the Society for Psychical Research, is interested in the idea of paranormal events being the result of 'place memories', through the ability of molecules of water to retain memory (1938–39). T. C. Lethbridge, the parapsychologist-explorer, is also interested in the idea that some form of memory connects inanimate objects through the 'ether' and ghosts are phenomena attributable to such memories embedded in place, appearing through invisible psyche-fields (1961). Lethbridge also considers water important in the conductivity of paranormal energies; he describes these fields using Greek mythology: water bodies (naiads), forests (dryads), mountains (oreads), earth (ge). Lethbridge thinks some places, notorious for a suicide or other trauma, accumulate an uneasy feeling about them, an eldritch – weird, uncanny – mood transmitted through water or a humid atmosphere. Perhaps, even with scientific scepticism, it is possible to imagine the spring water of the Lady's Bath and its masonry transmitting these bathing naiads having fun in the Wilderness as a powerfully persistent place memory, broadcast from an imprint sustained in the ecocultural field of this place.

Unfettered by the Cartesian doctrine that what is not physical must be mental, and with the kind of visions that may be described now as ESP, William Blake is writing as Powis Castle gardens develop. Blake's *Jerusalem: The Emanation of the Giant Albion* recognises the bathers as fairies or nymphs, dancing their way through folksong and country lore into a natural history of these lands despite their unreliable taxonomy, '... The Daughters of Albion, / Names anciently remember'd, but now contemn'd as fictions / Although in every bosom they control our Vegetative powers' ([*Jerusalem*: I. 37–9], quoted in Adlard 1972). The spirits that control the vegetative powers of this garden, despite centuries of work by gardeners, inhabit an imaginative, libertarian prospect of the natural world, seen from the refuge of a shared folk memory. Freudian they may be, but Blake's fairies are manifestations of undisciplined joy, of the kind Bertrand Russell believed could overcome the rages and unhappiness of the people, an 'instinctive joy' for a good world (in Adlard 1972: 1).

My own view of what a good world might be has been formed by instinctive joys with vegetational powers. I am about sixteen when my dad offers me a ride to Powis Castle to pick up his mother, my grandmother. She is a seamstress, a dressmaker to Lady Powis, and has a room in the castle where she lives for part of the year. I once went to a Christmas party for kids there but have a growing scepticism for the aristocracy and privilege and have no contact with the castle. My dad drops me off at the gardens, which are owned and managed by the National Trust, to wander around for a while. When I get to the pool at the edge of the Wilderness, I rifle through my pockets for a cigarette, find a crumpled but salvageable fag and a single match which I strike on the fly of my jeans. Through my heady nicotine hit, relief and smoke hanging in the air under tall trees reflecting in the water, I notice the crosiers of royal ferns, *Osmunda regalis*. I am enchanted by the unfurling fronds.

Ferns, pteridophytes, are vascular plants with roots, stems and leaves (fronds) but do not reproduce sexually with flowers and seeds, they are far more ancient than flowering plants and are cryptogams (secret-marriage) plants producing spores, as they have done since their Carboniferous ancestors of 300 million years ago were fossilised in coal. I think stumbling onto a ruined house in a wood when I am about twelve and discovering a sunken garden with the abandoned remains of a fern collection gone wild sparks my fascination for them. The romantic connection between ferns and ruins persists in my imagination and I am drawn to derelict buildings, tumbled masonry, ancient trees and scree slopes where contemplation of the juxtaposition between verdant life and decay leads to the kind of pleasure Rose Macaulay attributes to the self-projection of the tourist 'into the past, of composing poetry or prose, of observing the screech owl, the bat, and the melancholy ghost, and the vegetation that pushes among the crevices and will one day engulf' (1953: xvi). It is in this Gothic power of Nature to transform, to engulf historical forces, to crack open the industrial-era patina so that the spores of the ecoGothic can germinate. Ferns flourish in those fissures between the ideologies of science and the supernatural; they are of Blake's anarchic ecosystem taking root in the ruins of colonialism and nationalism; they pioneer the way for trees and woods, so familiar and yet so estranged from us, to reclaim an unthinkable transformation of society from spaces that hitherto did not exist. The ecoGothic is a taking notice of Nature's uncanny staring back. The prospect answers with its ruinous gaze penetrating the refuge with a disturbance, the uncanny described by Nicholas Royle as a 'critical disturbance of what is proper' (2003: 1), a crisis of the natural in our own nature.

Where flowering plants are objects of sunlight, ferns are, like Blakean characters, objects of shadow. Dark, mysterious, romantic and architectural, ferny ruins dripping with water-bearing memories make the ideal refuge. Although I do not collect them, ferns are a habit that has lasted longer than smoking. I may be a throwback to the Victorian fern craze which, although it did untold damage to botanical populations and leaves a legacy of nature-kleptomania, was a fantastically Gothic phenomenon. As objects of vegetation, ferns, not flowers, embody Ruskin's list of characteristics and 'moral elements' of the Gothic spirit behind Gothic architecture: '1. Savageness, 2. Changefulness, 3. Naturalism, 4. Grotesqueness, 5. Rigidity, 6. Redundance' (2004: 5) (as I write this, the most famous Gothic building, Notre-Dame cathedral, its roof timbers of thousand-year-old oak wood ablaze, stands in ruins on its island in the Seine). Ruskin also says of the Gothic, 'It is that strange *disquietude* of the Gothic spirit that is its greatness; that restlessness of the dreaming mind, that wanders hither and thither ...' (39). The ecoGothic collects ferns for their beautiful disquietude and cultivates them in gardens of the dreaming mind.

Osmunda, Osmund the Waterman (grows by water), the Royal Fern or Flowering Fern, is 'the most stately of British Ferns', according to the botanist Thomas Moore:

> It is a very handsome plant at all times, but especially when, in very luxuriant growth, its fronds loaded at their tips with the fertile panicles [of spores] are bent down gracefully until they almost reach the surface of the water by the side of which they are growing. Hence it should always find a space in cultivated collections.
> (Moore 1855: no page numbers)

Moore is a major influence on fern-crazed Victorians. His evangelism for plants as objects of desire is satisfied by collection and cultivation rather than observation in the wild and is at the core of the garden aesthetic. The garden draws prospect into refuge: in cultivating the wild, gardening is the performance of the movement of Nature into culture. This old dance between culture and cultivation has been performed at Powis Castle for as long as the gardens have been enclosed for protection against the crushing weight of the Marches' returning gaze.

As I follow my own historical steps, the *Osmunda* draws me further into that ecocultural field within the garden that so fascinated me fifty years ago when I stood smoking by the pool. I watch the cinnamon-coloured fiddleheads of the same plants begin to unroll from bases that have been trimmed of last year's dead fronds in a way that suggests a more fastidious degree of management than I would advocate for a 'wild' garden. There have been many changes since my time here. The climate is warmer and wetter, perhaps there is also less atmospheric pollution but the increase in mosses and lichens growing on tree branches in recent decades is very noticeable. Climate change has increased the diversity of plants growing on the terraces where they are largely free from frost. There also appear to be far fewer butterflies. Despite loving their dark, woody tangles, I began the process of taking out the naturalised *Rhododendron ponticum* decades ago; unknown to me then, it has to be grubbed up because it harbours Sudden Oak Death *phytophthora*, one of a growing number of plant pathogens that arrive in Britain as a consequence of the global trade in plants. The desire that sends botanists and plant hunters to collect the most beautiful and fascinating specimens of vegetation from around the world to grow in European gardens is a piracy whose bounty hides an ecological insurgency that will become killers of woods.

26 Royal fern (centre left) at the Horse Pool, Powis Castle Gardens

I do not know whether gardeners still live here in tied accommodation or if their way of life and sense of self is so intimately entwined with that of the garden's but I bet they are as enchanted with it as I am and those who work here long before us. When gardens are spoken about as symbols of privilege and power of the rich, the gardeners are forgotten; we are anonymous labourers who leave souls not names. The phenomenon of garden visiting replaces religious observances and the number of visitors to Powis Castle has risen hugely. The challenge for the National Trust is to manage its historical gardens to enhance the contemporary visitor experience and adapt to climate change without losing the magic.

There is no water in the Lady's Bath, and ferns in the grotto around it have gone, so maybe that place memory and its naiads are lost, for now. There is, however, much magic in the vegetation, in the plants and the atmospheres and moods they create. The Wilderness may be no more than a small Welsh oak wood with exotic and ornamental species bodged within it but the trees themselves have such charisma and presence. The geography of this tree collected from Sikkim or that from California, of this being a native of New Zealand or that of New York, of this symbolic and ritual plant of Hokkaido or that of Wales, these are stories we tell about ourselves. The geography matters less over time than the community of plants in this place, its collective, ecological being, its society. As historian Keith Thomas says of sociology, '[the sociologist] Durkheim may have been wrong when he suggested that when men worshipped God they were really worshipping society. But he would have been very near the truth if he had said it about the worship of trees' (1984: 223). Nature worship and the druidic tradition of divining knowledge from trees remains a powerful idea, as James Howell, a seventeenth-century Anglo-Welsh historian and writer, expresses:

> While Druyd like conversing thus with Trees,
> Under their bloomy shade I Historize.
> Trees were ordained for shadow, and I finde
> Their leafs were the first vestment on Mankind. (in Scoular 1965: 186)

Stirring from the druidry of winter trees, dressing in their spring foliage, the modern world's juxtapositions between beautiful and powerful vegetative spirits brought together in the woods produces a secular, off-hand, don't-make-a-fuss kind of veneration of trees. On an emotional plane, landscaped gardens, parks, arboreta, woods, evoke a magic of surrealism: the prospect of an irrational, dreamlike subconscious inhabited by quasi-supernatural beings observed from the refuge of psychology. As I perch on the Wilderness bench, listening to the oratory of ravens, breathing oak vapour, drinking intoxicants of magnolia and primrose, a feeling grows for what I think of as natural magic.

In the sixteenth and seventeenth centuries, poets and thinkers had an understanding of 'natural magic' which Kitty Scoular describes as 'a descriptive term on the borderline between mystical Paracelsan alchemy involving a supposed communion with the hidden forces of nature, and a more modern conception of scientific effort' (1965: 4). Poets from Spenser to Marvell are interested in the 'variety, enigma, metamorphosis' of both art and Nature and a possibility beyond truth that lies in 'the harmony of opposites', paradox, oxymoron and riddle, called synœciosis. Of Nature's riddles, providence – the benevolence of God or Nature – is the strangest for Renaissance poets, including George Herbert (1593–1633), born in Montgomery, if not exactly in this view (there is a hill in the way) then in its purview, before his family inherit Powis Castle. Scoular says Herbert's 1633 prayer-poem 'Providence' is paradoxical. In it, God's will is mysterious, 'Tempests are calm to thee; they know thy hand' (line 45), creation is full of creatures instructing humans in ways to exploit them, 'Birds teach us hawking; fishes have their net' (line 51), Nature's dangers may be turned to human advantage and the Earth's astonishing plentitude is full of shamanic power, 'And if an herb hath power, what have the starres? / A rose, besides his beautie, is a cure' (lines 77–8, quoted in Scoular 1965: 32–4). In the Middle Ages, providence is a divine horticulture, employing the gardener in a performance where cultivation (stock) and culture (scion) are grafted in the vegetative propagation of civilisation (chimera). Objects in Nature are expressed using incompatible opposites. In 'Providence', Herbert uses groups of verbs to describe the movement of light: 'glitter, and curle, and wind', 'stream and flow', 'hang and move', a metaphysical Nature expressed in a way that is more familiar now as metaphor and simile distilled from synaesthesia and the kind of descriptions that appear in contemporary nature writing.

I watch the light move through trees as birdsong; it occupies a space where natural magic morphed into nineteenth-century natural history and drew the paradox of Nature's utility and mystery into gardens such as the Wilderness Garden. Stories from living memory of the long nineteenth century tell of bowler-hatted head gardeners in white gloves, part druid, part engineer, directing the planting of trees and shrubs in the Wilderness, while cloth-capped gardeners like me, paid in beef and ale, dig the holes and hide a silver thrupenny bit under each new root ball, for luck, for the future. And for all its imperialist entitlement to Nature there are also nineteenth-century writers such as Richard Jefferies, whose *Journal* (1884) advises, 'Never go for a walk in the fields without seeing one thing at least however small to give me hope, the frond of a fern among dead leaves' (quoted in Mabey 1997: 136). What gives hope to a nature writer in today's emergency of climate crisis and extinction threat? That same fern frond growing from dead leaves – a mulch of discarded pages written about Nature. Something 'however small' leads to an inquiry into synœciosis – a possibility behind the paradox of Nature's providence (sacred) and its answering violence (profane). It is a gift from the Anthropocene of an ecology Timothy Morton may call 'dark-uncanny' (2007) and Graham Harman may describe as a world not manifest to humans but a reality beyond thinking (2011: 26). The ecoGothic, as a form of literature, is the conservation of the uncanny; I experience it as a mood; I am writing as an observer observed by the mood.

In the spirit of name-giving, I want to identify the mood that, as Howarth says, descends without reason, departs without cause, and is present when I sit on this garden bench to look at a view that is looking back at me. In writing this, I close my eyes and open Kitty Scoular's book, *Natural Magic* (ex-Wolverhampton University Library, plucked from a bargain bin in Hay-on-Wye), at a random page and move my finger down it. The page is a plate from Joachim Camerarius', *Symbolorum et Emblematum Centuriae* [1st edition] III. ixxxix, Nuremberg, 1590 (Scoular 1965: Plate III). It is a circular engraving, as if seen through a telescope, of a bat flying with the moon above and hills and woods below; the heading reads INTER UTRUMQUE, which reminds me of Mary Webb's liminal description of this land as 'betwixt and between' (Cole 1978: 145). My finger stops before it slips from the page at 'Z Vesper – '. I have no idea why this text appears here, perhaps it has something to do with evening prayer or meditation (probably nothing to do with motor scooters or cocktails). The letters are phantoms, they flit through a dusk that has nothing to do with time of day, in a borderland of possibilities between wild Nature and culture – *Z Vesper* – a riddle of uninvited synœciosis. I realise I am sitting in the nineteenth century, in a garden lush with desires of that time for aberrancy, deviance and acquisition. I am scanning the ruins of a medieval landscape for riddles and paradox – the raven's return from exile, the whimbrel's passing into myth – watching birds fly between the two realities. I feel edgy and restless and turn my back on the view. I walk through the Wilderness under oak trees whose calluses heal over chainsaw wounds I inflicted; I peel slivers of yellow birch bark from trees I planted to press in my notebook; I read Dymo Tape labels of the Latin names of trees I clicked out on cold winter days; I inhale the faint bubblegum fragrance from flowers of rhododendron I pruned; I visit the grave of Apollo, the cat I buried. I've climbed in its trees and dug in its earth; with saw and axe-mattock I have scratched the surfaces of the Wilderness. These are ways of knowing but I am just a fly-by-night, an outsider. I love the rest of the garden but keep returning to its edge as if coming up for air. However Powis changes and grows away from me, however my memories unfurl like fern fronds into a reality I become less part of, this place continues to exert a weird call on my attention.

A few days later I wake from a bad dream. In it I leave the bench under oaks to wander abroad but I am arrested and questioned about the murder of one of the gardeners in the 1978 photograph. I am in shock about the death of a friend and confused: why am I a suspect? Who are these people that dog my every step to apprehend me in derelict cottages in the hills and sheds in woods? How do they know a story of something that happens over forty years ago in a garden that exists only as a place memory now? I feel responsible for something I've left behind. I return to try and find it. Thoughts fly like birds into the *Z Vesper*. I am haunting myself.

WORKS CITED

Adlard, John. 1972. *The Sports of Cruelty – Fairies, Folk-Songs, Charms and Other Country Matters in the Work of William Blake* (London: Cecil & Amelia Woolf)

Appleton, Jay. 1975. *The Experience of Landscape* (London: John Wiley)

Cole, Gladys Mary. 1978. *The Flower of Light: A Biography of Mary Webb* (London: Duckworth).

De Gou, Piofu. 2019. 'Floating Dogs' (unpublished)

Glenny, Helen. 2019. 'Humans May Have an Ancient Ability to Sense Magnetic Fields', *BBC Science Focus*, 23 March, www.sciencefocus.com/news/humans-may-have-an-ancient-ability-to-sense-magnetic-fields [accessed 1 June 2020]

Harman, Graham. 2011. 'On the Undermining of Objects: Grant, Bruno, and Radical Philosophy', in *The Speculative Turn: Continental Materialism and Realism*, ed. by Levi Bryant, Nick Srnicek and Graham Harman (Melbourne: re-press), pp. 21–40

Harman, Graham. 2018. *Object-Oriented Ontology, a New Theory of Everything* (London: Penguin Books)

Heywood, Rosalind. 1975. *Telepathy and Allied Phenomena* (London: Society for Psychical Research)

Housman, A. E. 1896. *A Shropshire Lad* (London: Kegan Paul, Trench and Trubner)

Howarth, Jane. 1995. 'Nature's Moods', *British Journal of Aesthetics*, 35. 2: 108–20

Keane, Nigel and Sasdy, Peter (dir.). 1972. *The Stone Tape*, BBC Two, original release: 25 December

Lethbridge, T. C. 1961. *Ghost and Ghoul* (London: Routledge and Kegan Paul)

Lorenz, Konrad. 1961. *King Solomon's Ring* (1952), trans. by Marjorie Kerr Wilson (London: Methuen)

Mabey, Richard (ed.). 1997. *The Oxford Book of Nature Writing* (Oxford: Oxford University Press)

Macaulay, Rose. 1953. *Pleasure of Ruins* (London: Weidenfeld and Nicolson).

Moore, Thomas. 1855. *The Ferns of Britain and Ireland* (London: Bradbury and Evans), https://archive.org/details/b21495956_0001/page/n11/mode/2up [accessed 1 June 2020]

Morton, Timothy. 2007. 'What is Dark Ecology?', www.changingweathers.net/en/episodes/48/what-is-dark-ecology [accessed 1 June 2020]

Nietzsche, Friedrich. 1995. *Human All Too Human*, trans. by R. J. Hollingdale (Cambridge: Cambridge University Press)

Price, H. H. 1938–39. *Journal of the Society for Psychical Research*

Royle, Nicholas. 2003. *The Uncanny* (Manchester: Manchester University Press)

Ruskin, John. 2004. *On Art and Life* (1853) (London: Penguin Books)

Scoular, Kitty. 1965. *Natural Magic, Studies in the Presentation of Nature in English Poetry from Spenser to Marvell* (London: Oxford University Press)

Thomas, Keith. 1984. *Man and the Natural World: Changing Attitudes in England 1500–1800* (London: Penguin Books)

Index

EU authorised representative for GPSR:
Easy Access System Europe, Mustamäe tee 50,
10621 Tallinn, Estonia
gpsr.requests@easproject.com